# Gay Male Fiction
# Since Stonewall

The conflict between assimilationism and radicalism that has riven gay culture since Stonewall became highly visible in the 1990s with the emergence and challenge of queer theory and politics. The conflict predates Stonewall, however—indeed Jonathan Dollimore describes it as "one of the most fundamental antagonisms within sexual dissidence over the past century." How does gay male fiction since Stonewall engage with this conflict? Focusing on fiction by Edmund White, Andrew Holleran, David Leavitt, Michael Cunningham, Alan Hollinghurst, Dennis Cooper, Adam Mars-Jones and others, Brookes argues that gay fiction is torn between assimilative and radical impulses. He posits the existence of two distinct strands of gay fiction, but also aims to show the conflict as an internal one, a struggle in which opposing impulses are at work within individual texts.

**Les Brookes** is an Associate Lecturer at The Open University, tutoring in twentieth-century literature. Previously Brookes taught at Anglia Ruskin University, where he also gained his doctorate. Brookes has written for *Overhere: A European Journal of American Culture* and given papers at Warwick University and the Cambridge Centre for Gender Studies.

# Routledge Studies in Twentieth-Century Literature

# Gay Male Fiction Since Stonewall

## Ideology, Conflict, and Aesthetics

## Les Brookes

Routledge
Taylor & Francis Group
New York   London

First published 2009
by Routledge
270 Madison Ave, New York, NY 10016

Simultaneously published in the UK
by Routledge
2 Park Square, Milton Park, Abingdon, Oxon OX14 4RN

*Routledge is an imprint of the Taylor & Francis Group, an informa business*

Typeset in Sabon by IBT Global.
Printed and bound in the United States of America on acid-free paper by IBT Global.

*Library of Congress Cataloging in Publication Data*
Brookes, Les, 1943-
    Gay male fiction since Stonewall : ideology, conflict, and aesthetics / by Les Brookes.
      p. cm. — (Routledge studies in twentieth-century literature; 8)
    ISBN-13: 978-0-415-96244-5
    ISBN-10: 0-415-96244-7
  1. Gay men's writings, American—History and criticism.   2. American fiction—
20th century—History and criticism.   3. Gay men's writings, English—History and
criticism.   4. English fiction—20th century—History and criticism.   5. Male homosexuality in literature.   6. Gay men in literature.   I.   Title.
    PS374.H63B76 2009
    813.009'353—dc22
    2008007148


ISBN10: 0-415-96244-7 (hbk)
ISBN10: 0-203-89220-8 (ebk)

ISBN13: 978-0-415-96244-5 (hbk)
ISBN13: 978-0-203-89220-6 (ebk)

*For Phil, with love*

# Contents

# Acknowledgments

I began this book as a doctoral thesis at Anglia Ruskin University, where the Research Committee of the English Department supported me with generous bursaries for which I am extremely grateful. Support of a different kind came from friends in the Postgraduate Reading Group of the department, whose encouragement certainly played a major part in helping me to complete the project. The staff of the library were unfailingly helpful too, as were the staff at Cambridge University Library; and I would like to thank in particular Sue Gilmurray, the English Department's liaison officer at Anglia Ruskin.

For permission to quote from copyright sources, I am grateful to the following: Penguin Books Ltd and Farrar, Straus, and Giroux for extracts from Michael Cunningham's *A Home at the End of the World*; The Peters Fraser and Dunlop Group for extracts from *The Darker Proof* by Adam Mars-Jones and Edmund White, London: Faber and Faber. "An Interview with Edmund White" originally appeared in *Overhere: A European Journal of American Culture*, 18.1 (1998), and I would like to thank the editor, Professor Richard J. Ellis, for permission to reprint here as an appendix.

I hardly need to say that I am greatly indebted to Edmund White for allowing me to interview him, and for supplying me with the idea from which this book has grown. His openness, generosity, and friendship have been inspirational.

Sincere thanks also to the following, who helped me in various ways: Simon Avery, David Brown, Rychard Carrington, Mark Currie, Max Fincher, Paulina Palmer, Sam Pattenden, Rick Rylance, Val Scullion, Catherine Silverstone, Alan Sinfield, Rebecca Stott, Gina Wisker, Tory Young.

Finally, especial thanks go to Phil Bales, who has aided me at every step of the journey and never once complained.

# Introduction

Since no one is brought up to be gay, the moment he recognizes the
difference he must account for it.

—Edmund White, *The Faber Book of Gay Short Fiction*

The lights dimmed. The hubbub sank to a hushed expectancy. The film
began to roll. It was called *Victim*. I leaned closer to Abdullah, the handsome Hindu student who for the past few weeks had been the focal point of
my life. "It's about homosexuality," I whispered. But this was sham sophistication: I had no idea what the word meant. Nor was I about to be immediately enlightened, for the opening sequence of the film was merely intriguing.
Why was the young man so desperate to destroy the photographs of the older
man? Indeed, what was his involvement with this upper-class lawyer? And
why all this talk of suicide and blackmail? Then, as the mists of the scenario
began to clear, my moment of recognition arrived. In a Damascene revelation, the word I had whispered with such confident innocence at the start of
the film suddenly exploded with special meaning . . . and of course, at the
same moment, dropped out of the conversation. In the discussion I had with
Abdullah as we left the cinema, we were agreed. It was a fine film: intelligent,
well-acted, thought-provoking. We discussed many aspects, but we avoided
that word. Indeed we never uttered that word in each other's company again.
The recognition had gone deeper than we cared to acknowledge.

   After the film came the books. I had to know who I was; I needed
to forge a self and imagine a future. Along with a sociological study of
homosexuality and a life of Tchaikovsky, I devoured novels by Gore Vidal,
Angus Wilson, James Baldwin, and Christopher Isherwood. And the most
influential part of this reading was the fiction, for if recognition of difference was now forcing me, in White's words, to "account for it," it was to
the novelists that I turned, as pioneers of such accounts. Moreover, in this
respect, my experience was typical: the key role of literature, and especially
fiction, has long been recognised in the development of gay consciousness,
self-understanding, and sense of identity.[1] This is not surprising if we consider that literature has been almost the only place where one could learn
about homosexuality. Certainly, in the early 1960s, there was little to be

learned from parents, the wider culture, or mass media, a situation that has not much changed since that time. "The child who will become gay," David Bergman writes, "conceives his sexual self in isolation" (*Gaiety* 5).

There is a sense, then, in which this book is part of my continuing attempt to "account" for the difference. It focuses on fiction since Stonewall because the post-Stonewall period has been the most formative of my own sense of identity.[2] I had no gay friends, nor indeed any subcultural support, until I came to live in Cambridge in 1971. Here, in the immediate aftermath of the Stonewall riots, the organized gay life of the city was being politically galvanized. A new idea—gay liberation—was in the air, and a generation of students, radicalized by the events of 1968 and the counterculture generally, were staging discussions, confrontations, demonstrations. Some of these had recently returned from the United States, bristling with passionate commitment. At the same time, in London, the Gay Liberation Front (which was to burn itself out by the following year) was provoking large, exciting, anarchic "happenings." I thus found myself caught up in a thrilling, if dizzying, whirlpool of ideas, supposedly fomented by a remote and intangible weekend of rioting in Greenwich Village, which time had not yet hardened into symbol—ideas that are still at the center of current debates and that it is part of my purpose in this book to re-explore.

What was immediately evident to me, from my first experience of organized gay life, was that the subculture was riven by ideological conflict. Of course, this has always been the case, but in the early 1970s, it was perhaps especially and evidently so. We were, after all, experiencing the birth of a new consciousness and a new movement—a movement, in Jeffrey Weeks's words, "which stressed openness, defiance, pride, identity—and, above all, self-activity" (*Coming Out* 185). Ideological conflict was therefore inevitable at this moment of revolutionary change; and the basis of this conflict was the fundamental opposition between assimilationism and radicalism. The subculture of the early 1970s was in fact a battlefield: on one side were those who had no great quarrel with the social order, while on the other were those who wished to see it razed to the ground. The former were keen to show their allegiance to heterosexist norms, seeing such loyalty as evidence of their right to social inclusion—an attitude that underpins, for instance, Bruce Bawer's *A Place at the Table*, a book that I examine in Chapter 1. The latter group, on the other hand, were so determined to break free of these norms that relationships of more than a night's duration were condemned as showing abject deference to the heterosexual ideal of lifelong partnership.

Something of the flavor of this time and virulence of this debate is captured in the London Gay Liberation Front pamphlet, *With Downcast Gays: Aspects of Homosexual Self-Oppression* (1974), by Andrew Hodges and David Hutter. This vehemently rejects heterosexual marriage as the model of human relations, approved and upheld by "'responsible' gay activists" (11) and "homophile spokesmen" (14). Gay people, the authors suggest, should aspire to something better: namely, the pattern of relations they already enjoy. For nonmonogamous, long-term gay relationships, in which "the partners share loving companionship but find sexual pleasure outside the union," offer an enviable alternative to the "boring embittered cohabitation" (12) that many marriages become. Indeed, the main thrust of the argument in this pamphlet is that gay self-oppression (as indicated in an aspiration to achieve for gay partnership an equality of status with heterosexual marriage) stems from a servile need in gay people for social acceptance. If the authors admit to being critical of their fellow homosexuals, this is tautological: the rancor is evident in the severity of their judgments. At the heart of their essay, for instance, is a harsh and unforgiving appraisal of E. M. Forster, who is excoriated for ensuring that his novel *Maurice* was not published until after his death, for failing to speak out in support of gay people, and for valuing his reputation above the influence he might have brought to bear on the question of homosexual law reform.

*With Downcast Gays* contributes to a long-standing argument: an argument that Jonathan Dollimore describes as "one of the most fundamental antagonisms within the politics of sexual dissidence over the past century" (*Sex, Literature and Censorship* 4). In my view, it is *the* fundamental antagonism. On one side of this argument are those who believe that homosexuality is "a revolutionary force in western culture, with a power to subvert its heterosexist underpinning entirely" (3), while on the other are those who see no call for revolutionary change. These latter hold that gays and straights can happily coexist—indeed, that they are basically alike, and that any hostility between them is merely the result of ignorance and prejudice, which education and rational reform will sweep away. Moreover, if the queer radical position is rooted in a hatred of conformity and respectability, and a belief in the eternally oppositional nature of homosexual desire, the final implication of the assimilationist, liberal reformist position is that there is no reason to see the needs and aspirations of gays and straights as essentially at odds: no reason, in other words, to believe that gay people should not take their place as good citizens—parents, teachers, politicians—within the existing social order.

In practice, however, the divide is rarely as clear as this. It seems probable that most gay people—whatever their avowed stance, and often at a level below consciousness—are a mixture of radical and assimilationist impulses. This is apparent, for instance, from the failure of many queer radicals to recognize the full implications of their radicalism. Thus, on the one hand, these radicals declare war on contemporary society, while on the other they express indignation at the reaction that this provokes—an inconsistency that points to an inner conflict of pressures.[3] But assimilationists, too, often struggle with contradictory urges; their need to identify with the social order is often in tension with their need to assert and celebrate what is special about themselves: their sense of different, even unique, identity. Bruce Bawer, for instance, in an account of his own moment of recognition, writes that recognizing one's homosexuality is "a matter of realizing that you *are* different, that to most of society you *are* from the moon" (232). This realization, he suggests, can also be mysteriously comforting, "because you've always felt an odd, seemingly indefinable sense of being estranged from the world that's familiar to you" (232). Bawer seems to be struggling here with the paradox of his own standpoint, for a sense of "estrangement" from society would seem to preclude an urge to identify with it. Indeed, such feeling would seem to be the origin of an attitude of radical dissent.

These tensions, then, are the focus of this study. They have a long history, and are still at the heart of current debate. They have also been a fundamental part of my own experience, an experience mirrored and explored in the literature examined here. The central inquiry of this book, therefore, comes down to this:

> In what ways does gay male fiction since Stonewall engage with the longstanding conflict in gay culture and politics between assimilationism and radicalism: between the need for integration into the wider social scene on the one hand and the need to assert an independent identity on the other?

I should stress that "engage with" here implies reflect, explore, challenge. I see this fiction as having a shaping, forming, and actively contributing— rather than simply mirroring—role. If, then, I sometimes use the word *reflect* without qualification in later parts of this book, I would like these extensions of meaning to be borne in mind.

## CONTENT AND METHODOLOGICAL APPROACH

In this study I treat Stonewall as a turning point in gay self-awareness, but not as an absolute break with the past. As I indicate in Chapter 2, I approach the literature examined here as part of a continuing conflict, the roots of which are in the pre-Stonewall era. By "pre-Stonewall era" I mean the hundred-year span, 1869–1969, the former being the year in which the term "homosexuality" was invented, and hence from which many aspects of our current conceptualization of homosexuality could be said to date. Of course, the new consciousness that developed out of Stonewall inevitably came to express itself in a new kind of literature. This literature, however, although informed by the new consciousness, is not simply celebratory. Rather, it reflects the same tensions as pre-Stonewall gay writing. Indeed, if anything, it reflects a heightening of these tensions, particularly after 1981, with the arrival of the age of AIDS.

What very obviously changes after Stonewall is the sheer volume of gay male writing. The central entreaty of gay liberation, after all, was to "come out," and the vast expansion of gay literature in the post-Stonewall period is in part a response to this call, a response that has elements of both release (the "outing" of a long-repressed identity) and of creation (the forging of a new "self-identity").[4] But however we explain it, the now very large body of post-Stonewall gay writing can reasonably be described as comprising a modern gay literary movement—a movement, moreover, that encompasses a wide range of writing, including theory and sociological studies, as well as imaginative literature. However, such quantity and range of writing creates problems for the researcher: any attempt to address the question posed above, for instance, calls for careful selection and organization. Thus, for reasons of space and homogeneity, I have chosen to concentrate on fiction. Gay male writing since Stonewall embraces all forms, but fiction has been the vehicle best equipped to represent gay men's sense of place and role in society, and moreover the mode that has often subsumed the other elements of poetry, drama, memoir, and autobiography.[5]

The study opens with two chapters that are introductory. Chapter 1, as its title indicates, is an attempt to provide a contextual framework for the study as a whole. It looks not only at ideas (the ideological, theoretical, and conceptual underpinnings of the conflict mentioned in my title) but also at the history and evolution of gay culture in the post-Stonewall period, developments to which those ideas are bound and of which they are an integral part. It both sets the scene and establishes direction, immediately engaging the central question of my book through its focus on ideological conflict. The examination here of theoretical developments—from homophile movement, through gay liberation, to articulations of queerness—highlights the issue that fuels this conflict: the question of identity. These theoretical perspectives are not discussed in isolation, however; they are linked to the fiction explored in later chapters. Thus theory, history, and fiction are brought together as interactive forces.

Chapter 2 is retrospective. It supports my contention that the conflict between assimilationism and radicalism that is the focus of this study has a long history. Here, the opposing strains of post-Stonewall gay male fiction are traced back to fiction of the pre-Stonewall period. The assimilative strain is represented by E. M. Forster's posthumously published *Maurice* (1971), Gore Vidal's *The City and the Pillar* (1948), and Christopher Isherwood's *A Single Man* (1964), while the strain of radically transgressive fiction is traced from Oscar Wilde's *The Picture of Dorian Gray* (1895), through Jean Genet's *Our Lady of the Flowers* (1943), to William Burroughs's *Naked Lunch* (1959). Here, the impulse to make homosexuality fit into categories validated by heterosexuality is set against the sometimes violent iconoclasm of a very different strain of writing. This glance at the literary antecedents of the novels examined in my core chapters starts from the assumption that the later novels cannot be understood without some discussion of their lineage. It prefigures the later chapters in another way, however, for it explores the assimilative and radical impulses both as an opposition between writers and as a tension within those writers. It thus introduces the theme of internal conflict that is central to my argument.[6]

Against this background we move to the core of the book. In Chapter 3, I analyze three key novels of the 1970s: Edmund White's *Forgetting Elena*

(1973), Andrew Holleran's *Dancer from the Dance* (1978), and Larry Kramer's *Faggots* (1978). The twelve-year span between the outbreak of the Stonewall riots and the first reports of AIDS (1969–1981) is clearly a self-contained period requiring separate treatment. This long decade is often referred to as the golden age of gay liberation, and the best-known novels that come out of and reflect the new gay culture are American. But what is striking about these first flowerings of the new consciousness, these distillations of the gay liberation moment, is their ambivalence. The narrators of these novels observe the new gay scene with irony and sometimes revulsion, and the element of celebration in the writing is mixed with distaste. In short, the writers reveal an inner tension: an attraction to sexual outlawry and transgressiveness that is in friction with a residual allegiance to mainstream values and social norms.

The remaining chapters focus on fiction of the 1980s and early 1990s, fiction that emerges from, and reflects, a culture fundamentally transformed by AIDS. Each of these chapters opens, therefore, with a consideration of some aspect, or aspects, of the impact of AIDS. These include, in Chapters 4 and 5, the theoretical developments that evolved in the 1980s and 1990s, in part out of response to the epidemic (the growth of the constructionist thesis, queer theory), and in Chapter 6, the issues surrounding the writing of fiction about AIDS. As befits content, the analysis of opposing strains of fiction in Chapters 4 and 5 is structured around queer and postmodern challenges to the notion of gay identity, as exemplified in the work of, among others, Judith Butler, Michael Warner, and Steven Seidman. However, the exploration of sexual radicalism and transgression in gay fiction in Chapter 5 also draws, as appropriate, on theoretical writing by Leo Bersani and Alan Sinfield (their disagreement about Genet), David Punter (theories of the Gothic), and Julia Kristeva (her theory of abjection).

Chapters 4 and 5 should be viewed together, as forming a kind of binary opposition. I have positioned them here, between Chapters 3 and 6, as an indication of their centrality. They explore the assimilative and radically transgressive tendencies of gay writing separately, as productive of two quite distinct strains of fiction since Stonewall. Thus Chapter 4 looks at three novels—David Leavitt's *The Lost Language of Cranes* (1986), Michael Cunningham's *A Home at the End of the World* (1990), and Robert Ferro's *The Family of Max Desir* (1983)—in each of which the central character is a gay man, but a gay man viewed in relation to family, friends, and the heterosexual world, and as part of the wider social scene. Chapter 5, on the other hand, dissects a quite different set of novels: Alan Hollinghurst's *The Swimming-Pool Library* (1988), Clive Barker's *Cabal* (1988), Poppy Z. Brite's *Lost Souls* (1992), and Dennis Cooper's *Frisk* (1991). Here, the central characters are sexual rebels, at odds with the world generally and romantically drawn to life on the margins. These characters may see themselves as part of a marginalized group, to which they show some kind of tenuous affiliation, or as "loners," living so far outside the norms of society as to be beyond most forms of association. However, if these chapters explore opposed impulses and tendencies as they exist in tension between different strains of fiction, they also pursue my related theme of internal conflict by revealing this opposition as existing to some extent within the same text. The distinction between these strains of fiction, in other words, is not clear-cut: within individual texts, both strains are sometimes clearly at work, the conflicting tendencies simultaneously present. Consequently these chapters sometimes discover points of similarity between works of fiction that are otherwise wildly dissimilar.

Finally, how is this conflict between assimilative and radical impulses reflected in fiction about AIDS? Chapter 6 looks at Oscar Moore's novel *A Matter of Life and Sex* (1992) and the short stories by Adam Mars-Jones and Edmund White originally collected under the title *The Darker Proof* (1988). Of course, none of these texts presents AIDS as a moral warning. They nevertheless clearly reflect the conflict in their articulation and embodiment of very different perspectives. Thus, in Oscar Moore's novel, AIDS is stoically accepted as the inevitable fate of the sexual outlaw. Hence it also comes to signify his peculiar fate. Indeed, it figures finally as the special mark of the transgressor, as well as the source of his romantic fatalism. There is no sense here, however, of punishment or of getting one's just deserts. AIDS is not viewed as the outcome of moral degeneracy; it is seen, rather, as simply the natural consequence of a life of promiscuity. The narrative becomes the working out of a natural law, the fulfillment of a tragic destiny.

The short stories by Adam Mars-Jones and Edmund White, in contrast, reject such apocalyptic brooding. They struggle to keep a rational approach and sense of balance. Their tendency—as exemplified in "A Small Spade," "The Brake," and "Palace Days"—is to stand back and take a distant view. At times, they suggest an attempt to see AIDS as a phase of history, and indeed, in the case of White's story "An Oracle," to place it within a long historical perspective. Thus, to the extent that they present AIDS as part of the wider social scene and not as the distinctive mark of the sexual outlaw, and to the extent that they minimize its special horrors and make it accessible to the wider reading public, these stories show an inclination toward an assimilative position. I should stress, however, that this is a broad characterization, for these stories are not assimilative in the sense of seeing AIDS as a reason to abandon gay political agendas in surrender to moral panic. On the contrary, they suggest a reassertion of gay identity as part of a broadly radical stance, a stance given new energy precisely in face of the threat of AIDS. Conflicting tendencies are therefore at work here too, reinforcing the theme of internal tension that is present throughout this study.

## DEFINITIONS

At this point I feel I should offer clarification of some terms used in this book, terms that are problematic for a number of reasons, and not least because they have a wide range of possible meanings. Hence my aim here is not only to raise some attendant issues, but also to attempt some explanation of my own usage.

## Gay

The very word is charged with conflict, and vibrates with the tensions at the center of this inquiry, the tensions that inhere in and surround the question of identity. Adopted after Stonewall as a badge of positive self-identification, its current usage is so imprecise as to call into question its value as a meaningful term at all. Given its background, however, it is not inappropriately applied to the focus of this study. Its current usage, after all, however imprecise and contested, arose with and is inseparable from the emergence of the gay liberation movement after 1969. In other words, the fiction examined here, if we acknowledge the force of widespread practice over time, belongs to the "gay" period of homosexual history.

## Gay Male Fiction

As a category, this is equally contentious, and for related reasons. Thus some of the authors whose fiction is examined here would probably object to their work being classified in this way, their complaint grounded in the view that the category is reductive, limiting, or simply inappropriate to the kind of fiction they write. This objection clearly relates to that critical view of the label "gay" that sees it as a straitjacket—as a confining, rather than liberating, self-identification. I suspect that three such objectors would be David Leavitt, Michael Cunningham, and Dennis Cooper, the two former on the grounds that their writing belongs to the mainstream of fiction rather than to a ghettoized subdivision of it, and the latter on the grounds that his fiction exists in a category all of its own.[7]

So how would I define the "gay male fiction" of my title? I need to be careful here, but it seems safe to say that it refers, in general, to fiction by self-identified nonheterosexual men, who may or may not choose to call themselves gay. The category is thus a convenient shorthand term, which hopes to convey and even provoke an awareness of the inherent contradictions and ambiguities of such classification. It also recognizes that this writing, although perhaps of particular interest to gay men, may not be written exclusively *for* gay men, and indeed may aspire to the widest possible readership. As if to illustrate this instability, Chapter 5 includes a brief discussion of *Lost Souls* by Poppy Z. Brite, a novel that might more aptly be included in a study of women's vampire fiction. Nevertheless, this inclusion seems justified in the context of a chapter about sexual radicalism. For here the leading characters are all androgynes, who therefore problematize the sexuality and gender demarcations of my title and extend the range of the study generally, opening it up to the challenge of queer insights and readings, as well as to the contribution of popular and genre fiction.

## Ideology

I use this term in the sense of broad intellectual framework. Hence, in the sense used here, it comprises ideas, opinions, values, preconceptions, and general mind-set: that is, formal and conscious beliefs as well as "less conscious, less formulated attitudes, habits and feelings, or even unconscious assumptions, bearings and commitments" (Williams 26). I am aware of the history of the term both as a Marxist concept, criticizing bourgeois ways of thought as false consciousness, and, conversely, as a general term of abuse from conservative elements in society, disparaging any social theory (but in particular Marxist doctrine) as cold intellectual fanaticism. My concern here, however, is with a clash of broad sociopolitical and philosophical perspectives, based on neither abstraction nor dogma. Hence my use of the term is in no sense ironic or pejorative. It only remains to say that these tendencies may be implicit manifestations of ideology (as in the fictional texts explored here) or explicit expressions of it (as in the theoretical discourses used to interpret those texts).

## CHOICE OF TEXTS

In the history of homosexuality, the period "since Stonewall" has been one of meteoric change. It has witnessed the birth of modern gay culture, its brief flowering and near-extinction. It has also seen an explosion of gay literature documenting these changes, an outburst of creativity that could reasonably be described as constituting a modern gay literary movement. Part of my purpose here has been to explore this movement through the work of some of its leading writers. However, this study is not, nor was ever meant to be, a comprehensive guide to all this output. On the contrary, due to the sheer volume of writing in this period, the limitations of time and space, and the fact that my backward glance in Chapter 2 extends the range of literary production to more than one hundred years, I have had to be rigorously selective.

So what has guided my choice? One answer has already been suggested: in the main, these are texts that by common consent have established themselves, even in so short a space of time, as having some kind of landmark significance. So perhaps this is the place to comment on the fact that, while three of the twelve writers represented here are British, nine are American. The explanation for this is quite simple: gay male fiction since Stonewall *is* predominantly American—although why this is so is not entirely clear. After all, the scene before 1969 is very different. As Felice Picano writes: "In the beginning, there was the gay word and the word was—British! Oscar

Wilde, John Carpenter [*sic*], John Aldington Symonds [*sic*], E. M. Forster, A. E. Housman—you name the gay writer around the turn of the previous century and he was British" ("The British Are Coming" 38). Picano's tentative suggestions as to why the scene moves to the other side of the Atlantic after Stonewall (he mentions the influence of the pioneers, the male-male tradition in American literature, the untidiness of the country) are perhaps only partially convincing, although I think he quite rightly points to cultural differences between Britain and the United States as being the underlying cause. Dennis Altman also comments perceptively on these differences (and well before the emergence of post-Stonewall gay fiction) in his introduction to the first printing of *Homosexual: Oppression and Liberation* (1971):

> In American literature there is the continuing theme of men, often of different races, retreating into the wilderness, beyond society, in an implicitly homosexual relationship; this is very different from English novels, where the concern, even when homosexuality is involved, is much more with complex interactions within society. Even in postwar writing the difference persists: the homosexual in the American novel, as in Burroughs, Rechy, or even Baldwin and Vidal, is far more likely to appear an outsider than, as in the novels of Iris Murdoch or Angus Wilson, a participant in a world of social relationships. (19)

However, quality of writing and historical importance have not been the only determinants of the fiction I have chosen to focus on here, for I have also attempted to impose order on this wealth of material by pursuing a single line of inquiry. For reasons that those earlier hints of my personal history may make clear, I see the post-Stonewall period as one of ideological conflict. This conflict, I contend, is fundamentally a single conflict that ramifies into a series of related conflicts: for instance, essentialism/constructionism, sameness/difference, gay/queer—and crucially, assimilationism/radicalism. Furthermore, I see this fundamental conflict as an intensification of a long-standing antagonism—in fact, one that is as old as the concept of "homosexuality" itself, or, in other words, dates back to the late nineteenth century. The endurance of this conflict is not surprising if we consider how closely it relates to that fundamental issue of homosexuality, the question of identity. Throughout this study, then, my central concern is to show how this struggle (considered both as an antagonism between individuals and groups, and as an inner tension) is reflected and even embodied in my chosen texts.

There are thus some notable absences. The study treats no fiction by nonwhite authors, for instance, not even in Chapter 2, where a novel by James Baldwin might seem to cry out for inclusion, particularly given the importance of his work to me and my contemporaries. These omissions can be defended, however, on the grounds given above: that the study is not intended to be a survey, but rather the pursuit of a particular line of inquiry. The texts treated here have been chosen not just, nor even primarily, for their general significance, but to illustrate a theme. Moreover, the inclusion of a text by a French novelist—Genet's *Our Lady of the Flowers*—in a study of otherwise Anglophone fiction can be explained in the same way. The crossing of disciplinary boundaries here (along with the accompanying danger of suggesting that no other gay-themed fiction from Europe is worthy of attention) can be justified on the grounds that Genet is central to my argument, as I hope my discussions of his work in Chapters 2 and 5 make clear.

The theme of conflict, then, is what drives this study, and in exploring this theme I re-encounter some of my own formative influences—the post-Stonewall period, its conflicts, its literature—while continuing to reflect on questions with which I have been engaged for most of my life. Indeed the book is a personal journey in which I extend an argument with myself, an argument that dates from that moment in the early 1960s when I first recognized "the difference."

# 1 Gay Male Fiction Since Stonewall
## The Contextual Framework

In this opening chapter I want to take an extended look at the theoretical perspectives that underpin this study as a whole. But since these ideas are inextricably bound up with historical developments, history is also part of the framework examined here. Moreover, the chapter is interspersed with references to the fiction I shall be exploring in later chapters, so as to make clear the link between text and context, and not lose sight of my main focus. My discussion of theoretical and historical perspectives, in other words, is offered as context for the fiction. My starting point, given that focus, is of course Stonewall and the gay liberation theory that inspired and flowed from it. But gay liberation theory, as history shows, did not arrive from nowhere, and so I shall sometimes glance back at earlier ideas. This accords with my general thesis that the conflicts of gay male fiction since Stonewall have an ancestry stretching back to that period in the late nineteenth century when homosexuality first became conceptualized.

Gay liberation theory marks a change in the theorization of homosexuality in laying stress on the historical and social construction of identity. In this way it points to the future: to the refinements and later developments of social constructionist thinking in what is now called "queer theory." Indeed, Jeffrey Weeks has recorded his frustration (and that of other writers on sexuality whose work dates back to the late 1960s) at the failure of queer theory to acknowledge its debt to the past. He writes of having "our early efforts at understanding sexuality in general, and homosexuality in particular, refracted back to us through post-Foucauldian abstractions" and raises an eyebrow at the celebrity status of certain queer theorists who "are not saying anything fundamentally different from what some of us have been trying to say for twenty-five years or so" (*Making Sexual History* 53). Weeks, in accord with other experts in the field, sees Mary McIntosh's article "The Homosexual Role" (1968) as a founding document in the social constructionist theory of sexuality. However, it is Dennis Altman's *Homosexual: Oppression and Liberation* (1971) that is now seen as the cornerstone of that new body of theory that appeared as an accompaniment to the rise of the gay liberation movement in the early 1970s and as the distillation and central statement of gay liberation theory.

The central concern of Altman's book, as the author acknowledges in his introduction, is "the question of identity" (19); and this, writes Jeffrey Weeks in his introduction to the book, "has been the central concern of all subsequent lesbian and gay literature and politics" (6). The first publication of the book therefore chimed with the politics of the emerging gay movement, especially in its emphasis on the act of "coming out" and on the assumption of a potentially salvific identity that must be publicly avowed. Identity, in this context, is not a private matter; it is bound up with the transformation of society. It must be stressed, however, that Altman's notion of identity is not essentialist, even though he admits to some uncertainty about how a sense of identity is formed. As he states in his afterword to the 1993 reprinting of the book:

> Without fully understanding what I was writing, I was in fact a social constructionist without knowing the term—the ideas which were to be developed over the next two decades by scholars such as Jeffrey Weeks, Michel Foucault, etc., about the ways in which a homosexual identity is a particular historical construction are present in a not very clearly formulated way in my book. (253)

Thus the radicalism of Altman's book both reflects the revolutionary potential of the early gay liberation movement and looks forward to the elaborations of social constructionist thinking that have emerged in postmodern discourses.[1]

That revolutionary potential, however, soon gave way to an ethnic model of identity and politics that was predominantly white, middle-class, and male, and founded on notions of supposedly essential sexual categories. "As a movement committed to liberating humanity from the mutually exclusive and limiting roles of the heterosexual/homosexual and the feminine/masculine," writes Steven Seidman, "gay liberation came to an end by the mid-1970s" ("Identity and Politics" 117). Indeed, as Seidman goes on to imply, the extensions of social constructionist thinking currently known as queer theory are in part a reaction to this ethnic model. Altman connects with queer theory because, although, as he avows, he is much concerned with the question of identity, his notion of identity is not the ethnic one—or at least not finally, since, again like queer theory, he is more interested in questions than answers. It is therefore a gross misrepresentation of gay liberation theory (on the evidence of this book and other defining documents) to dismiss its underlying assumptions as crudely essentialist.[2] Certainly Altman promotes identity, but as a political rather than essentialist concept. The implication of his argument is that, for the transformation of society he desires to occur, lesbian and gay identities must first be constructed before they can be deconstructed. In other words, as Jeffrey Weeks puts it: "Such identities are . . . necessary fictions" (*Making Sexual History* 84).

The radical and socially transformative thrust of Altman's argument throughout the book is signaled early in the text. Thus, in his introduction, he writes: "The question [of identity] touches us all, for human liberation rests on our ability to liberate that part of ourselves that we have repressed. We all need to come out of our particular closets" (19). Homosexual liberation is therefore everyone's liberation, he implies, since each individual has a range of sexual responses much wider than concepts of sexual normality allow.[3] Although he confesses to confusion in his own mind as to how "we develop our various patterns of sexual response," he suspects that there is some truth in the claim that the adoption of homosexuality is in part an act of (perhaps unconscious) rebellion and involves "at least sometimes an element of deliberate choice" (25). This accords with his rejection of the notion that homosexual behavior is the result of inborn difference. Although generous enough to empathize with Radclyffe Hall's sense of natural outsidership as expressed in *The Well of Loneliness,* he opposes her essentialist position by firmly stating his belief that "the homosexual sensibility is entirely a product of social pressures" (46).

The final and controversial implications of Altman's position emerge in the conclusion to his book, which envisages "the end of the homosexual." In a transformed society, he argues, there will be no need for minorities; the homo–hetero distinction will wither and a "new human" will flourish, undivided and "able to accept the multifaceted and varied nature of his or her sexual identity" (241). Here, then, Altman's anticipation of theory pursued in contemporary queer/postmodern discourses becomes obvious and astonishing. It is important to distinguish this disappearance of the homosexual, however, from the disappearance envisaged in the preliberation theory of what is now known as the homophile movement—or, in other words, in the mainstream homosexual thought of those organizations that fought for social and political reform in the years before Stonewall.[4] The primary objective of the homophile movement was social assimilation. It did not, in general, celebrate difference. Hence, in this scenario, the disappearance of the homosexual amounts to self-erasure: to absorption into the current dominant heterosexual order and ideology. The disappearance of the homosexual envisaged by Altman, on the other hand, is clearly very different. What Altman envisages, strictly speaking, is not the end of the homosexual, but rather the end of the ideology within which the concept of "the homosexual" has been engendered: not self-effacement, but self-realization within a new economy.

Nevertheless, as we might expect, most people who identify as lesbian or gay feel a sense of resistance to Altman's unsettling vision of "the end of the homosexual." As Ken Plummer puts it: "[His] curious recognition . . . that a true liberation would also dissolve the very object of liberation . . . is the paradox of gay liberation" ("Speaking Its Name" 7). Of course, the same paradox also haunts queer theory. Indeed, this is the measure of Altman's closeness to postmodern ways of thinking. Moreover, the attempt by queer theorists to dissolve and reconceptualize categories of identification has, accordingly, aroused similar opposition. Thus Leo Bersani devotes a whole chapter of his book *Homos* (1995) to what he calls "the gay absence," and, in a passage that later alludes to the conclusion of Altman's book, writes: "Never before in the history of minority groups struggling for recognition and equal treatment has there been an analogous attempt, on the part of any such group, to make itself unidentifiable even as it demands to be recognized" (31–32). In Bersani's analysis of the queer debate, there is a subtle recognition of the complexities of the argument. Even so, for him, it is "not possible to be gay-affirmative . . . if gayness has no specificity" (61). The tensions surrounding this paradox are thus a constant, underlying presence throughout this study and surface at particular moments in discussion of both theoretical and fictional writing. I return to Bersani, for instance, at a later point in this chapter and again in Chapter 5.

As for the fiction I discuss in my core chapters, there is a clear divide between those novels that focus on gayness as a distinct identity and those that minimize its specificity. Thus, *Dancer from the Dance* and *The Swimming-Pool Library* are, we might say, ghetto novels: their prime focus of attention is the gay subculture. If Holleran and Hollinghurst are ambivalent in their attitude to this culture, they nonetheless show a strong sense of identification with it, as well as an urge to record its particularity, its distinctive "feel." They write primarily for a gay readership, and they make the sexuality of their characters central, as if to lay stress on this as the core feature of their identity. In contrast, Leavitt and Cunningham, in *The Lost Language of Cranes* and *A Home at the End of the World,* make only passing reference to the gay subculture. Instead, they examine the lives of a mixture of gay and straight characters, whose experiences are presented as similar, rather than special or unique. These writers, in other words, make themselves available to a wide readership by framing their gay characters in such a way as to weaken the specificity of their sexuality.

Altman, meanwhile, anticipates queer/postmodern debates and the issues of contemporary lesbian and gay culture and politics in other ways. Thus he recognizes the challenge of difference (especially between men and women, and people of different racial and ethnic groups) and highlights the problem in several substantial passages of his book. "The great dilemma that faces the movement," he writes, "is the difficulty of reconciling the individual development of a consciousness among oppressed groups with the task of building a coalition between them" (199). The subsequent history of the movement underlines the perceptiveness of this remark, for in the mid-1970s, with the formation of independent movements, lesbians and gay men effectively parted company, the tensions between and within certain groups evolving into full-blown separatism.[5] Race, too, has been a major issue since the early 1980s, with powerful protests from lesbians and gay men of color about black invisibility in gay public life.

In a sense, the challenge of difference, as Altman implies, leaves the movement again grappling with the paradox of liberation. Liberation, as conceived by Altman and later developers of social constructionist theory, is predicated on the erosion of the very distinctions of identity of the group to be liberated. Altman, representing the radicalism of the Gay Liberation Front as against the conservatism of the Gay Activists' Alliance, is opposed to the concept of "community" as envisaged by the homophile movement, which he sees as indicative of an inward-looking ghetto mentality. Transforming "the pseudo-community of the old gayworld into a sense of real community" (140) means reaching out not only to other oppressed groups in society but to society as a whole, since acceptance of homosexuality will help people "move closer to an acceptance of their intrinsic erotic and polymorphous natures . . . [and thus] ease relations between men and women" (244). If Altman pulls back from this utopianism in his afterword to the 1993 printing of his book (understandably, given the disappointments, the setbacks, the personal and community tragedies of the intervening decades), in the original text he pursues it with a generous and heartwarming lack of apology. Yet, with or without utopianism, the paradox remains: what happens to a movement with irreconcilable aims—with a desire on the one hand to recognize difference, and on the other to eradicate it?

The tensions of these opposed impulses are reflected in gay fiction generally, but surface perhaps most clearly, with regard to the literature examined in this study, in some well-known gay novels of the seventies. Thus, in *Forgetting Elena, Dancer from the Dance,* and *Faggots,* a fascination with gay identity and community collides with an impatient, sickened, and sometimes savage hostility to it. Similarly, elsewhere in gay fiction, a sense of singularity struggles with a sense of group identity. In other words, an assertion of difference, of independence, from the group (whether the gay or wider community) contends with a need to claim identification with it. In *The Family of Max Desir,* for instance, the struggle is enacted in the apparent irreconcilability of the novel's two contrasted modes of writing— the mundane realism of the family story as against the gothic fantasy of Max's personal narrative; and although Ferro attempts to heal the breach in his final chapter, the degree of his success here is open to question. In some gay fiction the tension is signaled in the total assertion of singularity and absolute denial of group identity. This line of fiction runs from *Our Lady of the Flowers,* through *Naked Lunch,* to *Frisk.*

Altman's book, informed by a Marxist Freudianism and inspired by the countercultures of the late 1960s, should also be seen as a precursor of more recent attempts to bring psychoanalysis and Freudian insight into the service of queer and antihomophobic discourse. As both text and afterword make clear, two of its strongest influences are Norman O. Brown and Herbert Marcuse, writers whose work has gone out of fashion. Indeed, as Jeffrey Weeks points out, Altman's own Freudianism was unfashionable in 1971, when the book first appeared in print. In the United States at this time, feminist and gay political voices were being raised against the backdrop of an Americanized school of Freud, which focused on "ego psychology" and "adaptation to social reality" (Fletcher, "Freud and His Uses"

90). Speaking often from bitter personal experience of conformist therapeutic practice, these voices drew attention to "the obvious role played by American Freud in the elaboration of a reactionary sexual ideology both in specialist psychiatric institutions and practices and in the wider culture" (90).[6] More recently, however, there has been attempt to recover Freud for radical sexual politics. Thus, following Juliet Mitchell's attempt in *Psychoanalysis and Feminism* (1974) to open up new feminist perspectives on the Freudian tradition and promote it as a useful tool in the analysis of gender and sexuality, a number of critics in similar fashion have begun to reframe the Freudian input to an understanding of homosexuality and to argue for its positive contribution.[7]

Altman's view of sexuality is thus in broad alignment with that of the radical psychoanalytic tradition and of contemporary queer theory. The essence of this view is its questioning of the idea that we are all unified sexual beings with a fixed sexual identity. This notion is deep-seated. Constituted by ideology, naturalized through cultural reinforcement, and installed at the heart of the homophile movement, it has become still further entrenched through the ethnic model of identity that has characterized lesbian and gay politics since the mid-1970s. Altman, following Brown and Marcuse, questions the fixity and unity of sexual identity by focusing on Freud's belief in "the essentially polymorphous and bisexual needs of the human being" (84). He puts emphasis on the way that Freud's theorization of the unconscious challenges the notion of subjectivity and sexual identity as stable and coherent. Hence, in his pursuit of the Freudian implications, he sees, like Freud, that our basic bisexual nature and polymorphous perversity is fundamentally at odds with our social identity: that beneath our fragile sense of wholeness lurks the danger of our unconscious desires. But if our original sex drive has been repressed, what accounts for this repression? Altman, in addressing this question, offers the need to procreate and the establishment of patriarchal society as primary explanations; but his Marxist-Freudian analysis also leads him to link the process to theories of economic development. He acknowledges, of course, that sexual repression and patriarchy exist in societies that are in no sense capitalist. "Nevertheless," he writes, "it is undoubtedly true that sexual repression was to prove highly functional for the rise of capitalism and industrialization which, at least in its early stages, demanded very considerable repression in the interests of economic development" (87).

## GUY HOCQUENGHEM: POSTSTRUCTURALISM AND REVOLUTIONARY SEXUAL POLITICS

If many of Altman's ideas are self-avowedly tentative, however, a more thorough attempt to combine psychoanalytic and Marxist theory in an examination of homosexuality appeared in the following year with the publication of Guy Hocquenghem's *Homosexual Desire* (1972). The essence of this dense and brilliant polemic is given in its opening line: "The problem is not so much homosexual desire as the fear of homosexuality." This statement clearly relates to the central claim in Mary McIntosh's essay "The Homosexual Role" (1968). Where homosexuality is concerned, McIntosh argues, the wrong question is being asked. Thus, rather than busy ourselves with what causes it, we should give our attention to the problem of why it arouses such hostility. But Hocquenghem takes this argument to new levels of elaboration. Drawing on the work of Gilles Deleuze and Félix Guattari, whose *L'Anti-Oedipe: Capitalisme et Schizophrénie* (1972) was first published in French earlier in the same year, he suggests that there can be no problem of homosexual desire because homosexual desire does not properly speaking exist. Indeed, he argues that the very expression "homosexual desire" is meaningless (with the implication that the very title of his book should be enclosed within quotation marks): that it denotes a merely artificial category, "a fallacy of the imaginary," since desire itself is undifferentiating, "an unbroken and polyvocal flux" (50). Moreover, he quotes from the *Three Essays on the Theory of Sexuality* to show this idea as part of Freud's own subversive position: "It seems probable that the sexual instinct is in the first instance independent of its object" (115). Indeed, he sees Freud's very use of the term "polymorphously perverse" as an expression of his belief that "sex is non-human, and that desire is fundamentally undifferentiated and ignorant of the distinction between homosexuality and heterosexuality" (74). But Freud, he argues, having revealed the impersonal flux of the libido, goes on to organize and entrap it within the guilt-inducing confines of the Oedipus complex: to "[enchain] it as the Oedipal privatisation of the family" (73).

Hence, in Hocquenghem's account, psychoanalysis (particularly as conceived by Freud's followers, but encouraged by tendencies in Freud's own writing) becomes a means of shoring up the family, and by extension the social order, both of which are in danger of disintegration from the effects of capitalism. Indeed, in a phase of history when the family is becoming increasingly deprived of its essential social functions by the ever-expanding threat of capitalist individualization, the Oedipus complex represents "the internalisation of the family institution" (74). It is thus the origin of the anti-homosexual paranoia that Hocquenghem analyzes in the opening chapter of his essay: paranoia that becomes, within his analysis, a symptom of society's repression, and consequent displacement or sublimation, of its own homosexuality. But of course such repression, assailed from within and without, is in constant danger of breakdown, and all efforts to force the contaminated, scapegoated homosexual beyond the pale only serve to install him "at the centre of waking dreams" (52). Society thus fuels its own persecutory delusion, for the more it strives to banish its homosexuality to the margins, the more it ensures the return of that homosexuality to declare its centrality. Or as Hocquenghem so graphically puts it: "The homosexuality which [society] represses and sublimates keeps springing from every pore of the social body" (61).

The relatedness of these ideas to those of our current debates about sexuality is therefore perhaps only too obvious, and lends support to that view of Hocquenghem's essay that sees it as perhaps the first example of what we now call queer theory. The link is clearly established, for example, in Jonathan Dollimore's claim that one dimension of his study *Sexual Dissidence* is to see why "homosexuality is so strangely integral to the selfsame heterosexual cultures which obsessively denounce it" (28). But the central thrust of Hocquenghem's argument is again recalled in Judith Butler's discussion of the way that heterosexuality's act of elaborating itself, its compulsion to repeat, "is evidence that it is perpetually at risk, that is, that it 'knows' its own possibility of becoming undone" ("Imitation" 23). Moreover, his theme of sublimation is extensively explored in Eve Kosofsky Sedgwick's literary study *Epistemology of the Closet,* where the affinity of ideas becomes explicit in the book's proposition that "many of the major nodes of thought and knowledge in twentieth-century Western culture as a whole are structured—indeed, fractured—by a chronic, now endemic crisis of homo/heterosexual definition" (1).

How, then, are Hocquenghem's ideas reflected in the fiction I explore in this study? In many of these novels, fear of homosexuality is signaled by the fact that gay freedom can be achieved only within the confines of the ghetto; and even there, it may need to be sublimated: channeled into aestheticism or artistic expression (as in *Forgetting Elena* and *Dancer from the Dance*), or belief in universal brotherhood and transcendental love (as in *Faggots*). In *The Lost Language of Cranes,* however, David Leavitt explores this theme rather differently in his presentation of Owen and Philip, father and son, both of whom attempt to sublimate their homosexuality in relationships that aspire to (ultimately self-defeating) heterosexual ideals. Again, Hocquenghem's theory of the interdependence of homosexuality and heterosexuality is well illustrated in *The Swimming-Pool Library,* where Will (the vulnerable gay grandson of a homophobic high-court judge) is both representative of the ruling class and its dominant ideology, and also the enemy within. He is the "faultline" in the system that puts it "at risk," that allows the possibility of its "becoming undone."

*Homosexual Desire* is a unique synthesis, however, for as commentators have noted, its theoretical discourse, which draws to a large extent on French poststructuralism, is also energized by a strong gay activist approach, making it, as a result of such combination, perhaps once again the earliest example of its kind. Thus it offers not only an analysis of the Oedipal family and of reproductive sexuality in modern capitalism, but also a revolutionary project of resistance to this power structure through "anti-capitalist and anti-Oedipal struggles" (Weeks, "Preface" 24). Central to this project is Hocquenghem's theory of the sublimated anus, which is the particular focus of Chapter 4 of his book. Our phallocratic society, he declares, is organized in hierarchic obedience to "the great signifier." Indeed, the way our social relations are structured in orderly, pyramidal deference to this despotic organ represents "the triumph of Oedipus" (96). But most important, what results from such phallic investment is the general downgrading, even discounting, of all other forms of sexuality—and, in particular, the privatization of the anus.

Now clearly, for Hocquenghem, this privatization of the anus is deeply bound up with the repression of homosexuality generally, since he also argues that "[homosexuality] primarily means anal homosexuality, sodomy" (98). However, as Jeffrey Weeks points out, this statement is not to be taken literally: Hocquenghem is using the word *anal* here (as elsewhere he uses the word *phallic*) in a symbolic sense. To privatize the anus, for Hocquenghem, is thus to privatize homosexuality. And to privatize homosexuality is to individualize it, to deny it access to the public sphere. Moreover, he argues that the reason anal desire cannot be allowed to emerge socially (in a society based on individual identity, on the boundary between self and other) is that it would involve loss of identity and individual control. It is the phallus, after all, that signifies the difference between the sexes, that dispenses identity and confers status. The anus, on the other hand, does not discriminate between the sexes, and indeed works against such signification, dissolving identity and difference. Consequently, it must be privatized—that, is, allowed to exist only "as something which is socially elevated and individually debased . . . torn between faeces and poetry, between the shameful little secret and the sublimated" (100). The central dynamic of Hocquenghem's revolutionary project is therefore the recovery (or desublimation) of anal desire, as constituting a direct challenge to the private–public division on which our society is based.

How, though, is such recovery to be achieved? Hocquenghem's answer is that anal desire (which, as I have said, becomes, within his system of signifiers, another name for homosexual desire) needs to be what he calls "grouped," the term derived from his suggestion that homosexual relations constitute a "group" mode of relations "as opposed to the usual 'social' mode" (110). "Grouping," in this sense, denies the individualized notion of identity that characterizes the "social" mode of relations: it rejects "the false coherence of the 'molar' self . . . [and leads] us to an experience of the self at the 'molecular' level of our desiring machines" (33). Indeed, group desire of this kind, through its rejection of guilt and sublimation, amounts to a denial of Oedipus and the whole Symbolic Order. It thus replaces the pyramid of phallic hierarchy with a system that resembles a circle, with a mode that is annular. In short, Hocquenghem's concept of homosexual grouping is a challenging and valuable defense of promiscuity, a call for the kind of "sexual communism" that he suggests we can glimpse "in Turkish baths, for example, where homosexual desires are plugged in anonymously, in spite of ever-present fears that the police may be present" (111).

With regard to the fiction I discuss in later chapters of this study, Hocquenghem's concept of homosexual "grouping" and the desublimation of sex is well reflected, as we might expect, in fiction of the 1970s: in *Dancer from the Dance* and *Faggots,* for instance. These novels capture the liberationist moment and its driving idea (realized at various gay venues in New York and San Francisco, and suggested in Hocquenghem's essay) of sex as revolutionary statement. As Edmund White remarks: "Young people now have no idea that our promiscuity then was a form of idealism, that we really did want to find new ways of relating" (Brookes 37).[8] Even Reed Woodhouse, who is unapologetic about "the ghetto's ethic of cheerful hedonism," admits to an attempt at the time to motivate and justify such behavior politically, citing a series of essays in Boston's *Fag Rag,* an early liberationist newspaper (102). Of course, since the coming of AIDS there has been widespread and contentious re-examination of such ideas, with the result that Hocquenghem's revolutionary concept, though still at the center of controversy, is less well reflected in gay fiction of the 1980s and 1990s. Moreover, if novels of the AIDS era do engage with these themes, they tend—as in *The Family of Max Desir* and *The Swimming-Pool Library*—to do so retrospectively.

Hocquenghem's stress on anonymity and decentering, on group rather than individual and social identity, helps to explain why Jonathan Dollimore finds in his writing "the anarchic joy of anti-humanism" (*Sexual Dissidence* 212). Yet his antihumanism, Dollimore argues, is nevertheless based on an essentialist model of desire, and hence it links to that view of sexuality as redemptive—a vision that may now seem "misguided, deluded and deluding" (217), even if, as Dollimore goes on to suggest, we need to temper our denunciation of it with a knowledge of its history. Nor is Jeffrey Weeks uncritical. In his 1978 preface to the first English-language edition of *Homosexual Desire*, he too draws attention to some of the book's limitations. Thus, while generally welcoming Hocquenghem's notion of homosexual "grouping" as a useful challenge to the centrality of reproductive sexuality, he finds that it tends to overstatement. Styles and attitudes born out of reaction to social oppression, he argues, cannot answer to the need of gay people to devise "life-styles and forms of relationship which break away from heterosexist norms" (40).

Again, in his assessment of Hocquenghem's theory of antihomosexual paranoia, Weeks allows that it is cogently argued, but also feels that it leaves too much unaccounted for. First, if we attribute homosexual repression to the perceived threat to the family and the general social order in capitalist economies, how do we explain the partial liberalization of attitudes that has occurred in some of those economies? Second, even if we accept that "homosexual" and "heterosexual" are artificially constructed categories, how do we account for the fact that certain individuals come to identify with the former category rather than the latter? Weeks suggests that Hocquenghem's account of Oedipal processes ignores external (that is, familial, educational, and media-created) pressures, and asks to what extent these affect orientation: to what extent these determine whether an individual "[enters] the symbolic order as a 'homosexual' rather than a 'heterosexual'" (37).

Nevertheless, there is general agreement that *Homosexual Desire*, whatever its shortcomings, has a more than historical significance. Indeed, the

1993 reprinting of the book is itself a declaration of this viewpoint, a declaration confirmed by the decision to reprint, in the same volume, Weeks's preface of 1978, with its concluding remark that "the questions he [Hocquenghem] raises, both implicitly and explicitly, are important now" (45). Jonathan Dollimore makes a similar point: if the book is "situated somewhere before the current repudiation of desire as revolutionary," he writes, "[it is] also too close, too implicated in the present, to be assigned to the past" (*Sexual Dissidence* 212). Moreover, this claim to the book's continuing relevance is, as we might expect, enthusiastically endorsed in Michael Moon's new introduction to the 1993 reprinting. Moon sees the book as a valuable contribution to the theory of homosexuality, and as a rousing document from our radical past, the significance of which extends into the present. "For, over twenty years after its first appearance," he writes, "this book of Hocquenghem's still requires to be read not only as a treatise but also as a manifesto, a powerful incitement to join an intense political struggle whose time has come" (10).

## THEORY AND HISTORY

I have been drawing attention to the continuities between gay liberation theory and contemporary queer/postmodern discourses, but what of the discontinuities? If, in reading the work of the early gay liberationist writers, what surprises us is the extent to which they anticipated our current debates, what we are also forced to recognize are the dramatic changes that have occurred in the three decades that now separate us from the brief life span of the Gay Liberation Front and the literature that emerged from its heady ferment of ideas. Altman touches on some of these changes in his Afterword to *Homosexual* (255–59). Thus he speaks of his overconcern to "connect the gay movement to a general radicalism" (256), a concern that could not have foreseen the future fragmentation of the movement along gender lines and according to differences of race, class, sexual practice, and cultural-political affiliation. Although he sees links between the militancy of gay liberation and the current mood of upfront activism, he also sees, from his vantage point of the 1990s, that a new generation, which "has come to adulthood in the period of AIDS and Reaganism" (257), is unlikely to share his earlier millennial vision of a transformed society, of "a liberated humanity free from constraining normative structures" (Seidman, "Identity" 116). In general, postmodernists do not share the millennialism and vanguardism of liberationist discourse, Stephen Seidman observes; and he characterizes gay liberation theory as "a post-Marxian left discourse that leans in a postmodern direction yet retains much of the modernist legacy" (116).

On the ground, what transpired in the decades after 1969 was not the revolutionary transformation of society envisaged by Altman and other liberationist writers but rather "the vast expansion of the lesbian and gay world" (Weeks, "Introduction" 10). Altman, in his afterword, again puts his finger on a significant aspect of this development in his reference to the commercialization of this world—or of "the male part, at least" (257)— while recognizing that the growth has been more than purely commercial. Consequently, if the aim of the movement, as Altman defines it, is its own demise ("gay liberation will succeed as its raison d'être disappears" [246]), this expansion and consolidation of the lesbian and gay community, through the mobilizing strategy of identity politics, would seem to indicate a move in the wrong direction. But this would be to overlook the resilience of the movement and its adaptability to change, particularly in the definition of terms such as "identity" and "community." The so-called ethnic model of identity among lesbians and gay men, which grew out of Stonewall and quickly established itself, was being forced to face the challenge of diversity and difference from as early as the mid-1970s. Moreover, the realpolitik that in our own time has replaced the utopianism of the early seventies is a movement of struggle, negotiation, and local initiatives, based on recognition of unresolved and perhaps irresolvable tensions.

Whatever the ultimate effect of this resilience and adaptability, there is a sense in which the rapidly expanding lesbian and gay world of the 1970s became the victim of its own success. It is easy to forget that by the early 1980s, as Alan Sinfield puts it, "gayness was becoming quite fashionable" (*Wilde Century* 185). The growth of subcultural organization, community building, and networking, the increased visibility of homosexuality, and the popularity of certain gay (or at least sexually ambiguous) pop/rock performers, such as Boy George, Divine, Frankie Goes to Hollywood, and Bronski Beat, had by this stage produced a level of social tolerance that inclined gay politics toward a social assimilationist program rather than the liberationist ideals of the previous decade. However, such runaway success inevitably provoked a right-wing backlash, a backlash that was suddenly invigorated at this time by the arrival of the AIDS epidemic, following the first diagnosed instances in 1981. Moreover, it is undoubtedly the case that the elaborate expansion of the gay male subculture in the 1970s (and the ideology of sexual experimentation with multiple partners that accompanied it, particularly in the large urban centers of the United States) created the conditions that facilitated the rapid and tragic spread of HIV and AIDS in the gay male community generally.

To return to Sinfield's point, he suggests that by the early 1980s, and before the full impact of AIDS, homosexuality was beginning to gain advantage over heterosexuality as a viable basis for human relations. "The idea was that we were doing better with the sex-and-love questions," he writes, referring specifically to gay men—although, by implication, lesbians are included in that "we" (*Wilde Century* 185). Gay men, he suggests, were perceived as leading patterns of life that avoided the tensions and inequalities of heterosexual relations. Moreover, this perception was justified, he implies, for gay men had indeed evolved ways of combining casual sex with nonmonogamous long-term partnerships, were attempting to liberate themselves from the effects of possessiveness, jealousy, and gendered role-play, knew how to stay friendly with former lovers, and were generally less impeded by barriers of age and class. Thus, "for right-wingers AIDS was a godsend (so to speak). It countermanded, precisely, that alleged gay advantage. It had all been a fantasy, 'the family' should set the limits of important emotional experience, and gays have only 'pretended' families" (185).

Indeed, the effect of AIDS, as Sinfield suggests, was to force lesbians and gay men back again onto a defensive footing, as disparaging or pathologizing religious and medicalized models of homosexuality, which had lost some credibility in the previous decade, were reinstated. Or at least this was one of its effects, since there were many, and some that with hindsight we can only perceive as positive. One such effect was the strengthening of community ties (between gay men, and between gay men and lesbians) that resulted from response to the crisis, a response that also testified to the goodwill, infrastructure, and mobilizing power of the movement. On the other hand, another effect (of both AIDS and backlash) was to reveal the limits of an assimilationist gay political agenda based on minority rights and inclusion. This, in turn, sparked a renewal of radical activism, as well as an urge to develop and promote a theory of sexuality and gay politics in accord with the changed perspective that the AIDS crisis and the ensuing backlash had generated.[9]

Of course, the beginnings of such theory already existed; and not only, as we have seen, in the writings of Altman and Hocquenghem, but also in the pioneering sociology of Mary McIntosh, Michel Foucault, Mario Mieli, Jeffrey Weeks, and Ken Plummer. This theory, like sociology in general, begins from a constructionist understanding and has a denaturalizing intent. In other words, it reframes the issue of homosexuality by asking a new and challenging set of questions about it. Where formerly homosexuality had been seen as the natural condition of a social minority, these writers approach it as an ideological construct, the meaning of which is historically and culturally determined. This idea is inscribed in the very title of Plummer's book, *The Making of the Modern Homosexual*, with its implication that our modern concept of "the homosexual" is a fabrication, a product—and furthermore a product specifically of our time and culture, of modernity. It grows out of Mary McIntosh's aforementioned remark that the failure of successive generations of medical researchers to locate the natural origins of homosexuality results from the fact that "the wrong question has been asked." Moreover, it argues, as she does, that this question is linked to the conception of homosexuality as a condition, a conception that "[operates] as a form of social control in a society in which homosexuality is condemned" (34).

## QUEER THEORY

When, in the 1990s, such questioning, prodded still further by French poststructuralism and Lacanian psychoanalysis, developed into a strain of social constructionist thinking called "queer theory," it not only challenged mainstream heterosexual thinking, it also shook the foundations of mainstream gay culture and politics. But why such impact? After all, if the central challenge of queer theory is its questioning of the assumption of a unified homosexual identity, this challenge, as we have seen, had existed since the late 1960s. The answer is that the earlier challenge was on the whole quiet and modest (McIntosh), embryonic in conception and form (Altman), or located in a distinctly European philosophical tradition and inspired by currently unfashionable and mistrusted French psychoanalytic theories (Hocquenghem). By the early 1990s, on the other hand, this same challenge, strengthened by the now widely discussed writings of Michel Foucault, had become seemingly irresistible. Poststructuralism and psychoanalysis were now at the center of English-language debates about sexuality. Moreover, these changes were occurring against the background of a culture and politics still reeling from the convulsive effects of the AIDS disaster. A large measure of the impact of queer theory is thus attributable to the dramatically different context from which it emerged.

The paradox of queer theory resides and resounds in its very name. Thus it suggests a move both to reclaim the word *queer* and to employ it as a term beyond reclamation: to give positive resonance to a label of disparagement and abuse, while at the same time declaring its resistance to rehabilitation, its marginality to all forms of mainstream culture. Ambiguity, however, is central to queer's self-identity; and furthermore it promotes such indeterminacy as a strength. Speaking of her willingness to appear at political events under the sign of lesbian, Judith Butler, whose *Gender Trouble* (1990) is arguably the single most influential book in the emergence of queer theory, writes: "but . . . I would like to have it permanently unclear what precisely that sign means" ("Imitation" 14). The remark indicates the main thrust of queer theory and of her own work in particular: it underwrites that notion of identity—common to both—as existing in time rather than space, as a performative act of becoming rather than a state of being. Butler's work situates itself within the discourse of feminism; nevertheless, its insights into the formation of genderized identities within a regulatory construct that privileges heterosexuality have had an equally penetrating effect on attempts to understand lesbian and gay subject positions.[10] Thus, the following summing-up of the theory of performativity that her book elaborates has a clear relevance to identity formation in general: "Gender is the repeated stylization of the body, a set of repeated acts within a highly regulatory frame that congeal over time to produce the appearance of substance, of a natural sort of being" (*Gender Trouble* 33).

How does the fiction I examine in this study reflect queer notions of sexual identity? The first thing to say is that, to some extent in all this fiction, the identities of the gay characters are presented as dependent on social construction and historical contingency. The unnamed, amnesiac narrator of *Forgetting Elena,* for instance, can discover his identity only through careful scrutiny of the social and historical circumstances in which he finds himself. Again, Malone in *Dancer* and Fred Lemish in *Faggots* are characters constituted by the particular social scene and historical moment in which they are fictionally "framed." Even Philip, in *The Lost Language of Cranes,* is presented as having an identity produced by a particular ideological moment: post-Stonewall gay identity politics. Furthermore, this is an identity that Edmund White, in his short story "An Oracle," puts into historical perspective, thus foregrounding its constructedness. But the queer notion of homosexuality as dangerous, fluid, and marginal/central to mainstream culture is perhaps best reflected in *The Swimming-Pool Library, Cabal, Lost Souls,* and *Frisk.* In these novels, indeterminacy rules: our grasp of who the characters are—particularly in terms of their sexuality—is, in the Judith Butler sense, "permanently unclear."[11]

Queer theory has been the conceptual strain of a queer nexus of developments—a queer movement—in lesbian and gay culture and politics since the early 1990s. In the United States, the aforementioned renewal of radical activism was initially spearheaded by the groups ACT UP and Queer Nation. If the immediate provocation, particularly in the case of ACT UP, was the public neglect of AIDS, the more general stimulus was the resurgence of belief in the revolutionary potential of dissident sexuality; and of course this belief entailed a corresponding condemnation of assimilationist politics and complacent lesbian and gay accommodation to bourgeois ways of life.[12] I mentioned earlier that mainstream gay politics and culture was being forced to confront the challenge of difference from as early as the mid-1970s. In respect of racial difference, this challenge gathered strength during the 1980s with the publication of a number of personal narrative testimonies.[13] At the same time an equally powerful challenge was being mounted against the categories "lesbian" and "gay" by people of diverse experiences and political-sexual persuasions, for whom these groupings had become a regulating and restrictive (rather than liberating) disciplinary force.[14]

One such challenge came from women who were critical of what they saw as the attempt by traditional lesbian feminists to impose their "spiritualized" understanding of female sexuality on women in general.[15] By the late 1980s this challenge had become a general protest by both male and female sex rebels—sadomasochists, butch-fems, transvestites, drag queens, and other people of "deviant" sexuality—about the stifling of their sexual practices and desires by the straitjacket of assimilationist identity politics. Bisexual people—previously vilified by many people on both sides of the gay–straight divide for their alleged promiscuity, treachery, immaturity, and cowardice, and as carriers of AIDS—began to speak out loud and clear in their own defense. Yet even *this* confounding of the binary was not enough to accommodate the growing recognition of human sexuality as infinitely various. As Susie Bright, admirably summing up the mood of this queer moment, puts it: "It's preposterous to ask sexual beings to stuff ourselves into the rapidly imploding social categories of straight or gay or bi, as if we could plot our sexual behaviour on a conscientious, predictable, curve" (Garber 83).

## LONG-STANDING AND PROLIFERATING CONFLICTS

The developments outlined above—the continuing catastrophe of AIDS, the right-wing backlash, the renewed activism, the queer challenge, the challenge of difference—now constituted a general "crisis" to which there were widely differing responses. Indeed, the age-old and ever-present quarrel between reformists and radicals now flared up once again. The essence of the reformist position, as has been commonly observed, is its self-evident belief in the power of reason. Based on the assumption that mainstream attitudes to homosexuality are simply irrational, it holds that knowledge and enlightenment will bring acceptance. "[It] only needs a few more of us to come out," writes Alan Sinfield, paraphrasing the reformist argument, "so that the nervous among our compatriots can see we aren't so dreadful, and then everyone will live and let live; sexuality will become unimportant" (*Wilde Century* 177). For queer radicals, on the other hand, this is a misreading of mainstream society, which quite rightly recognizes in homosexuality a threat to its basic values and structures, and which therefore develops attitudes of hostility toward it that are not unreasonable or paranoid. In short, the threat is real, the radicals claim, and a good thing too: mainstream assumptions need to be challenged; society needs to be transformed.

The transformation of society is a concept that takes us back to the early gay liberationists with whom I began. Indeed, as this study should make clear, the quarrel between radicals and reformists is, and always has been, an energising presence in gay politics and culture, although the strength and popularity of each group relative to the other has shifted with change of circumstance. Thus, in the early 1970s, with homosexual organization still at an early stage of development, the dominant voices, like Altman's, were radical. By the end of the decade, however, in a more tolerant climate and from the different basis of a much-strengthened subculture, the mood had swung toward reform and away from full-scale radical social change. Then, in the late 1980s, in the midst of a devastating epidemic and a much less generous climate, radicalism returned, although not of course without opposition, so that in the somewhat calmer waters of the 1990s, following the advances in medical understanding of the disease and the corresponding reduction of hostility in public attitudes, voices were once again being raised in favor of moderation and reform.

Two such voices can be heard in a couple of widely-sold and much-discussed books of the 1990s—Bruce Bawer's *A Place at the Table* (1994) and Andrew Sullivan's *Virtually Normal* (1995)—the very titles of which are a clear indication of the assimilationism they argue for. Bawer distinguishes between what he calls "subculture-oriented gays" and "mainstream gays" (35), the latter group being part of general (rather than gay) mainstream society; and he clearly identifies with this latter group. These gays, raised in middle-class homes, "want to spend their lives in similar homes and neighborhoods, and don't see why being gay should prevent them from doing so" (35). There is an echo of this in the introduction to *The Penguin Book of Gay Short Stories* (1994), where David Leavitt writes of wanting to be openly gay without the need to cut himself off from "the totality of the world I'd grown up in," of the attendant risk of doing himself "real psychic violence," of the possibility of celebrating identity "without having to move into a gulag" (xxii). Moreover, Philip, Leavitt's protagonist in *The Lost Language of Cranes,* is not a subculture-oriented gay, and his coming-out story very much includes his middle-class parents, Owen and Rose. Indeed, it has been argued that Rose, who learns in the course of the narrative that both her son and her husband are gay, is the emotional center of the novel (Woodhouse 145–55). She is certainly the most vulnerable of these three characters, and her plight dominates much of the action. The attentions of the novel are thus generally directed at the concerns of a mainstream readership, and away from those of the subculture.

Bawer, while conceding his indebtedness to the gay subculture, is generally critical of it. In this way he is close to the queer radicals, who are also critical of it and sometimes for similar reasons. Like them, he protests against the tendency of the subculture to become a regulatory and disciplinary force, and excoriates the narrowness of its constituency and its failure to represent him. He writes of the frustration of "being made to feel . . . that one must think and dress and act in a certain way . . . have certain artistic interests and political views and a certain sense of humor, and that, if one does not, one is a traitor to one's kind" (43). It is important to stress, however, that Bawer and the queer radicals reach their critical standpoints from quite different bases. After all, Bawer's concern here is not so much with loss of individuality (he seems to have no objection to the regulatory and disciplinary power of the heterosexual mainstream) as with attachment to an oppositional political grouping. In other words, he approves of identity politics, so long as they promote an identity he approves of. The concern of the queer radicals, on the other hand, is to question the very notion of "identity," both as a means to lay bear its constructedness and its use as a tool of regulatory regimes, and as a strategy to undercut the self-identity of dominant ideology.

Bawer hides his assimilationism—and hence his own regulatory tendency—behind a declared belief in diversity. He writes: "It [the gay subculture] believes there are correct and incorrect ways of being gay" (38). But so does Bawer—indeed, spelling out his own view of the correct way to be gay is the entire purpose of his book. When he speaks of "a spectrum of gay 'lifestyles'" (33) and attempts to give some indication of its range, we are left in no doubt as to which end of the spectrum wins his approval. Thus he describes a gay couple, with a lifestyle "indistinguishable from that of most heterosexual couples," whom most people "would not even recognize as gay" (34); and given his earlier characterization of himself as a "neocon-servative intellectual" and "monogamous, church-going Christian" (25), these remarks suggest that the very existence of gay men at the other end of the spectrum—men whose "manner of dress would probably draw stares on the main street of the average American town or city" (34)—is, for him, a matter of regret.

No doubt he would retort that this is not what troubles him, but rather that the subculture is representative of only one lifestyle, and one very differ-ent from his own and that of most "mainstream gays." But, as Alan Sinfield has argued, this is to misread the subculture, which has a much wider con-stituency than he thinks. Bawer characterizes the subculture as the haunt of radicals: his composite "subcultural gay" is a man whom most Americans would consider "aggressively non-conformist . . . uncomfortably left-wing" (34). Les/bi/gay people, however, "manifest the same range of political atti-tudes as straight people," Sinfield remarks (*Gay and After* 114).

Moreover, in speaking of himself as a spokesperson for what he calls the "silent majority" of homosexuals, who "tend not to consider [themselves] 'members' of anything" (26), Bawer misjudges that majority, for whom he and the subculturalists are much closer than he supposes. "Both Bawer and Queer Nation belong to the privileged upper tenth of the gay com-munity," observes John Weir, who implicitly objects to Bawer's use of the term "mainstream" ("Going In" 32). For him, the gay mainstream is a sub-merged, amorphous group beyond the recognition of urban-based arbiters of gay culture and politics. Weir no longer calls himself gay, because for him the term has come to signify the blindness to class and race differences that springs from a position of privilege. For him, the real silent majority of gay men, contrary to what Bawer imagines, "are poor, provincial and clos-eted, in the Marines, or at home with Mom and Dad and *Reader's Digest*" (Sinfield, *Gay and After* 115).

Weir is thought-provoking and indeed provocative in his suggestion that subcultural gays, anti-subcultural gays, and queer radicals are all assimi-lationist at heart and hence fundamentally alike, any differences between them being a matter of "style, not ideology" (32). Moreover, his remarks are in rough accord with a strain of criticism in contemporary theoretical writ-ing that takes issue with the spurious radicalism of some kinds of academic and metropolitan sexual politics—indeed, that sees this "radicalism" as both dishonest and, contrary to its tone and image, deeply conformist. Leo Bersani, for instance, has frequently pointed out that radical sex does not necessarily produce radical politics: that, on the whole, gay men, as he puts it, "are no less socially ambitious, and, more often than we like to think, no less reactionary and racist than heterosexuals" ("Rectum" 205). Showing a brave willingness to confront some of the myths of gay activist rhetoric, he argues that the lesbian and gay community is now strong enough to be able to dispense with the strategic necessity of telling lies about itself. Jonathan Dollimore is equally critical of the stress on gay political conformity and of the power of what he calls "the gay/academic thought police" (*Sex, Literature and Censorship* 6). He remarks that too much attention to political correctness leads to conferences where speakers, for fear of giving offense, have very little of significance to say: "Instead they tell the audience what it wants to hear in the desperate hope of becoming its favourites, or at least of avoiding the dreaded reproach of discrimination-by-omission" (6). The "radicalism" of such politics, Bersani and Dollimore suggest, is skin-deep, more concerned with conformity than confrontation, and hence (to return to Weir) more a question of style than ideology.

Will Beckwith, the narrator of *The Swimming-Pool Library,* is a character who vividly exemplifies Bersani's point that radical sex does not necessarily produce radical politics. Indeed, the novel suggests a determined attempt by Hollinghurst to challenge some of the very myths that Bersani confronts in his essay—or, as the latter calls them, the "lies" we have been telling about ourselves: "lies whose strategic value I fully understand, but which the AIDS crisis has rendered obsolescent" ("Rectum" 206). Will's social advantage as a wealthy, white, upper-class male is compromised only by his sexuality. But what he learns to some discomfort in the course of the novel is the degree to which he is prepared to compromise the expression of his sexuality in the maintenance of that advantage. His sexual relations are tolerable, he finds, provided they do not threaten the patriarchal power structure—or, better still, are used in the service of that structure. Moreover, the novel shows that the kinds of sexual relations he enjoys are determined by the reactionary, sexist, and racist attitudes of his class. Will is attracted to power: to the exercise of it, and to those who wield it.

## Anti-Gay

The essay from which the above-quoted remarks of John Weir are taken is one of a collection, edited by Mark Simpson, called *Anti-Gay* (1996). As deliberately provocative as its title suggests, this collection, when it first appeared, aroused exactly the storm of controversy it intended. Presenting itself as an antidote to the assimilationism of Bawer and Sullivan, *Anti-Gay* attacks, among other things, the repackaging of homosexuality as "a traditional family value" (26). The general complaint of the contributors, however, is that gay culture and politics have become stultifying; such clinging to the middle ground, they imply, inevitably leads to mediocrity and suspension of the critical faculties. Yet the book is in no sense a queer manifesto. Indeed, in his preface, Simpson denies that the book is a manifesto of any kind. Instead, he offers it as the beginnings of "a new dialectic," an "anti-thesis" to "the awful gay thesis that we appear to be trapped in right now" (xix). The Queer movement, in its early days, was perhaps part of this new dialectic, Simpson argues, but unfortunately its moment quickly passed. Initially, he claims, it did pose a threat to both gay and straight mainstream—especially through its challenge to the gay–straight divide—but then almost immediately it became assimilated by both. Gay, in short, took from queer "what it wanted and disregarded and suppressed the threatening stuff" (xvi). *Anti-Gay,* then, as its title implies and as Simpson confirms, is antigay rather than queer, a stance unchanged by the fact that two of its contributors, Lisa Power and Peter Tatchell, argue *for* gay, while nevertheless retaining the right to be self-critical.

Simpson's preface to the book, as this account already suggests, preempts certain lines of criticism by establishing clear boundaries and stating the limits of its ambition: it is not a manifesto; it does not pretend to a greater inclusiveness than gay; it does not promise to be anything except a "collection of malodorous essays by various disgruntled non-heterosexuals" (xix). It might therefore seem superfluous to complain of the book as a whole that it lacks coherence; that it demonstrates exactly the same kind of concern with style over ideology that Weir complains of; that its tone is often sour and bitchy rather than constructively critical; and that in general it is clearer about what it is against than what it is for. Nevertheless, it is not inappropriate to take issue with the main thrust of its critique, nor with the particular arguments of its various contributors. Thus Alan Sinfield has responded forcefully to its central claim that gay culture is mindless, uniform, and trivial. He argues that the contributors to *Anti-Gay* are deliberately taking this narrow view in order to be provocative. In fact, he observes, the gay subculture is made up of people as diverse as those that make up straight culture; indeed, the two are "shaped broadly by the [same] patterns of gender, class, race, age and education" (*Gay and After* 16). And this is surely a fair point: if mindlessness, uniformity, and triviality are the most publicized aspects of the gay subculture, then that is because these aspects have mass appeal and hence attract publicity.

Although *Anti-Gay* is not a queer manifesto—and indeed, as we have seen, contains writing that takes a critical view of queer radicalism—there are elements of the queer critique in it. Thus the book puts its main weight on the challenge of difference and diversity; on bisexuality's threat to the gay–straight paradigm and the bigotry it provokes; and on transgression, viewed as an exhilarating, anarchic, purely oppositional rather than teleological experience. Simpson, for instance, writes of the initially quite liberating effect of "[the] strong strain of punkish transgression running through queer" (xv); and Toby Manning urges all those who are sick of the official mediocrity of the gay world to immerse themselves in the alternative of a transgressive culture that "operates outside the mainstream's rules, jettisons its rationales, and rejects its bourgeois morality, as part of a broader, oppositional movement of outsiders" (109). Manning offers Rimbaud, Genet, Burroughs, and Dennis Cooper as key figures here, but insists that transgressive culture is not just literary: there is also film (Fassbinder, Jarman), the visual arts (Mapplethorpe, Bacon), and music (Velvet Underground, Patti Smith), as well as the punk subculture of "queercore" bands, fanzines, queerzines, and queer filmmakers (108–15).

The problem with the book, however—a problem impossible to overlook, even if some of the contributors try to preempt such criticism by open admission of the limitation—is that its transgressive stance, as already suggested, is too often a matter of gesture. Indeed, Elizabeth Wilson would take this critique to a deeper level of argument. She suggests that transgression is fundamentally, and therefore always, gestural: that it is rooted in "a desire to shock" and hence "can only be a tactic, never a total politics" (110, 116). Wilson is not an assimilationist: our watchword should be "transformation," she maintains, not "transgression" (116). Nevertheless, her argument, as we might expect, does not appeal to those committed to gesture, outrage, or revolutionary absolutism—or even to those who are simply impatient with the politics of compromise and gradualism.[16] Wilson does not reject transgression out of hand: she concedes that gesture and aesthetic forms of protest have a part to play, provided they do not become a substitute for politics. The role of transgression is to insist that "we are there, that we exist," she argues; but when detached from "some idea of how society ought to be," it becomes merely self-referential, a goad to evermore shocking extremes of behavior, leading "eventually to entropy" (116).

Wilson's argument has considerable force, and Manning comes close to admitting its validity when he allows that transgressive cultural strategies could be dismissed as "individualistic and no more than gestural, doomed to remain on the margins, unable to effect real change" (114), especially since he fails to come up with any strong argument to counter this kind of dismissal. Moreover, his point that "many of the visible signifiers of queer (nipple rings, tattoos and punk styles)" have become fashion accessories and thus "stripped of their original meaning" (115), seems to invest those signifiers with a lost meaning beyond gesture, while offering no counterclaim to the possible objection that they were never anything but fashion accessories from the start. Nevertheless, queer, he insists, has been neutralized, and hence "[a] new term is badly needed for the kind of genuinely radical transgressive culture" (115) that he wishes to promote. But the problem is that he fails to make that culture actual in his writing, to say what in practice it might be; and his failure here is symptomatic of the general failure of *Anti-Gay* to propose viable alternatives to the current "gay thesis." Indeed, his call for a new term to replace "gay" and "queer" seems to bear out Wilson's point that transgression "can define no final goal," being rather "a process of continuously shifting boundaries" (110).

How can transgression get beyond its tendency to be limited by that which it would transgress? How can it avoid entrapment in repetition and circularity, break free from its habit of biting its own tail? In addressing this problem Alan Sinfield echoes a point that Elizabeth Wilson makes in her essay: that transgression is concerned with defining difference and separation, rather than demanding inclusion. "[The] transgressor claims some kind of intensity of experience from which the mainstream of society is cut off," she writes, and goes on to suggest that the transgressive impulse is perhaps therefore "ultimately élitist" (111). Sinfield is clearly nagged by similar doubts. "The ineluctable problem with transgression as an idea," he writes, "is that it is individualist and voluntarist; too closely allied to the romantic gesture out of an exalted, solitary engagement within the profoundly troubled self" (*Gay and After* 142). Like Wilson, Sinfield is bothered by the thought that transgression can define no final goal, that its process of revolt is potentially endless. Indeed, his questioning of that process is summed up in his very chapter heading: "How transgressive do we want to be?" (129–45). Moreover, his argument suggests that he too sees transgression as a tactic rather than a total politics, a tactic to be used "against the straightgeist, the State and capital, not each other" (144). The role of transgression, he implies, is bound up with its relationship to fantasy: fantasy exists, and within the world of fantasy may be given free rein; but in the world of sociality its expression must be negotiated and contained; it should not "determine our socio-sexual relations" (144). Of course, as he recognizes, such negotiation could be seen as a negation of queer sexuality; he, however, prefers to view it as a channeling of antisocial impulses "into responsible subcultural routines" (144).

The fictional exploration of transgressive ideas through fantasy is well illustrated in many of the novels I discuss in this study. Indeed, my core chapters suggest a line running from *The Picture of Dorian Gray*, through *Our Lady of the Flowers* and *Naked Lunch*, to *Cabal, Lost Souls*, and *Frisk*. Robert Ferro's *The Family of Max Desir* is rather different, however. Occupying an intermediate position between social realism and transgressive fantasy, this is the novel that perhaps best illustrates Sinfield's idea of negotiation and containment. Thus, in those parts of the novel that explore Max's secret "desire," fantasy is indeed allowed free rein; but in the strand of narrative representing social reality, these impulses are channeled into social responsibility. In other words, the novel makes a clear distinction between fantasy and reality, while exploring the interplay between them. *Frisk* explores this interplay too, but is much more disturbing. Here, Cooper plays a game with the reader, deliberately blurring the distinction between fantasy and reality, and asking the question, "What *is* the relationship between the world of mundane respectability and that of our most violent anti-social impulses?" *Frisk* is a metafiction: a novel about fictionality, and what the stories we tell each other through fiction mean.

## LEO BERSANI

The focus of Sinfield's critique of transgression is given in the subtitle of his chapter, "What *about* Genet?"—a chapter that he offers as an attempt to confront a subcultural myth that he feels gay men have neglected. His quarrel is not only with Genet but also with Leo Bersani, whose admiration for Genet he wishes to challenge. As I give a fairly lengthy account of this dialectic in Chapter 5 of this study, I shall confine myself here to a brief overview of Bersani's position, as given in his essay "Is the Rectum a Grave?" (1991) and his book *Homos* (1995). Bersani is an antiassimilationist, who views queer theory's reformulation of traditional notions of sexual identity as a development to be "both welcomed and resisted" (*Homos* 2). It was inevitable, he suggests, that the attempt to fit diverse human subjects into a clearly defined homo–hetero dyad would eventually reveal itself as "inherently a disciplinary project" and hence "become suspect" (3). He nevertheless insists that resistance to such formulation can be effective only if the resisting subject retains some kind of specificity; attempts to "[play] subversively with normative identities" may otherwise have "assimilative rather than subversive consequences" (5). In short, lesbians and gay men, in rejecting the whole concept of identity, are risking annihilation through collusion with "the homophobic project" that wants to erase them (42).

Once again we are brought back to the disturbing paradox of gay liberation: to the tension inherent in the notion of the disappearing homosexual, and to how keenly Altman in 1971 anticipated contemporary debate. I remarked earlier that Altman's vision of "the end of the homosexual" has to be kept distinct from the social assimilation that the homophile movement saw as its ultimate goal. For homophiles, "the end of the homosexual" meant absorption into the status quo; for Altman it means the end of a world in which differences matter. For homophiles, it was homosexuals who had to accommodate themselves to society; for Altman, it is society that has to change in order to accommodate homosexuality. Bersani's response to the paradox, on the other hand, is to reject all forms of accommodation. In his account, homophile, liberationist, and queer strategies all ultimately reduce to the same abject plea for tolerance. For him, the disappearance of the homosexual, whether the result of a reformist or radical erasure of identity, is rooted in "our anxiety to convince straight society that . . . we can be, like you, good soldiers, good parents and good citizens" (42).

Bersani's antiassimilationism requires a radical "redefinition of sociality" (7)—indeed, a redefinition so radical that it contradicts the very notion of sociality, since it posits a way of relating that seeks to "bypass the social" (179), to "[erase] cultural relationality itself" (153). Sociality, as conventionally understood, is founded on a system of differences, against which Bersani sets the radical identity of homo-ness (sameness). Beneath our artificially created social identities, he suggests, "[we humans] exist . . . in a vast network of *near-sameness*" (146). In other words, in a sense and at a level that we might call racial, we correspond to each other, even if the correspondence is not strictly accurate. Through fear of otherness, however, we exaggerate our differences in heteroized social identities, while at the same time nurturing "a hopeless dream of eliminating difference entirely" (146). Thus the disruptive sense of sameness that Bersani offers as an alternative to existing forms of identity politics rejects "heteroized sociality" (7) in favor of a depersonalized sense of "shared being" (147). But how, in the real world, would such radical identity be expressed? Bersani seems unclear. Instead, he turns to literature, and in the final, climactic chapter of his book explores the anticommunitarian impulse and gay outlaw dynamic that informs the concept through an examination of writings by Gide, Proust, and Genet.

There is a link between Bersani's concept of radical sameness and the ideas he puts forward in his essay "Is the Rectum a Grave?" This is the pernicious effect of social identity, which, he claims, idealizes and romanticizes our view of sex. Thus, in the essay, he attacks what he calls "the redemptive sex project," which is the tendency he sees in much contemporary discourse (he instances not only Foucault, Weeks, and Watney, but also the prominent lesbian proponents of S/M sex, Gayle Rubin and Pat Califia) to deny sex as we know it; to render it anodyne; to present it as "less disturbing, less socially abrasive, less violent, more respectful of 'personhood' than it has been in male-dominated, phallocentric culture" (215). Although strongly opposed to the antipornography project of Catherine MacKinnon and Andrea Dworkin, he gives them credit for at least having had the courage "to be explicit about the profound *moral revulsion* with sex that inspires the entire [redemptive sex] project" (215).

We do not need to redeem sex, he argues; rather, we need to see and value it for what it is: "anticommunal, antiegalitarian, antinurturing, antiloving" (215). If social identity and sexual pleasure have become almost indissociable, we must nevertheless make the attempt to dissociate them. This means changing the way we choose to enjoy sex. Thus, if the effects of male power translate sexually into "relations of mastery and subordination" (216), we must abandon this phallocentrism and ego-based struggle, along with the temptation to deny "the *value* of powerlessness in both men and women" (217). Powerlessness, in the sense Bersani intends here, is not a temporary and shallow self-experiment, but rather a radical, ecstatically painful and exuberant discarding of the self, a profound self-shattering that is also intensely antirelational. It pertains, he suggests, not only to Freud's speculation, especially in *Three Essays on the Theory of Sexuality,* that the supreme moment of sexual pleasure erases the object of desire, but also to its even more radical corollary that the experience entails "a shattering of the psychic structures themselves that are the precondition for the very establishment of a relation to others" (217).

I commented earlier in this chapter on the way Bersani's exploration of the disintegrating effect of sexual pleasure—as Jonathan Dollimore points out (*Sexual Dissidence* 209)—shares and extends the insights of Hocquenghem's *Homosexual Desire*. Like Hocquenghem, Bersani is concerned to desublimate sex, to confront the lies we tell about it, and the attempt to romanticize it. His critique of "the pastoralizing, the idealizing, the redemptive project" (221) links up with Hocquenghem's sardonic commentary on "the triumph of Oedipus" (*Homosexual Desire* 96). In his effort to account for the extremes of hostility toward gay men that the AIDS epidemic has incited, he focuses on the way that sex, through the very process of sublimation, becomes a power struggle. Thus, for him, as for Hocquenghem, it is the exalted self, the civilized ego, which creates the sex war of oedipalized rivalry and competitive jealousy. He, too, sees our society as dominated by the rule of the phallus, and argues, in a polemic that closely resembles Hocquenghem's, that gay men should eschew the masculine ideal that glorifies sex-as-power, and that makes "of the inevitable play of thrusts and relinquishments in sex an argument for the natural authority of one sex over another" ("Rectum" 218).

So, in respect of identity, what kind of change is Bersani calling for? This, I have to say, is not easily stated. His challenge to traditional notions of gay identity is accompanied by a warning against the wholesale rejection of identity. But is it clear what kind of alternative he is offering? As I have said, his notion of radical homo-ness is explored in the final chapter of his book through the work of writers who, in his own words, "are drawn to the *anticommunitarian* impulses they discover in homosexual desire" (*Homos* 7 emphasis in original). The communitarian impulses that drive the politicized lesbian and gay community, he argues, have left that community imprisoned, oppressed, and devalued in a social structure based on a hierarchized system of differences (53). His alternative is an identity based on a notion of gayness (or homo-ness) as inherently disruptive. This would be a force "not limited to the modest goals of tolerance for diverse lifestyles, but in fact mandating the politically unacceptable and politically indispensable choice of an outlaw existence" (76). He stresses that he is not urging a return to "immobilizing definitions of identity": specificity of this kind, he insists, need not commit us to a notion of "a homosexual essence" (76); indeed, the disruptive character of such identity will be positively enhanced by its very lack of fixity.

Nevertheless, what is striking here is the closeness of Bersani's concept of radical homo-ness to the notion of identity as formulated by certain queer theorists. Thus, despite all his misgivings about queer theory's questioning of gay specificity, he too sees value, as a basis for effective political strategy, in the disruptiveness of an unfixed identity. Indeed, his suggestion that resistance and subversion are best found in the "indeterminateness," "mobility," and "ambiguities of being gay" (76) shows a clear link to Judith Butler's remark that "[the] deconstruction of identity is not the deconstruction of politics; rather it establishes as political the very terms through which identity is articulated" (*Gender Trouble* 148). Furthermore,

Bersani's general opposition to traditional notions of identity and assimilationist politics is reflected in Michael Warner's observation that the distinguishing mark of queer theory is its rejection of "a minoritizing logic of toleration or simple political interest-representation in favor of a more thorough resistance to regimes of the normal" (Warner xxvi).

Finally, how are Bersani's ideas reflected in the fiction I discuss in later chapters? Actually, I have already indicated some of the ways in my earlier discussion of Hocquenghem's ideas, which so closely resemble Bersani's. But I should like to add to these some comments about Edmund White's short story "An Oracle," a story that explores the link between sexuality and social identity. The central character here is Ray, who welcomes the offer of a holiday in Crete as a chance to reorient himself after the death from AIDS of his long-term partner, George. In his encounter with Marco, the Greek youth with whom he falls "in love," Ray experiences a profound self-shattering, a psychic dissolution similar to that suggested by Bersani in the passages quoted above. Ray's "civilized" ego here receives a salutary blow, for in returning the gift Ray offers him, Marco punctures the dream Ray has been nurturing of idealized "love" between them, based on the pattern (although with Ray now in the dominant role) of his unequal, power-based relationship with George. The story leaves us with a sense that the encounter with Marco has changed Ray permanently, that he has finally shaken off the influence of George, and is now poised on the brink of regeneration, having glimpsed the value of a new kind of intimacy between men—an intimacy uncontaminated by the power-driven distortions and sublimating tendencies of social identity. I return to this story in Chapter 6.

## ALAN SINFIELD: *GAY AND AFTER*

I began this chapter with "the question of identity," which Dennis Altman sees as the central concern of his book *Homosexual: Oppression and Liberation*, and which Jeffrey Weeks claims "has also been the central concern of all subsequent lesbian and gay literature and politics." Moreover, as if to underline Weeks's claim, it has clearly been the focus of this chapter generally. I therefore propose to end it with a consideration of Alan Sinfield's engagement with the question, as given in his book *Gay and After* (1998), one of the most thoughtful appraisals of the current situation in the wake of recent challenges to the concept of "gay identity."

Sinfield accords with Bersani in at least one major respect: he too sees a threat to gay-affirmativeness in the loss of gay specificity. Even if we allow that categories such as "gay," "lesbian," and "heterosexual" do not demarcate *essential* differences, he argues, we can nevertheless not escape the fact that they do demarcate "differences that our societies find necessary in their current formations" (*Gay and After* 190). Like Bersani, he is concerned by the general tendency of discourse about sexuality to become increasingly detached from the social and political realities of life. He insists that we must engage with current formations, even as we challenge them, since to avoid what they represent is to retreat into abstraction and political ineffectiveness. In other words, we must bear in mind what these formations mean in terms of the scope for our lives: "for to write as though cultural categories were a semiotic game, without location in the actual structures which make some people powerful and others weak, some rich and others poor, some legitimate and others shameful, is to attempt a merely abstract, and conservative, exercise" (190).

Where Sinfield and Bersani part company is in their view of sexual dissidence. Thus Sinfield is clearly disturbed by Bersani's view of the homosexual "role" (to use Mary McIntosh's word) as one of permanent opposition and outlawry, of banishment from "genial human society" (129) and "everyday amiability" (142). Where Bersani sees sexual dissidence as a force that operates beyond, outside, and *against* social identity, Sinfield argues that we must stage such revolt from within and *on behalf of* the social. Hence he writes that he wants to "reassert the general potential of political action" (142). For if we cannot ignore the dark forces in each one of us, he implies, it is dangerous and self-deceptive to invoke them as a viable substitute for the difficulties of political confrontation and negotiation. Indeed, he suggests that we need to recognise these dark forces for what they are: fascistic impulses to which many people, and perhaps all of us, are drawn. In this respect, his position is close to that of Elizabeth Wilson, who also writes about the trangressive, homoerotic appeal of fascism (114). To be fair, Bersani recognizes the link too: "social revolt," he writes, "is doomed to repeat the oppressive conditions that provoked the revolt" (*Homos* 172). But, as Sinfield points out, Bersani's way of avoiding the problem is through a rejection of social identity altogether, and a corresponding stress on the value of the antirelational and anticommunitarian. For Sinfield, "this cannot be; there is no human life beyond the social" (*Gay and After* 141).

Sinfield admits that the two leading ideas of his book "are pulling in different directions" (6). Thus, on the one hand, he asserts his belief in the subculture through a call for more purposeful subcultural work, while on the other registering an awareness that "the kinds of subcultural cohesion that we have developed since Stonewall are losing effectiveness" (6). Moreover, his book ends with this tension still unresolved—or rather with a restatement of how the first idea (the call for a stronger subculture) derives from and is a response to the ongoing tension that springs from the second (the challenge of diversity). Sinfield's claim is that we need a more determined subculture precisely *because* we are now aware that sexuality is "more mobile and various than it has been convenient, historically, for our subcultures to handle" (199). He argues that there is strength in diversity, but that such strength can be mobilized only through the medium of a more informed and critical activism. This means acting together, in *collaboration*—a word that he identifies and uses as a positive term that needs to be reclaimed: rescued from its historical vilification as "a euphemism for treachery" (142). It also means eschewing the kind of transgressiveness that is merely individualist, voluntarist, and gestural, that reflects the limited viewpoint, the romantic self-absorption, of "an exalted, solitary engagement within the troubled self" (142): the kind of transgressiveness, in short, that Bersani sees and admires in Gide, Proust, and Genet. In a dangerous world, he warns, we cannot afford the risk of trying to manage "without the social support and political organisation that derives from subculture" (199). Collective decision making, however difficult in such a diversely populated constituency, is thus still our best hope for the future: decision making about "who we are, where we want to be, and what strategies are going to help us get there" (142).

As I hope the earlier part of this chapter shows, the debate between Bersani and Sinfield (which resurfaces, as I say, in Chapter 5 of this book) renews a long-standing argument, and indeed brings it up-to-date. If the fictions examined in my core chapters are reflections of this argument, however, they reflect it not as a matter of clear-cut opposition, but in ways that reveal confusion, cross-affiliation, and internal struggle. Thus the eponymous hero of *The Family of Max Desir* shows both a need to invest in the responsible routines of social identity (Sinfield's collaborative ethos) and an urge to surrender to the transgressive appeal of thrilling sexual fantasy (Bersani's radical homo-ness). Likewise, Dennis, the narrator of *Frisk*, is mainly drawn to those antirelational, anticommunitarian impulses of homosexual desire that Bersani promotes as the essence of a new radical concept of what it means to be gay. Nevertheless, Dennis's impulses, in spite of himself, *are* relational, as Sinfield finds to be the case with Genet. For although Dennis, like Genet, seeks "to remain outside a social and moral world" (141), his urge reveals itself as inseparable from a strong relational drive. Indeed, in the very violence of his compulsion to destroy the identities of his victims he shows himself to be haunted by them. But I shall restrict myself here to these few illustrative remarks rather than anticipate my fuller discussion of these tensions in subsequent chapters.

## SUMMARY

In this chapter I have attempted to trace the main lineaments of the conflict between assimilationism and radicalism within gay culture and politics since Stonewall. Post-Stonewall developments have been my main focus, although I have occasionally glanced back at earlier expressions of the conflict. Taking an eclectic approach, I have brought history, theory, and fiction together here as interactive forces. The chapter shows how the radicalism of the early theorists of the gay movement (Altman, Hocquenghem) was counteracted by the very success of the movement, which, in the euphoria of that success, moved away from radical politics toward a more assimilationist attitude. It also looks at the return of radical politics in the 1980s in response to the emergency of the AIDS epidemic, the consequent right-wing backlash, and the crisis of gay identity that has grown out of AIDS and the development of queer, constructionist, and postmodern discourses (Butler, Sedgwick).

These events, I argue, produced an intensification of the conflict. Thus the return of radical politics in the 1980s was followed in the early 1990s by the rise of a new brand of well-articulated assimilationism (Bawer, Sullivan). Moreover, my discussion of the ideas of Bersani and Sinfield that concludes the chapter—theorists who have attempted a general overview of the current situation from a broadly literary perspective—shows the conflict between assimilationism and radicalism as an issue of urgent ongoing debate, as well as giving some indication of its more recent expression. I have also interspersed the chapter with brief pointers to the main focus of this study: the representation of this conflict in fiction. As well as in the internal tensions of individual texts, the conflict, I argue, is reflected in two distinct strains of fiction since Stonewall, strains that have their traceable antecedents in fiction of the pre-Stonewall era. This earlier fiction is therefore the background to this study, and hence the focus of my next chapter.

# 2   Divergent Lines of Dissent
## Wilde to Stonewall

They [gay authors] fall into two groups. There are those, following
Shakespeare's Coriolanus, who say defiantly, on their expulsion from
society, "There is a world elsewhere" and, when banished, retort, "I
banish you!" . . . The second group of writers, people like Forster,
Isherwood and Leavitt, are reformers rather than rebels.

—Mark Lilly, *Gay Men's Literature in the Twentieth Century*

Genet's books are the exact opposite of a literature of indignation
and rebellion. The author has no intention of making accusations
or unmasking society. He is a true believer in the bourgeois order,
not a critic.

—Hans Mayer, *Outsiders*

Gay literature is fraught with paradox.

—Bruce Bawer, *A Place at the Table*

The central conflict explored in this study of gay male fiction since Stonewall—the conflict between assimilationism and radicalism: between a fundamental acceptance of social and sexual norms and an outright rejection
of them—can also be traced in gay male fiction from before Stonewall. I
shall therefore attempt such a retrospective here in order to show the lineage of the fiction discussed in the core chapters and to provide the study as
a whole with some literary and historical background. However, in accordance with the study as a whole, I shall do this not through a survey, but
through a brief examination of a few representative texts: texts that date
from the late nineteenth century (Wilde's *The Picture of Dorian Gray*,
1891) to the mid twentieth (Isherwood's *A Single Man*, 1964).

The first thing to say is that this chapter reaffirms the theme of internal
tension that runs throughout this study: the conflict identified above exists
both between these texts *and* within them. Thus, although chosen for their
tendency to represent one side of the conflict or the other (and grouped

accordingly) not one is purely representative of either side. This is because, on the one hand, all gay male writing, however assimilative, exists in some degree of opposition to the dominant culture, while on the other, even the uncompromising self-determination of Genet cannot break entirely free of the ideology that envelops and engenders it, and consequently falls short of the pure transcendence to which it aspires. In other words, the lines of conflict explored here, as throughout this study, are not clear-cut. Points of similarity may exist between texts that are otherwise radically dissimilar, and there may be a crossing of lines that corresponds to—and thus reveals the extent of—their ideological ambivalence.

One way in which these chosen texts reveal their differences is in the degree to which they incline toward realism or fantasy. Realism, as theorists often remark, is a notoriously problematic term. Thus the kind of realism that has been the dominant form of narrative in fiction since the middle of the nineteenth century is, for many poststructuralist and Marxist critics, an expression of dominant bourgeois values and ideology. This is particularly so for Roland Barthes, to whom I shall return at a later point in this study. What we call realist fiction, these critics claim, is an author-manipulated, illusionist trick, offering the appearance of reality and a single, author-imposed meaning.[1] Hence the implication of their argument is that such fiction, when found in the context of gay male writing, has a similar tendency to underwrite dominant ideology. A further implication is that fantasy in gay male writing is bent on shattering the illusion that realist fiction works so hard to create.

I have already given some brief indication in the previous chapter of how fantasy in gay male fiction is often the means of exploring transgressive ideas. Moreover, such fantasy sometimes has elements of Gothic fiction (monstrous and supernatural beings, bizarre happenings, strange psychological states) and hence shares some of the current reputation of this latter genre for radical reinscription. This may help to explain its wide appeal, for as numerous novels and films testify, contemporary Gothic fantasy, particularly in the form of horror or vampire fiction, is hugely popular. In fact, several writers have produced full-length critical studies in an attempt to explain the phenomenon.[2] However, the unambiguously subversive role that is frequently assigned to Gothic fantasy in contemporary critical accounts, which is the alleged source of its current voguishness, has been questioned. For a fair assessment of Gothic writing, Chris Baldick and Robert Mighall argue, we need to maintain a critical detachment from it and hold its qualities in balance: "The psychodynamic model employed in this phase of Gothic Criticism in fact requires that a text include both radical and reactionary impulses in conflict with one another" (226). This accords with my own already-stated view that the texts examined in this chapter, whatever their general tendency, are marked by internal conflict. Baldick and Mighall also refer to the work of Rosemary Jackson, who, in drawing attention to "the difficulty of reading

Gothic as politically subversive" (96–97), argues that most Gothic fiction is in fact conservative in tendency:

> Drawing upon the left-formalist tradition of Barthes and Kristeva, in which formal disjunction or "openness" is equated with radicalism and formal "closure" is assumed to be ideologically regressive, Jackson divides Gothic texts into the majority, in which the "threat" to bourgeois subjectivity is contained, and those few . . . whose open structures obstruct such conservative recuperation. The notion that Gothic writing is in some way uniformly or automatically an expression of "revolutionary" impulses . . . is now more commonly qualified by a discrimination between conservative and "subversive" varieties of Gothic. (Baldick and Mighall 226–27)

Challenging the Barthesian suggestion that Gothic writing represents an alternative to the bourgeois values and ideology enshrined in realist fiction, Baldick and Mighall conclude that Gothic fiction, in general, is itself a bourgeois genre, neither "excitingly subversive" nor "scandalously reactionary" but "just tamely humanitarian" (226–27). But no doubt, like Rosemary Jackson, who instances Maturin's *Melmoth the Wanderer* and Stoker's *Dracula,* they would admit exceptions to this overview.

In any case, what Baldick and Mighall are concerned with is that tradition of Gothic writing in English that derives from the novels of Horace Walpole and Ann Radcliffe, a tradition to which only Wilde's *The Picture of Dorian Gray* could be said to belong. The other novels I have grouped with Wilde's—Genet's *Our Lady of the Flowers* and Burroughs's *Naked Lunch*—occupy a quite different space, although clearly there is a strong strain of Gothic in both, and certainly the macabre, fantastic, and supernatural elements they flaunt mark them off from the mainstream realist tradition to which the other novels treated in this chapter incline. Their sheer originality and idiosyncrasy makes them marginal to any tradition, however, and hence they cannot be included in comments about the nature of Gothic writing in general.

Actually, if these two novels belong anywhere, it is to the experimental tradition in fiction, for they come out of, and extend, the modernist movement of Gertrude Stein, Joyce, Gide, and others. In these novels, a highly individual perception of reality bursts through the confining walls of fiction, shattering formal conventions and invading forbidden territories. Accepted notions of character, based on the concept of the unified self, are replaced, as in the fiction of D. H. Lawrence, by explorations of unknown modes of being. These are novels of fluid psychological states and shifting viewpoints, and consequently the creatures we find in them bring to mind Lawrence's own words in a letter to Edward Garnett: "You mustn't look in my novel [*The Rainbow*] for the old stable ego of character. There is another ego, according to whose action the individual is unrecognisable, and passes through, as it were, allotropic states which it needs a deeper sense than we've been used to exercise, to discover" (Lawrence 18). Moreover, in place of linear narrative, the reader is faced with an extension of (or variation on) the stream of consciousness technique developed by Joyce and other writers in the early decades of the twentieth century—or, in other words, with a mosaic of seemingly chance impressions, lacking an omniscient center and vivid with the challenging confusions and contradictions of immediate experience.

## SANE, CIVILIZED, UNAPOLOGETIC

In that they are centrally concerned with homosexual relations, the three novels I want to examine in this first part of the chapter—E. M. Forster's *Maurice,* Gore Vidal's *The City and the Pillar,* and Christopher Isherwood's *A Single Man*—are daring, controversial, groundbreaking fictions. Nor would it be true to say that they are untouched by modernist ideas and experiment. Thus all three, in their Freudian awareness of the irrational and the workings of the unconscious mind, use poetic imagery, symbolism, and myth as structuring devices. Moreover, *A Single Man* is clearly indebted to Joyce and Virginia Woolf for its aesthetic principles and method of organization, being, like *Mrs Dalloway,* a much smaller scale, more domesticated, and less labyrinthine *Ulysses.* Nevertheless, in form and substance, these novels are closer to the mainstream realist tradition of Euro-American fiction inherited from the nineteenth century than to twentieth-century avant-gardism. Despite hints of mystical awareness, nihilistic terror, and tragedy, they reflect a viewpoint grounded in the scientific rationalism and liberal humanism that dominates our post-Enlightenment Western ideology. They thus hold to a sense of order through a notion of character based on the concept of the autonomous, unified self, and by retaining the central organizing consciousness of an omniscient narrator.

What they also have in common, accordingly, is an insistence on the basic normality and ordinariness of homosexuality. The protagonists of all three, as the writers themselves claim (or suggest within the narrative), are embodiments of this principle. "Maurice is Suburbia," Forster writes in the terminal note to his novel, and his self-conscious decision to create such a character, he implies, was a deliberate act of provocation that called for an effort of will and imagination: "In Maurice I tried to create a character who was completely unlike myself or what I supposed myself to be: someone handsome, healthy, bodily attractive, mentally torpid, not a bad businessman and rather a snob" (218). Similarly, Vidal claims that an attempt to subvert the popular view of homosexuality lay behind the creation of Jim Willard, the central character of *The City and the Pillar.* "It was part of American folklore," Vidal writes in the afterword to the revised edition (with reference to 1946, the year his novel was written), "that homosexuality was a form of mental disease" (208). Like Maurice, Jim Willard and Bob Ford confound the stereotypical notion of male homosexuality—that effeminate, Wildean model of the queer man that became established in the twentieth century and still prevails.[3] Conspicuously sound in mind and body, and uncomfortably close to the American ideal of manhood, they constitute a very deliberate calculation on Vidal's part, as he openly admits in his preface: "I knew that my description of the love affair between two 'normal' all-American boys, of the sort I had spent three years in the army with during the war, would challenge every superstition about sex in my native land" (3). *The City and the Pillar* did shock America, and the shockwaves it produced were compounded later in the same year by the arrival of *Sexual Behavior in the Human Male* (1948), the first of two reports by Alfred C. Kinsey and others, based on interviews with more than ten thousand white American men and women.[4]

George, Isherwood's protagonist, has a related significance, which is inscribed in the text rather than a matter of direct comment by the author. Underlining its debt to Joyce and Woolf, the novel squeezes George into the narrow frame of a single, average day, a twenty-four-hour period in which ordinary events are transformed into moments of epiphanized meaning and insight. Like Leopold Bloom and Clarissa Dalloway, George is both unique (the "single" man of the novel's title) and archetypal. This is made clear in the novel's opening paragraph, where the waking George, emerging from the undifferentiated state of being we all inhabit during sleep, slowly acquires the name, features, and social identity that give him his place in the world: "Waking up begins with saying *am* and *now*. That which has awoken then lies for a while staring at the ceiling and down into itself until it has recognized *I*, and therefore deduced *I am, I am now*" (7). Similarly, in the novel's closing pages and at the end of his waking day, George sinks back into sleep, where (in a condition that, as Isherwood reminds us, resembles death) the trappings of his identity fall away and he becomes a "non-entity" (158). These allusions to the Vedantic idea of the oneness of life, the universal consciousness that subsumes the ego of individual identity—a philosophy that Isherwood embraced in 1939 and that influenced all of his later writing[5]—erase George's aura of separateness and convert him into an Everyman.

Another common feature of these novels, and perhaps a necessary concomitant of their insistence on the basic normality of homosexuality, is their concern with the ideal of the lifelong love relationship, an ideal central to Western cultural and spiritual values, Judaeo-Christian in origin, and essentially heterosexual. Forster again nails his colors to the mast in the terminal note to his novel: "I was determined that in fiction anyway two men should fall in love and remain in it for the ever and ever that fiction allows" (218). This remark suggests that *Maurice* is a metaphorical working out of the author's own search for an ideal friend, a search inspired, as the terminal note again makes clear, by Whitmanesque and

Carpenterian notions of male comradeship. For many readers, however, the novel's single-minded pursuit of this ideal, maintained without a corresponding ballast of realism, leaves it ultimately open to the charge of sentimentality.[6] Hence, in this respect at least, it contrasts sharply with *The City and the Pillar,* where the protagonist's equally single-minded pursuit of the same ideal is presented from the start as romantic delusion. There are two versions of Vidal's novel. In the ending of the original version, Jim Willard murders his boyhood friend, Bob Ford, at the moment when his dream of reciprocal love between them is brutally shattered and his devotion to Bob revealed as fallacy. In the revised version, written in response to criticism of the original ending as melodramatic, Jim overpowers Bob and rapes him. This version is not only less melodramatic, it is more convincing. Though somber, it avoids the sense of absolute finality, together with the aura of false romanticism, that mars the original. It also hints at possibilities of self-renewal. The important point, however, is that both versions end with Jim's symbolic destruction of the mirage that has acted as an impediment to his spiritual growth.[7]

*A Single Man* is different. Here, the ideal that Maurice and Jim pursue as a possibility becomes a realization, and a realization strengthened by perspective, since the lifelong love relationship at the center of the novel is viewed retrospectively and when effectively at an end. In focusing on a single day in the life of an elderly college lecturer, whose lover of many years is now dead, Isherwood is able to view that life comprehensively and show an enduring love in all its phases, both in life and beyond death. In this way George becomes representative, for in taking the long view, in drawing back to give us the full trajectory, the novel obscures the particularity of his experience and plays up its generality: its closeness to the "universal consciousness" of Vedantic philosophy.

The emphasis on the normality of homosexuality in these novels is controversial not only from the standpoint of dominant ideology (from which standpoint homosexuality is by definition an abnormality) but also from the perspective of contemporary queer theory (from which perspective the very concept of "normality" is itself problematic). For queer theorists, the concept of normality is bound up with essentialist notions of sexual identity: with belief in fixed categories, natural conditions, and transhistorical essences. Queer theory not only demonstrates "the impossibility of any 'natural' sexuality, it calls into question even such apparently unproblematic terms as 'man' and 'woman'" (Jagose 3). The protagonists of these novels thus embody the contradictions of contemporary debate about sexuality, for they conform to the conventional model of manliness while practicing a form of sexuality that confounds that model. Consequently, from the standpoint of dominant ideology, these novels are both reassuring and unsettling. Outwardly respectful, yet quietly treacherous, they defer to that ideology on the one hand and subtly undermine it on the other.

In their focus on the normality of homosexuality, these novels reflect (or would seem to reflect) the ideology of the homophile movement, which is the name given to that somewhat loose collection of disparate organizations, committees, and initiatives that campaigned for law reform and a better understanding of homosexuality in the years before Stonewall.[8] Originating in Europe at the end of the nineteenth century, this movement laid stress on homosexuality as a natural phenomenon and took as its basis the "scientific" findings of late nineteenth-century sexology, which the father of queer theory later characterizes as the fruit of the urge at this time to classify and compile (Foucault, *History* 17–35). At least, this was the general thrust of a movement that inevitably encompassed within its disparateness a number of conflicting ideologies—ideologies, moreover, in which there is a tendency to self-contradiction. For instance, the homophiles argued that homosexuality was congenital in an attempt to remove it from the category of sin or illness, and took as their premise a belief in the natural origin of all forms of sexuality. But this created a problem for them: for if "normal" heterosexual relations, together with the male–female binary, the sex/gender system, and the characteristics conventionally ascribed to men and women, all have their origins in nature and are indeed the central constituents of the natural sexual order, how does homosexuality fit into this scheme of things? The homophiles responded to this with the claim that homosexuality was the natural practice of a third or intermediate sex. But in making this claim they tended to subvert their own argument and strategy, since a third sex, within an essentially binaric view of sexual difference, is inevitably an aberration, and thus contradicts the alleged normality of homosexuality, denies that homosexual people are just like everyone else.

Furthermore, as I suggest above, there are indications that the very concept of sexual normality was challenged by groups within the homophile movement.[9] The ideology of the Mattachine Society in its early years, for instance, had a strong Marxist slant, which analyzed the oppression of homosexuals from an essentially social constructionist standpoint. Hence, it viewed the concept of normality as the creation of forces in society that have a vested interest in the suppression of difference. But when such analysis became dangerous—in a United States gripped by McCarthyism—the Mattachine Society changed dramatically. In short, its oppositional stance became assimilationist: or, as one historian has put it, "accommodation to social norms replaced the affirmation of a distinctive gay identity" (D'Emilio, *Sexual Politics* 81). The affirmation of a distinctive gay identity becomes instead the central motivating drive of the later and more militant gay liberation movement. Yet the evolution of this movement parallels that of the former, as the ethnic model of gay identity it promotes becomes absorbed into the mainstream, to be eventually reconfigured (in light of Foucauldian and later developments of social constructionist theory) as itself a form of accommodationism.

Like the homophile movement, the three novels examined here exhibit a *prima facie* accommodation to social norms, though an accommodation that simultaneously challenges those norms by drawing attention to the contradictions of its own position. In short, the insistence on the normality of homosexuality in these novels implicitly questions the very concept of normality. This tendency to self-contradiction, as we have seen, is echoed in the negotiations of the homophile movement, whose central ideology and strategy instituted what Foucault calls a reverse discourse. In this discourse, "homosexuality began to speak in its own behalf, to demand that its legitimacy or 'naturality' be acknowledged, often in the same vocabulary, using the same categories by which it was medically disqualified" (*History* 101). But again, to attempt to legitimize homosexuality within a system of oppositions, the logic of which denies that legitimacy, inevitably raises fundamental questions about the legitimacy of the system itself.

Thus, in *Maurice,* accommodation to social norms proves ultimately unviable, for Maurice's aspirations to ordinariness are finally defeated by the realization that he must necessarily seek his destiny outside ordinary society. Hence, for much of its length, the novel seems torn by an inner dialectic. On the one hand, its insistence on the basic normality of Maurice suggests a fundamental acceptance of the social order within which the character's homosexuality figures as an aberration, an aberration that eventually forces him into marginalized existence as a social exile in the greenwood of the novel's ending. Yet, on the other, in Maurice's growing awareness of alternative modes of being and his eventual defiance of this oppression through abandonment of his conventional lifestyle, the novel vehemently rejects those norms and issues a challenge to the very concept of normality. The assimilative motivation of the novel, in other words, is accompanied by (and ends with) a daring assertion of difference.

For there is danger in Maurice's ordinariness, which, like that of Jim Willard in *The City and the Pillar* and of George in *A Single Man,* is double-edged, for it at once domesticates homosexuality and brings it unsettlingly close. Its threatening aspect emerges in the scene where Maurice, in his second year at Cambridge, meets Risley for the first time. In this scene, Maurice, initially sensing the need for a self-defensive strategy, carefully defines himself in opposition to Risley, deliberately pointing up his ordinariness in contrast to Risley's advertised homosexuality and outrageous defiance of masculine codes: "Finding Risley adored music, he began to run it down, saying, 'I don't go in for being superior,' and so on" (32). Later, however, finding himself exhilarated by the man's playful seriousness, he wonders whether he should see more of him. Thus Maurice first observes Risley from the minoritizing viewpoint of dominant ideology, from which viewpoint the latter's exoticism can be kept at a safe distance.[10] At this distance, like the third or intermediate sex of homophile ideology, it can be tolerated as a distasteful but ultimately harmless natural aberration. Safely minoritized in this way, Risley belongs to a separate species of person and becomes a special kind of individual, no part of whose "total composition [is] unaffected by his sexuality" (Foucault, *History* 43).

But the problem for Maurice, as for the reader who shares his secret, is the knowledge that he and Risley belong to the same species. For in that case, why, in their total composition, are they so apparently different? The minoritizing and essentializing view of homosexuality is based on the notion of the self as a unified entity, to which all parts give coherent expression. According to this view, Maurice and Risley have selves that are essentially similar, a correspondence that should be evident from "even the ostensibly least sexual aspects of [their] personal existence" (Sedgwick, *Epistemology* 2). Yet, as if to confound such theory, this is not at all evident: Maurice and Risley express their supposedly similar "essential selves" quite differently. Hence the danger of Maurice's ordinariness: for viewed in conjunction with Risley's exoticism, it raises the question of what the "essence"—or, to use Foucault's word, the "naturality"—of homosexuality is.

Indeed, in this context, Maurice's conformity to the norms of masculine behavior, which from the gender-inflected viewpoint of conventional understandings of sexuality so disturbingly fails to match or signal the species he belongs to, raises the question whether homosexuality has any kind of foundational essence or natural origin: for the assimilated masculinity of Maurice's "total composition," like the apparently quite different "naturality" of Risley, suggests an identity "performatively constituted by the very 'expressions' that are said to be its results" (Butler, *Gender Trouble* 25). Consequently, in the contrasted identities of Maurice and Risley, the novel seems implicitly to contradict its ostensible aim of legitimizing homosexuality through a process of naturalization, and instead to invoke the Butlerian notion of performativity. In other words, the opposed genderized identities of the two men, especially given their shared sexuality, suggest, in light of Judith Butler's analysis of the construction of gender, effects of reiterated performance rather than expressions of a permanent, preexistent core of being.

The inner dialectic of the novel, however, is also suggested in the presentation of Clive—or, more accurately, of Clive in relation to Maurice. For in the development of the novel the roles of the two men, vis-à-vis each other, become reversed. Clive, who has a reputation "for brains and also for exclusiveness," is initially associated with the "queer fish" Risley, for Maurice meets him accidentally on a visit to the latter's rooms, a visit sparked by a Risley-inspired need to "break all the undergraduate conventions" and seek "an adventure" (36–37). Moreover, the adventure of the subsequent Maurice-Clive relationship leads, via Plato and Tchaikovsky, to a declaration of love, an expulsion from the college and a two-year period of "as much happiness as men under that star can expect" (91). The shallowness of Clive's defiance of social norms, however, and the fundamentally conformist nature of his character, are signaled early in the text. Thus Clive dictates the terms within which the relationship is to be conducted, terms that confine the relationship to an idealized concept of male friendship derived from a reading of Plato.

This is made clear from the conversation he and Maurice have on the day of the latter's arrival at Penge. To Maurice's question "what was it in me you first cared about?" Clive replies "it was your beauty." Yet when, in response to this, Maurice reveals his less than spiritually pure concept of beauty, Clive turns crimson and advises a change of subject (85–86). Similarly, when Maurice, having failed to follow the high-flown rhetoric of their conversation, asks "I say, will you kiss me?" (86), Clive shakes his head. And here, the irony of Forster's reference to the establishment of "perfection in their lives" indicates the extent to which his view of Clive has turned sourly satirical (87). Thus Clive's description of himself as "a bit of an outlaw" (84) is entirely accurate, for the limits of his outlawry are quickly reached.

Nevertheless, his abrupt conversion to heterosexuality is a puzzling moment in the text. Does Forster take this event "at face value," as Stephen Adams suggests (113)? Or is the reference to "a blind alteration of the life spirit" (106) a further instance of Forster's ironic presentation of this character? Claude Summers accepts the conversion as genuine, but argues that Forster's final condemnation of Clive is due to "the eagerness with which he embraces the 'beautiful conventions' that earn social approval" (*Gay Fictions* 93). Adams, on the other hand, sees Clive's sudden change of sexual preference as more obviously the expression of "a nervous crisis," and as ultimately the result of a conscious choice—the choice of "a 'safe' passage through life" and of "security over passionate fulfilment" (113).

In my view, the ambiguity of the text here arises precisely from what I have been calling its inner dialectic. Robert K. Martin sees an opposition in the novel between "two kinds of homosexuality—one that is identified with Cambridge and Clive, and one that is identified with Alec and the open air" (35). Structured around this opposition, the novel divides into two parts: the first "dominated by Plato and, indirectly, by John Addington Symonds and the apologists for 'Greek love,'" and the second by "Edward Carpenter and his translation of the ideas of Walt Whitman" (36). In the developing imagery of the novel the Symonds-Cambridge kind of homosexuality, which initially figures as a liberating force, becomes associated with the élitist notions and false Hellenism of the early homophile movement, within which male–male sexual relations are reframed as a "superior" kind of love, uncontaminated by any kind of distasteful physicality. Hence it is also associated with the sophistications and artificialities of advanced civilization: the divisive forces in society that obstruct the free-flow of natural feeling between people and frustrate the "only connect" of Forsterian affirmation.[11]

This persuasive analysis of *Maurice* relates to my earlier comments about the tension in the novel between its assimilative and radical impulses. Thus the homosexuality associated with Clive, Cambridge, and the apologists for

"Greek love" in the novel is clearly based on a minoritizing account. In the above-mentioned conversation with Maurice, for instance, Clive remarks:

> Look at that picture, for instance. I love it because, like the painter himself, I love the subject. I don't judge it with the eyes of a normal man. There seem two roads for arriving at Beauty—one is in common, and all the world has reached Michelangelo by it, but the other is private to me and a few more. (86)

Clive speaks of himself here as a man gifted with special, private insight: insight granted to a select few of the human race, beyond the reach of the normal man and different from, probably superior to, that of the common herd. Like the homosexual condition to which it is causally related, you either have it or you don't. This is an odd attitude, given the historical perspective that informs it, because such perspective would seem to promote an understanding of homosexuality as invention rather than condition.

The minoritizing account, which sees homosexual orientation as the condition of a fixed minority, lays emphasis on difference, the difference that by definition marks any discrete identity. But, paradoxically, it is also assimilative, since it derives from an acceptance of the sexual norms that create that identity and that define homosexuality as the interest of a minority. The result of such acceptance is that Clive, like Symonds and the apologists for Greek love, is fearful of arousing "either disgust or desire" (86). Hence he luxuriates in a form of spiritualized sexuality that is so physically undernourished as to be effectively refined out of existence. This "self-erasure," as John Fletcher calls it ("Forster's Self-Erasure" 65), is eventually rejected in the novel, as Clive, the representative in the early chapters of Cambridge values and enlightenment, becomes, in Fletcher's words, "the embodiment of stupidity of heart, emotional tepidity, and expediency" (83).

Thus what Forster finally affirms is the homosexuality identified with Alec and the ideas of Carpenter and Whitman. For the novel is clearly organized around the contrast between Clive and Alec, even though historically, as Fletcher shows (65–67), the distinction between the attitudes to homosexuality of Symonds on the one hand and of Whitman on the other is not as clear-cut as Robert K. Martin suggests. Hence, with the rejection of the homosexuality associated with Clive, and the affirmation of that identified with Alec, the novel becomes radical: the latter kind of homosexuality, after all, is based on a defiance of social and sexual norms, arising from an acceptance of "the social and political consequences of homosexuality" (Martin 42). If Clive's kind of homosexuality is associated with the minoritizing exclusivity that imitates the hierarchy of sexual norms, Maurice's relationship with Alec reflects the inclusivity, based on social and sexual equality, that characterizes the Carpenterian and Whitmanesque love of comrades.

Moreover, the wider dimensions of the novel's radicalism have been explored by Debrah Raschke, who argues that Maurice's break with Clive is also a break with Platonic philosophy. Drawing on David Halperin's exposition of the Socratic-youth relationship in ancient Greece (*One Hundred Years* 29–38), she sees the novel as an engagement with "the difficulty Platonic philosophy poses as a paradigmatic homoeroticism" (153). The survival of the Maurice-Alec partnership, she claims, is shown as dependent on a rejection of the Platonic separation of mind and body, a separation that, in its association of the latter with femininity and passivity and in its constituting of sex as a polarizing experience between social superior and inferior, is indicative of the asymmetry and power structure of sexual relations in ancient Greece: "Maurice and Alec's relationship, which in its initial stages is not free of class, ends with the refusal of those hierarchies and with Maurice's stressing the desire for mutuality, for *sharing* his body" (154).

But the oppositional pull of the novel, and its final radical turn in favor of "Alec and the open air," is also reflected in its imagery. At first sight, the association of Alec with primroses, animality, and the greenwood suggests the Foucauldian concept of reverse discourse, whereby homosexuality seeks to legitimize itself through a demand that its "naturality" be acknowledged. In the wider context of the novel, however, the imagery surrounding the Maurice-Alec relationship points to a more radical insight. For here the Maurice-Alec relationship is seen against the backdrop of the Clive-Maurice and Clive-Anne relationships, both of which suggest an attempt to denaturalize sexuality in all its forms. Thus, in an early episode of the novel, the burgeoning love of Clive and Maurice is projected through an image of motorcycle and sidecar: "Forster's cold term [for the cycle] ('machine') signalling the opposition between nature and the products of an industrial society" (Martin 40). The link here is significant because, in the Foucauldian account of sexuality, it is the age of the machine that, in its thirst for a science of sex, "produces" the homosexual.

Likewise, Clive's marriage to Anne is presented, in its association with the imagery of Penge, as the centerpiece of a constructed identity: for the dilapidated Penge epitomizes the crumbling defenses of a fabricated set of values, which, like the motorcycle and sidecar, are the products of an industrial society rather than the offshoots of a natural order.

Hence the greenwood, to which Maurice and Alec finally escape, symbolizes not a place of exile but a place of new growth. It is "Another Country," to borrow the defiant title of James Baldwin's novel, although here the vision is of England—an England purged of its snobberies and prejudices, its divisive social and sexual categories.[12] For, with no sense of regret at their exclusion from society, the lovers look forward to the construction of a new way of living and relating:

> He was bound for his new home. He had brought out the man in Alec, and now it was Alec's turn to bring out the hero in him. He knew what

the call was, and what his answer must be. They must live outside class, without relations or money; they must work and stick to each other till death. But England belonged to them. That, besides companionship, was their reward. Her air and sky were theirs, not the timorous millions' who own stuffy little boxes, but never their own souls. (208–09)

Ultimately, then, it seems untrue to describe Forster (as Mark Lilly does, in the citation at the head of this chapter) as a reformer rather than a rebel, for in this angry and deeply personal novel, he too, like the Coriolanus that Lilly invokes, renounces the world vehemently. Moreover, like Baldwin, he speaks from a "deep loathing of contemporary society" and from an attitude that combines a "vigorous iconoclasm with implied . . . suggestions for a different world" (Lilly xi).

## MASCULINE LOVE

Nevertheless, the iconoclasm of *Maurice* does not extend to an outright attack on the masculine–feminine binary structure, even if, in its occasional nods toward the notion of constructed identity, it hints at such an attack. The brave, new world of the greenwood suggests a vision of masculine love, in which, in John Fletcher's words, the "virile doubling" of Maurice and Alec is celebrated at the expense of the "feminized and inverted" Clive ("Forster's Self-Erasure" 90). Indeed, as Fletcher observes, it points to an underlying structural logic in the novel "whereby the formation of the masculine couple requires the exclusion of the unmanly intellectual with his disavowed paternal affiliation" (90). This suggestion is reinforced by Forster's terminal note to the novel, for as the account of the visit to Millthorpe makes clear, the final vision of the novel was inspired by the homosexuality of Edward Carpenter, with its belief in outdoor physical labor, its roots in the poetry of Whitman, and its emphasis on conventional notions of masculinity.

In this respect *Maurice* compares interestingly with *The City and the Pillar*. Thus, in choice of protagonist, both novels suggest a bold attempt to confound what Judith Butler calls "[the] cultural matrix through which gender identity has become intelligible," a framework which requires that "certain 'identities' cannot 'exist'—that is, those in which gender does not follow from sex and those in which the practices of desire do not 'follow' from either sex or gender" (*Gender Trouble* 17). Yet, in both novels, the radical intent is undercut by signs of nervousness and confusion. As John Fletcher convincingly argues, Forster's choice of a protagonist who is the antithesis of himself suggests an act of self-erasure; and this goes some way to explaining why the "imperative" happy ending of the novel vibrates with a sense of loss, for the novel's radical turn in favor of the rebel lovers necessitates the exclusion of Clive, whose background and intellectuality point to a strong authorial identification. As the representative of society and civilized values, Clive is a father figure. Yet he also stands in opposition to Carpenterian principles: "Anything effeminate in a man, or anything of the cheap intellectual style, repels me very decisively," Carpenter wrote in his self-analysis for Havelock Ellis (quoted in Fletcher, "Forster's Self-Erasure" 73). The novel's rejection of Clive is therefore both a necessity and a matter of regret, Fletcher argues; and hence its radicalism is accompanied by feelings of nostalgia and "unsatisfied yearning" (84).

In *The City and the Pillar,* Vidal's assault on the imprisoning myths of masculinity similarly fails to break free of them. Here, as in *Maurice*—and in accordance with the main thrust of homophile ideology—the vision of homosexual love is grounded in nature. The vision is realized in an episode that comes very early in the novel and on which Jim becomes fixated. This is the episode in which he and Bob make love in the woods on the banks of the Potomac. In its evocation of a homoerotic Eden, this pastoral idyll is an echo of the greenwood in *Maurice*. It is a nostalgic vision, which seeks escape from the corruptions of the world and in which commentators have seen multiple allusions. Bernard F. Dick, for instance, reads it as part of an attempt to demythologize the American Wilderness novel by revealing "the homoeroticism implicit in much classic American literature, including *Huckleberry Finn* and *The Last of the Mohicans*" (Summers, *Gay Fictions* 118). But as Claude Summers points out, the details of the scene suggest a much wider network of literary reference, and he instances numerous other analogues including the *Idylls* of Theocritus and the eleventh section of Whitman's "Song of Myself." He also mentions the commentaries of Roger Austen and Stephen Adams, for both of whom "[the] fact that the lovemaking is preceded by wrestling is suggestive . . . of the Hylas ritual in classical literature" (119).

But what exactly is Vidal's attitude to this episode? Everything here— the pastoral setting, the bathing in the river, the wrestling and lovemaking "between two 'normal' all-American boys"—confirms his avowed intent to show the "naturalness" of homosexuality. Moreover, the scene is imbued with his belief, explicitly stated in the afterword to the revised version of 1965, that "there is of course no such thing as a homosexual" (207). In other words, there are intimations here, as there are in *Maurice,* of homosexual identity as social construction. Bob's remark, made during a pause in the lovemaking, that "boys aren't supposed to do that with one another" (33) could be seen as an early indication of his "true" orientation, an interpretation suggested in Summers's reading of the novel. However, it could also be read as an expression of alarm, signifying his fear of the stigma of homosexuality. Thus, for Stephen Adams, "it prefigures the masculine 'ideology' which will dictate their future" (19). Adams's reading of Vidal's novel, when read in conjunction with his reading of Forster's, highlights the parallel between them: for just as Clive's conversion to heterosexuality in *Maurice* implies, however Forster glosses it, "a choice of security over passionate fulfilment" (113), so Bob's capitulation in Vidal's novel to "convention, domesticity and a future in insurance" (23) suggests a flight from dangerous impulses.

It therefore seems reasonable to suggest that this pastoral idyll on the banks of the Potomac represents for Vidal what the greenwood represents for Forster. In *Maurice,* as the terminal note makes clear, the greenwood represents both an ideal and a reality. It is a vision, but a vision grounded in the actuality of Millthorpe. If some critics see it as a sentimental vision, this is not because it evokes an impossible dream but because its actuality is insufficiently realised in the text. It is true, as Stephen Adams observes, that Maurice values the greenwood "above all as a refuge" (117). But the greenwood, as vision, should also be seen as Forster's notion of what a society might be. Moreover, Forster remains loyal to his vision ("A happy ending was imperative") in spite of the inauspicious circumstances in which he was trying to embody it in fiction. In *The City and the Pillar,* on the other hand, Vidal seems torn by an inner conflict that leads him to betray his own ideal. "What begins as a 'commonsense redefinition of the homosexual-ist in American life,'" writes Adams (quoting from Vidal's afterword to the revised version of his novel), "transforms itself into a study of self-deception" (21). Moreover, the text suggests that Vidal sees the self-deception he is studying as his own, that he is "depicting the impossibility of his own dream too" (19). While recognizing this conflict in the text, Adams appears to defend Vidal's defection on the grounds that, in Jim, the ideal petrifies into romantic fallacy: "Nature suggests flux, change and growth, but Jim loses this capacity to respond freely and flexibly to experience" (21).

Claude Summers maintains a similar line of defense, seeing the novel as, in part, a successful and necessary attempt to explode "that staple of American literature, the myth of innocence" (*Gay Fictions* 118). He argues that Vidal's central characters are all cases of self-absorption, self-delusion, and emotional immaturity: dupes of "false idealization" (119) and "false romanticism" (128). Of course he recognizes that, in associating Jim with these deficiencies of character, Vidal runs the risk of underwriting the Freudian diagnosis of homosexuality as arrested development, but he nevertheless defends this aspect of the novel on the grounds that its target is not homosexuality *per se* but American romanticism in general. This defense, however, ducks the issue of Vidal's muddled purpose: it ignores the confusion between his need to validate homosexuality—his driving thesis "that homosexuality is a normal variation of human behavior"—and his desire to unmask "a hypocritical and falsely romantic society" (129). Adams acknowledges the problem when he writes that "[the] attempt to demonstrate the 'naturalness' of homosexuality is . . . in conflict with the form Vidal gives to his novel" (21). In concentrating on the self-deception of his central characters, he argues, Vidal is forced to "compromise his sympathetic portrayal of homosexuality" (21).

But Summers too, in spite of his general line of argument, seems at least aware of the problem. He remarks of the novel, for instance, that "it both reflects and challenges the sexual attitudes of its time" (129); and these conflicting characteristics, as he intimates, point to an insecurity in Vidal's own position. The insecurity is reflected not only in Vidal's eagerness to strike out at too many targets at once, but also in the way his bold attempt to subvert the myth of homosexuality is vitiated by his tendency to confirm stereotypes. Jim, as the site of conflicting attitudes, is the central problem here, for he is both the vehicle of Vidal's attempt to demonstrate the "naturalness" of homosexual relations and a study in self-deception. Consequently, Vidal both identifies with him and views him with critical detachment. Moreover, in reading the novel, it is difficult to separate these opposed attitudes, to know which predominates at any point.

For instance, we are told that most of the men Jim meets in the homosexual milieu of Hollywood behave "like women" (64), but that Jim is eager to know about them, "if only out of a morbid desire to discover how what had been so natural and complete for him could be so perfectly corrupted by these strange womanish creatures" (65). The problem is how to read this passage. Does it suggest that the misogyny and homophobia displayed here is not only Jim's but also Vidal's? On the one hand, the latter's choice of a protagonist who, in all but sexual preference, conforms to masculine stereotype suggests an identification with these attitudes. Yet on the other, they are clearly offered as part of the novel's critical presentation of Jim: they underpin his aloofness, his fear of confronting his own sexuality, his need to pose and "pass for straight," his failure to form lasting relationships. Hence the impression the novel gives us of insecurity and muddled purpose: for in the alternation between subjective and objective viewpoint in the presentation of Jim, an act of self-validation on Vidal's part collides with a process of critical self-scrutiny.

This brings us back to the notion of self-betrayal. For the novel never quite makes clear why Jim should be condemned for his devotion to Bob. Nor do the commentaries by Summers and Adams. Summers argues strongly that the ideal embodied in Jim's sexual initiation by the river is a false one, but his attempt to show why it is false never quite convinces. Jim's devotion to Bob, he suggests, becomes an inability to distinguish dream from reality. He admits that part of Vidal's purpose is to "validate the archetypal search for a lost partner" (*Gay Fictions* 119), but he glosses the novel's betrayal of this ideal as a warning against the ambiguity of dreams: "They may signify psychological truth, yet they can also distort reality" (120). Thus, for Summers, Jim's rape of Bob, in the violent climax to the definitive version, signifies the salutary death of the dream; and the novel ends, he suggests, on a note of muted optimism, with Jim having taken a crucial step toward self-knowledge.

Adams, too, appears to endorse the novel's thesis that Jim's devotion to Bob is an impediment to growth. However, unlike Summers, he clearly detects in the novel an unresolved conflict. For Summers, the novel is structured to show the value of experience as against the debilitating effect of a fixation on innocence. But for Adams, the project fails, since what it finally reveals is that Jim has learned nothing from experience. Jim takes revenge on Bob for his capitulation to heterosexual conformity, his betrayal of the dream, but does so through a display of male aggression, an act of rape that "confirms that he himself is trapped within the same system of values" (24). If, for Summers, the climax of the novel breaks the circularity of Jim's experience, for Adams, it confirms it:

> His anger is not transformed into an awareness that he must revise the values by which he lives or into a compassionate sense of fellowship with others in his situation. Indeed, he wallows in drunken self-pity and we are left with the image of him amusing himself by scorning the advances of some "little fag." "Endless drifting, promiscuity, defeat"—such was the future he conjured up for himself as an "ordinary" homosexual, as if this were the only alternative to Bob. It is appropriate, therefore, that he should reappear in one of Vidal's subsequent novels, *The Judgment of Paris* (1958), hustling in Paris, a poseur to the last. (24–25)

So although Adams here avoids the issue of whether the memory of Bob may have symbolic value to Jim as an enshrined ideal, he does make clear the inadequacy of the "reality" the novel evokes by way of contrast. Hence, in the process, he supports both his own claim that there are opposing tendencies at work in the text, as well as Summers's contention that the novel's radical intent is compromised by "Vidal's accommodationism" (*Gay Fictions* 129).

## SINGULARITY AND VEDANTIC ONENESS

*The City and the Pillar*, like *Maurice*, dramatizes a crisis of identity, and in this respect it also resembles Isherwood's *A Single Man*, even if here the crisis is different in being that of a protagonist in late middle age. This crisis arrived with the invention of the term "homosexuality" in 1869 (with its consequent, attendant notion of the "homosexual" as an identifiable type of person) and its continuing existence is borne out by the fact that an uneasiness with identity categories is the defining characteristic of contemporary queer theory. Thus Judith Butler writes: "I'm permanently troubled by identity categories, consider them to be invariable stumbling blocks, and understand them, even promote them, as sites of necessary trouble" ("Imitation" 14). However, unlike *Maurice* and *The City and the Pillar*, *A Single Man* is not a *bildungsroman*, as Claude Summers rightly points out (*Gay Fictions* 203); and George, Isherwood's fifty-eight-year-old protagonist, is certainly more at ease with his sexuality than Maurice Hall or Jim

Willard. On the other hand, Summers surely goes too far in claiming that George's homosexuality is "a simple given in the novel, not the source of agonizing self-examination" (203). For there *is* a good deal of pain in the novel, and much of that pain is the result of George's awareness not only of his awkward status in the local community but also of his problematic relationship to society in general.

*A Single Man* is centrally concerned with the conflict between "identity" and "difference." Throughout the novel George's need for community is seen in creative tension with his—and our—sense of his individuality and uniqueness. He is both alien and essential to the society in which he lives and works, for the more his neighbors, colleagues, and students are inclined to reject or marginalize him, the more he returns to haunt them. He thus illustrates the mutual dependence of homosexuality and heterosexuality: the way the one cannot exist without the other. George's neighbors, Mr. Strunk and Mr. Garfein, seem heterosexually secure in their suburban kingdom, but George senses that in truth they are very afraid: "afraid of what they know is somewhere in the darkness around them, of what may at any moment emerge into the undeniable light of their flashlamps, nevermore to be ignored, explained away. . . . [And among] many other kinds of monster . . . they are afraid of little me" (20–21). This passage recalls not only Eve Kosofsky Sedgwick's use and enlargement of the term "homosexual panic" (*Epistemology* 182–212) but also Judith Butler's observations on the way heterosexuality is driven to parodic imitation of itself in panicked response to anything it perceives as a threat to its stability:

> That heterosexuality is always in the act of elaborating itself is evidence that it is perpetually at risk, that is, that it "knows" its own possibility of becoming undone: hence, its compulsion to repeat which is at once a foreclosure of that which threatens its coherence. That it can never eradicate that risk attests to its profound dependency upon the homosexuality that it seeks fully to eradicate and never can or that it seeks to make second, but which is always already there as a prior possibility. ("Imitation" 23)

For Messrs. Strunk and Garfein, George is "the unspeakable that insists, despite all their shushing, on speaking its name" (21); and their sense of being perpetually at risk is illuminated by Butler's reflections on psychic identification and the self–Other distinction, in which she develops her argument about performativity. For Butler, "the self is from the start radically implicated in the 'Other'" ("Imitation" 26). Thus, Mr Strunk's attempt to nail George down with a word—"*Queer,* he doubtless growls" (21)—suggests, in Butler's elaboration of Freud's theory of incorporation, "a hateful effort to replace or displace" (27). Moreover, his use of the term "queer" reveals the very source of the theory of sexuality and psychic self-positioning under which Butler writes in an endeavor to resignify. Mr. Strunk's attitude to

George, Butler would say, is an attempt to achieve and maintain a sense of coherent identity through a process of separation and loss. Yet, paradoxically, this process is also an act of incorporation, since the "Other," always already installed in the self, "establishes the permanent incapacity of that 'self' to achieve self-identity" (27). The passage thus reveals Mr. Strunk as dependent on George for his very being, for "the disruption of the Other at the heart of the self is the very condition of that self's possibility" (27).[13]

The struggle between identity and difference that is central to the novel is presented in subtle and complex ways. George's profound sense of singularity, underscored in the title of the novel, resists identification not only with the wider Los Angelean society of the novel's setting but also with the minority group of which George recognizes himself a member. As Gregory Woods comments, "George has no gay friends" (*History of Gay Literature* 345). Yet, in apparent contradiction, he is shown as always conscious of belonging to a minority—indeed, as having a keen awareness of minorities in general and especially of the relationship between individuals, minorities, and the wider community. George's singularity is revealed in the sometimes savagely satirical interior monologue, the free indirect discourse, that forms the novel's main method of narration; and his venom is directed at those forces in American society—"our Country of the Bland" (26)—that, trained in the technique of "annihilation by blandness" (21), would strip him of his singularity. George nurtures eccentricity, seeks out offbeat places, cultivates odd friendships, cherishes his English background, and in general displays the kind of gay affirmativeness that resolutely resists the notion of "the positive role model." Frequently absurd and sometimes touchingly vulnerable, he indulges his misogyny and hatred of families. But his self-honesty can also be admirable: clear about what he values in his friendship with Charley, for instance, he refuses to let her attempts to domesticate him threaten that friendship.

The novel's stress on singularity, on George as metaphor for the isolated self, is balanced by a corresponding emphasis, again conducted through George, on the human need for identity and community. As my earlier remarks indicate, these contrasted views of the human condition are metaphysically suggested in the very framing of the novel, which begins and ends with an allusion to the Vedantic idea of the oneness of life, the universal consciousness that unites all humankind. George's isolation, embodied in his role as homosexual outsider, reinforced by his constant awareness of Jim's recent death, and dramatized in his visit to the hospital (where Doris, his fast-fading link with the past, is dying of cancer), is countered by an urge to reconnect with life and humanity—an urge that surfaces sporadically throughout the novel and with particular force in the final pages. Thus the factory-functional, death-dealing blandness of the university is offset by George's sudden, spontaneous surrender to feelings of lust for two young men playing tennis on the campus courts. Again, emerging from the hospital after his visit to the dying Doris, he is "almost indecently gleeful" to find himself in "the ranks of that marvellous minority, The Living" (87). He also delights later in the leisurely camaraderie of the gym, where nobody "is too handsome or too hideous to be accepted as an equal" (91).

The need for community—what we might call the assimilative tendency of the novel—is most strongly asserted, however, in the final sections of the novel. In his midnight swim with Kenny, for instance, George strips away barriers of difference to reveal his naked vulnerability, as he and Kenny merge in a sea "symbolic of the oceanic consciousness that is the novel's higher reality" (Summers, *Gay Fictions* 211). Later, he upbraids Kenny for his failure to lower his own defenses, to get beyond an attitude of shallow curiosity about George—in short, to relate seriously to people: "I mean, what is this life of ours supposed to be *for?* Are we to spend it identifying each other with catalogues, like tourists in an art gallery? Or are we to try to exchange *some* kind of a signal, however garbled, before it's too late?" (148)

This integrative drive of the novel is also evident in the naked mingling of bodies that constitutes George's subsequent masturbatory fantasy, in which the tennis players return, not as individuals, but as undifferentiated specters in a universal orgiastic embrace. Moreover, George falls asleep—a sleep in which he merges with all the living and the dead—vowing to fly to Mexico for Christmas: "It is Now that he must find another Jim. Now that he must love. Now that he must live—" (155).


## EXOTIC, MARGINAL, MONSTROUS

The novels we have just been looking at, whatever their challenge to convention, rest on a fundamental acceptance of social and sexual norms. The novels we turn to now, on the other hand, are based on an outright rejection of those norms, and linked by an emphasis on homosexuality as defiance, rebellion, willful transgression, and deviancy. Mark Lilly sees gay male writing in general as driven by the notion of freedom, and specifically, of freedom as the forbidden fruit that invites disobedience (16–32). This reference to the Book of Genesis evokes the primal myth of Western literature, and suggests a lineage running through Milton, Byron, and Wilde to the Beats and beyond.[14] Enacted in the story of the Fall, as in the line of literature it inspires, is the conflict between the aspirations of the individual and the constraints of the human condition: a struggle also reflected in the Classical–Romantic opposition that is central to cultural analysis and critical terminology, as well as in the Dionysian–Apollonian opposition of the Nietzschean theory of tragedy. Descendants of Milton's Satan, of Byron's various personae, and of Zarathustra, the characters in the novels examined here are existential outlaws, resisting conformity and nihilism, and struggling to fulfill themselves in a self-created moral universe.

But whatever its qualities for inclusion here, there is general critical consensus that *The Picture of Dorian Gray* is a muddled text, and that the muddle arises in part from the conditions in which it was written and in part from Wilde's ambivalence toward his sexuality. In its suggestion of a Faustian pact, the story reworks yet another of our cultural myths about the urge to escape human limitation. Critics differ, however, in what they see as the central thrust of the novel. "It is really about the jealousy and pain, the fear and guilt of being a homosexual," writes Jeffrey Meyers (20). For Mark Lilly, on the other hand, this is a gross misreading, grounded in heterosexist bias. In Lilly's view it is foolish to take at face value the way Wilde uses "the vocabulary of official culture" in this novel (28), where the references to "sin," "vice," and "evil," he argues, are a form of moral probing, a way of questioning the meaning and validity of those words. The novel should rather be seen, he suggests, as an existential rejection of socially sanctioned morality: "A more appropriate way of looking at the excesses and debaucheries of Dorian Gray . . . is the deliberate, proudly-perverse owning to titles conferred by society" (29). Hence, in Lilly's account, Dorian becomes a forerunner of Genet, defiantly living up to an enforced reputation and taking furious revenge on an unjust world: "It expects of me nothing good. Very well . . . I will become what they thought I already was" (29).

Joseph Bristow argues similarly, but elaborates by placing the novel within the particular context of the Labouchère Amendment to the Criminal Law Amendment Act of 1885.[15] Wilde's novel, he writes, "risked opening up a metaphorical space in which male same-sex desire could be articulated as a potentially beautiful thing that the law rendered ugly by granting such desire a grotesque and incriminatory definition—namely, gross indecency" ("Wilde" 44). Its central metaphor, he claims, must be read against the background of late Victorian legislation on sexual relations, which, in seeking to preserve youth, created the "corruption" it was designed to eradicate. Contained within the metaphor, he suggests, is the distinction between public and private behavior: between the open display of "morality" on the one hand and the secret enjoyment of "vice" on the other. Like Lilly, Bristow rejects the overt meaning of the tale and instead reads it as an interrogation of the language and morality of official culture. What fuels the oppositional thrust of this novel, both critics maintain, is the doctrine of aestheticism that underpins it: for aestheticism in this text becomes itself a metaphor for a whole cluster of energies—passion, same-sex desire, sensuality, hedonistic self-indulgence—outlawed by conventional morality. This metaphor is a recurring one in gay male fiction. It returns in *Forgetting Elena,* for instance, a contemporary re-engagement with the theme of *Dorian Gray* that I discuss in the next chapter.

Bristow and Lilly argue convincingly about the central drive of the text, yet as they themselves suggest, there remains, within and surrounding it, the aforementioned sense of muddle. As Lilly points out, the novel's preference for aesthetics over ethics is itself an ethical act that contradicts the statement (given in the group of aphorisms Wilde added as a preface) that there is "no such thing as a moral or immoral book." Indeed, Wilde's defense of his novel, made in response to horrified reaction to it, attempts both to transcend conventional moral judgements *and* to affirm them. The preface (which Wilde appended to the novel for its first publication in book form; it was originally published serially in *Lippincott's Magazine*) is part of this defense and relieves the artist of all moral responsibility. Yet Wilde also revised the novel to calm the moral objections that had greeted its earlier publication, and even insisted that he had written a conventionally moral book: "And the moral is this: All excess, as well as all renunciation, brings its own punishment" (*Letters* 259). These contradictory responses to the charges brought against it reflect, as Claude Summers remarks, "the incompatible impulses of the novel itself, which mocks conventional morality while enacting a moralistic fable" (*Gay Fictions* 43).

Wilde's incompatible impulses—his antiauthoritarianism and his need for social acceptance—make him the embodiment of the conflict explored in this study. Indeed, the tensions, both internal and external, of his life and work exemplify, in a symbolically significant way, the predicament of homosexual people and movements generally. These tensions are especially evident in *The Picture of Dorian Gray,* where the iconoclastic pull of the writing is constantly at war with the constricting moralism of the plot and formal structure. The opposed energies of the tale, however, are not equally weighted: Dorian, as Summers remarks (44), is strong, youthful, and glamorous, while the good characters—Basil, Sybil, Alan Campbell—have their goodness called to account by the suggestion that they are mere victims of their own weak passivity and mindless conformity, exemplars of Lord Henry's dictum that "Conscience and cowardice are really the same thing, Basil" (6). Hence, the impression *Dorian Gray* finally leaves is quite different from the moral Wilde appends to it as an afterword. For here, excess and renunciation are not equally punished, and where the good characters die horribly, Dorian enjoys, as Summers puts it, a "preternaturally extended youth and beauty bought at the trivial price of a disfigured portrait" (44). In short, the appeal of the Faustian dream in this novel is stronger than "the superimposed lesson of the dangers of narcissism" (44).

There is clear support for this view in Alan Sinfield's remark that "Wilde's fable is ultimately complicit with Dorian's narcissism" (*Wilde Century* 103). Sinfield sees the novel as an attempt to articulate an inchoate, emerging, still dimly perceived and unformulated, queer sensibility. Hence, he suggests, the hostility of the initial reviewers, who perceived the underlying tenor of the book with "varying degrees of knowingness" (104). But he too, like other commentators, finds the text muddled and ambivalent, seeing a revelation of its inner conflict in Dorian's murder of Basil Hallward, who, as the keeper of Dorian's conscience, becomes intolerable to his protégé while still alive. Thus "Dorian arrives at disaster not because he abjures conventional moral principles but because he remains under their sway" (100). Nevertheless, the main thrust of the novel, he implies, is its invocation of an alternative moral vision based on aesthetic principles and focused on youth and beauty—a vision that, perhaps in its very defiance of conventional moral precepts, "answers to a fantasy in gay male subculture" (104).

As Sinfield and others point out, the pervasive suggestion of same-sex passion in *Dorian Gray* is heightened by its specific nonrepresentation in the text. As Neil Bartlett writes: "Only one of [Dorian's] vices is hidden, only one sin cannot be named" (*Who Was That Man?* 94). The central concern of the novel is thus evoked by its absence, becoming the more insistently present in the very act of not being mentioned. Of course, defining the nature of Dorian's life, as Joseph Bristow observes, "would have risked prosecution" ("Wilde" 53), although, as history shows, it is also possible to risk prosecution through intimation of what is not defined. But whatever the case, it is clear that the necessity of presenting its central concern in coded form threatens the novel's coherence. Moreover, it seems likely that the extreme hostility it initially aroused was provoked, in part, by its obliquity: by its never quite saying what it seems to want to say. Although some critics, as their remarks show, caught its drift only too well, for the majority of its early readers, Sinfield suggests, the meaning of the novel became plain (as it does retrospectively for us today) only in the context of what emerged later in the sensational trials of 1895. At which point the text springs "into miraculous coherence" and the book becomes "deafeningly queer" (*Wilde Century* 104–05).

In general, post-Stonewall gay and antihomophobic commentaries on *Dorian Gray,* while recognizing the deep ambivalence and muddle of the novel, lay stress on its radically subversive undercurrent; and this is the emphasis I want to place on my reading of it here. For the motive force of this text, which resonates beyond the contrived melodrama of its plot, is its push for an alternative society and a new moral order. To reduce this alternative to "decadent hedonism," as Mark Lilly does (32), is to ignore the wider implications of Wilde's aestheticism, which, as I note above, subsumes many different kinds of subversive impulse within its metaphoric allusiveness. "Wilde's transgressive aesthetic," writes Jonathan Dollimore, "subverted the dominant categories of subjectivity which kept desire in subjection, subverted the essentialist categories of identity which kept morality in place" (*Sexual Dissidence* 68). Similarly, Claude Summers points up the perversely dynamic and visionary aspect of Wilde's work, drawing attention to those passages in *Dorian Gray* that lament mankind's distrust of the senses: "As he looked back upon man moving through History, he was haunted by a feeling of loss. So much had been surrendered! and to such little purpose!" (130). Indeed, in Summers's view, the novel is ultimately a protest against "an unsatisfactory reality and a tragic history, linked to asceticism and medievalism," in which homosexuality figures as "a powerful and fatal attraction, guilt-inducing and dangerous, yet enormously creative and potentially salvific" (*Gay Fictions* 51).

## JEAN GENET: SUBVERSION FROM WITHIN

Some of the issues raised in these contemporary accounts of *Dorian Gray* are also central to any consideration of *Our Lady of the Flowers*. Thus the creative tensions of Genet's novel, as of Wilde's, arise from an apparent acceptance and simultaneous rejection of cultural norms and conventional moral principles. As Mark Lilly writes, in a remark that could equally apply to Wilde, "Genet's vision of the world is based on ambivalence and unresolved paradoxes" (84). In *Our Lady,* this inner tension is most obviously manifested in the violent incongruity of the novel's subject matter and means of expression. Genet's low-life protagonists—his pimps, prostitutes, thieves, and murderers—often bear sanctifying or hallowed names: Divine, Gabriel, Our Lady. Moreover, the essentially squalid action of the novel, often articulated through the language and imagery of religious experience, is presented as spiritual drama. This clash of sacred and profane implies both reverence and irreverence: on the one hand, respect for life as imbued with the will of the universal law maker; yet on the other, satirical disrespect toward earthly interpretations of that will.

In an attempt to identify the specific nature of Genet's trangressive reinscription, Jonathan Dollimore turns to Genet himself in *Our Lady:* "We are, after all, familiar enough with the tragedy of a certain feeling which is obliged to borrow its expression from the opposite feeling so as to escape the myrmidons of the law. It disguises itself in the trappings of its rival" (*Sexual Dissidence* 96). Genet, Dollimore argues, is concerned, like Wilde (although in ways very different from Wilde) with questions of authenticity and selfhood. He, too, "subverts the depth model of identity via the perverse dynamic" (313). But while always aware of identity as disguise, Genet internalizes the disguise and reauthenticates it. Thus authentic selfhood is first "denied and then re-constituted in perverse, parodic form" (314). Subverting not from without but from within, Genet blows the sacred apart with (and the oxymoron here is itself Genetesque) "a strange knowing innocence" (315). This subtle overturning of hierarchies, Dollimore implies, is more insidiously subversive than blatant resignification, for "[what] transpires is not the sacrilege which pays testimony to the sacred (i.e. containment), but a sacrilege inscribed within the sacred" (314–15).

Genet's concern with authentic selfhood, with identity as disguise, emerges in his attitude to the masculine–feminine binary structure and treatment of sexual stereotypes. He writes: "He [Darling] liked selling out on people. Dehumanizing myself is my own most fundamental tendency" (70). Just as Darling here, "thrilled by a prankishness . . . born from within: 'I'm a double crosser'" (70), accepts and even revels in the dehumanizing title of "traitor," so Genet owns up to and even glories in the sexual stereotyping with which society has already dehumanized him. This is clear from the scene in Graff's café in Montmartre, with which the narration of Divine's life in Paris begins (61–63). Here, Divine, making her entrance in the early hours of the morning, clearly relishes the sensation her outrageous presence provokes. Moreover, in the course of the scene she progresses from object of ridicule to creature of awesome veneration. Indeed, at the point when the café empties of customers fleeing her presence, she has transmogrified into a thing of mystery and myth:

> The cafe disappeared, and Divine was metamorphosed into one of those monsters that are painted on walls—chimeras or griffins—for a customer, in spite of himself, murmured a magic word as he thought of her: "Homoseckshual." (63)

As Stephen Adams points out, the attitude of Genet/Divine here—an attitude fundamental to the novel and to Genet's work as a whole—is disturbingly odd and perverse (185–86). It does not look to find the authentic person beneath the stereotype. Rather, it exalts malicious stereotype, "converting [it] into an idealised state of being" (186). Its glorification of effeminacy and male passivity is thus radically antiassimilative, and accords with Genet's deep and solitary sense of alienation from society, his aloofness from (and disdain for) political movements, and his desire to remain in a state of permanent revolt. Yet, as Adams observes, in its rejection of compromise, in its refusal "to purchase liberation at the expense of others by equating self-respect with manliness" (184), and in its proud adoption of "terms that were formerly pejorative" (186), Genet's position does relate (paradoxically, in view of his apoliticism) to the radical strain of gay political consciousness that emerged after Stonewall.

Genet's subversion of identity, through his glorification and simultaneous exposure of stereotype, is also clear from his treatment of the other characters in the novel. Thus Divine is attracted to, and sexually involved with, a group of males who identify with the conventional model of masculinity, and hence define themselves in opposition to her queenliness. This, together with her "abject submission to the cruelty of the pimps who live like parasites on her" (Adams 188), suggests a deference to the hierarchy of the masculine–feminine binary, and by extension, a passive acceptance of social and sexual norms. Yet this deference and passivity is subtly treacherous, and, as with the novel's attitude to authority in general—to the law, both secular and religious—it subverts artfully, from the inside. Thus Divine is in thrall to the manliness of the men she is involved with and at the same time acutely aware of the theatricality of their assumed roles. Moreover, she sees that their virile posturing is dependent on her worship of it. The effect of this is a constant transference of power, whereby Divine sometimes seems stronger than the men who "control" her.

The very nicknames given to these street hoodlums are an instance of this role-reversal: Darling Daintyfoot, Our Lady, Angel. But delicacy, transience, and vulnerability are also suggested in the characterization of these roughs through the recurrent use of the flower image. Similarly, in the scene of lovemaking between Divine and Darling, the latter's passive role is emphasized. He becomes Divine's doll or plaything: "She takes care of his penis. She caresses it with the most profuse tenderness and calls it by the kind of pet names used by ordinary folk when they feel horny" (88). A large part of what makes these men so touchingly vulnerable, Genet implies, is their anxiety about their masculinity; and in the guise of Divine he is slyly satirical about their concern to avoid any taint of homosexuality or effeminacy. Thus Our Lady in drag, as he accompanies Divine and Gorgui to the cabaret at The Tabernacle, "knows that all his pals will have a laugh, that not a single one will snicker; they esteem him" (172). Nevertheless, he takes delight in being a sexual turn-on for his mates, and is himself sexually excited by the pleasure he gives them:

> Our Lady is acclaimed by his pals. He had not realized that his firm buttocks would draw the cloth so tight. He doesn't give a damn that they see he has a hard-on, but not to such a point, in front of the fellows. He would like to hide. (172)

Divine's belief in these men—these gods of her secular worship—exists alongside a tender and compassionate recognition of the hollowness behind their rough male swagger and self-aggrandisement. This fundamental ambivalence of the novel, this wavering between faith and doubt, is perhaps most clearly intimated in Divine's recollection of her attempt, as the child Lou-Culafroy, to steal the communion hosts from the chapel of the Virgin (136–38). Here, a naive belief in miracles, suggesting both fear and an eager reaching out for assurance—"Blood will flow from the hosts if I take one!"—coexists with a nihilistic urge to test belief to the point of destruction: "And the miracle occurred. There was no miracle. God had been debunked. God was hollow. Just a hole with any old thing around it" (138).

Genet's revenge on society, for the cruel branding he has received at its hand, is to acknowledge proudly the evil attributed to him—indeed, like Divine, to glorify evil and hence achieve sainthood, as she does, through sacrificial and single-minded pursuit of it. Moreover, with this gesture of absolute refusal and grand revolt, Genet, in the guise of Divine, aspires to the heroic stature associated with the other great rebellions of folk myth, of which the Fall is the prototype. The gesture remains finally a gesture, however, since it can never break entirely free of the morality it would disown. Genet's difficulty becomes clear from his stance on homosexuality, for in order to maintain his position of permanent revolt, he has to insist that homosexuality is inherently evil. Part of this insistence, in Leo Bersani's words, is his "original and disturbing notion that homosexuality is congenial to betrayal and, further, that betrayal gives homosexuality its moral value" (*Homos* 153). I return to this idea in Chapter 5, in my discussion of the debate surrounding Genet's novel *Funeral Rites;* but here I want to remark that the link between homosexuality and treachery that Genet alleges is denied within *Our Lady* itself. Thus there is nothing evil or treacherous in Culafroy's love for Alberto, for instance, or in Divine's brief idyll with the doomed soldier, Gabriel. In these relationships, as Stephen Adams puts it, "homosexuality threatens to become a moral positive" (193).

Moreover, as Adams argues, the ambivalence and unresolved paradoxes of the novel become clear in other ways. Thus the novel's insistence that homosexuality is inherently evil is undercut by its attack on those forces in society that convert the possibility of love between men into "gestures of a brutal power play" (192). The positive values of the novel, however, are most clearly embodied in the heroic character of Divine, who sacrifices herself to the ideal of absolute moral solitude. "She is the vehicle of those sensitive, delicate qualities that Genet fails so completely to destroy in himself," Adams writes, "and until her author determines—by her gesture of killing a child—that she should join the 'Elect' of murderers, she subverts the equation of homosexuality with evil as surely as she undermines the domination of her 'masters'" (193).

## BURLESQUE, PARODY, AND VIOLENT TERROR

Internal tensions, such as we find in *Dorian Gray* and *Our Lady*, are also evident in Burroughs's *Naked Lunch* (1959), although here they assume a dramatically different form. Like Wilde and Genet, Burroughs is an enraged iconoclast and satirist, vehemently and energetically striking out at all forms of social control and manipulation. Moreover, his writing, like theirs, suggests an aspiration to escape the confines of the self into an alternative vision of existence. Thus the carnage and brutality of *Naked Lunch* is occasionally interrupted by brief snatches of tenderness and affection, a strain of the writing that points to the lyrical homoeroticism and visionary fantasy of his later novel, *The Wild Boys* (1971). But whereas, in *Dorian Gray* and *Our Lady*, the restricting patterns of life figure as barriers to the realization of the homosexual self, in *Naked Lunch*—where addiction (of many kinds, but especially drug dependency) becomes an all-embracing metaphor for the human condition—homosexuality, in general, figures as part of the self the writer aspires to escape.

Burroughs's relentless pursuit of excessive sexual fantasy in his writing is double-edged, being on the one hand an anarchic revolt, an indulgent, liberating protest against the confines of existence, yet on the other a punishing, curative bid to escape the addictions of life—and, ultimately, the addiction *to* life. His vision is notable for its impersonality, and derives from his commitment to a philosophy he terms "factualism": "All arguments, all nonsensical condemnations as to what people 'should do' are irrelevant. Ultimately there is only fact on all levels, and the more one argues, verbalizes, moralizes, the less he will see and feel of fact" (quoted in Tytell 112). Hence, in contrast to the writers discussed in the first part of this chapter, his resistance to the very idea of love. Love, the above remarks suggest, is a mere word, the product of more nonsensical babbling. Burroughs is committed to facing, and making his readers face, his version of the "facts": the unpalatable truths about ourselves and the human condition generally. As he writes in the introduction to his novel: "The title means exactly what the words say: NAKED Lunch—a frozen moment when everyone sees what is on the end of every fork" (7).

Burroughs's obsession with our enslavement to sex in *Naked Lunch* embodies the central tension of the novel. His rehearsal and repetition of particular sexual fantasies is both a defiant gorging on forbidden fruit and an attempt to cure the craving through surfeit. Moreover, this tension is written into the very fabric and form of the novel, since the cut-up technique used here (whereby written texts are literally cut up and randomly rejoined to form new texts) suggests an act of simultaneous creation and destruction—or perhaps of creation *out of* destruction.[16] Burroughs's friend and disciple, Allen Ginsberg, sheds light on this, in some remarks made in an interview with *Gay Sunshine:* "In fact, the cut-ups were originally designed to rehearse and repeat his obsession with sexual images over and over again . . . so that finally the obsessive attachment, compulsion and preoccupation empty and drain from the image." Ginsberg also illuminates the paranoid, science fiction cosmology of *Naked Lunch* when he adds that Burroughs viewed the body as perhaps "the by-product of a large scale conspiracy by certain forces . . . trying to keep people prisoners in a prison universe made out of parent matter" (quoted in Adams 98). These remarks suggest that the obsession with imagery of sexual excess in the novel is both the feeding of a desperate habit with an urgent fix *and* a final death wish attempt to break free of corporeal imprisonment and erotic compulsion altogether.

This central tension of the novel is clearly encapsulated in what is perhaps its most insistent and disturbing motif: the image of the hanged man. Here, Burroughs crystallizes his obsession with "terminal sex" (to borrow Stephen Adams's expression) into a hypnotic fantasy that fuses feelings of extreme pleasure and pain: sexual ecstasy, terror of life, horror of death. The involuntary arousal of the hanged man—and particularly the culminating simultaneity of ejaculation and snapping neck—is thrillingly macabre, while the spectacle as a whole acts as a dense configuration of Burroughs's paranoia about the loss of the autonomous self through the power of sex to invade and control the body. Thus, in the earliest rehearsal of the fantasy, sex itself seems to be obscenely reified in the grotesque figure of the Mugwump, to whose rape, torture, and execution the "slender blond youth" (69) gives himself in enthralled surrender. But after rising to an excited climax—"A final spasm throws a great spurt of sperm across the red screen like a shooting star"—the sequence suddenly collapses, ending with a suggestion of postorgasmic self-loathing, as Burroughs confronts his squalid subjection to the tyranny of vile fantasy: "The boy falls with soft gutty suction through a maze of penny arcades and dirty pictures" (70).

Terminal sex attains its orgiastic climax, however, in the section of the novel called "A.J.'s Annual Party." In this scenario of a blue movie (briefly introduced by the monstrous impresario, The Great Slashtubitch, whose thuggish name and character are thematically indicative) Mary, Johnny, and Mark attack and destroy each other in an escalating cycle of sado-mas-ochistic lust. Here, the wild surrealism of the narrative suggests an urgent attempt to escape bodily limitation altogether, to explode all the confines of physical existence. Thus the characters adopt different positions and swap gender roles: Mary, for instance, fellates and rims Johnny, and then assaults him with a rubber penis. They also devour and metamorphose into one other, dissolve and reappear, die and resurrect. Moreover, the sequence as a whole suggests an urge to exploit the body not only to the limits of sex-ual pleasure/pain but also to the point of terminal exhaustion. The hanging that features as the centerpiece to this cycle of violence, for instance, cul-minates with Johnny's leap into space: "Masturbating end-over-end, three thousand feet down . . . he screams all the way against the shattering blue of the sky . . . to shatter in liquid relief in a ruined square paved with lime-stone" (86). Eventually he becomes "a limestone statue, a plant sprouting from his cock, lips parted in the half-smile of a junky on the nod" (87). The tension here between Burroughs's enslavement to sex and his urge to break free is demonstrated in the indissoluble mix of compulsive, repetitive imagery (Johnny is resurrected after his fall in order to rerun the cycle) and death wish, for in these pages ecstatic conflagration becomes inextricable from the "liquid relief" of ultimate burnout.

Leaving aside their significance as evidence of internal tension, how else should we interpret these overtly pornographic and shockingly violent scenes? I said at the beginning of this section that what links the novels examined here is their outright rejection of social and sexual norms. In *Naked Lunch*, this rejection is expressed through Burroughs's above-noted paranoid fear of, and assault on, all forms of social and sexual control. The novel's cut-up, deliberately disconnected narrative method, which Stephen Adams reads as an act of self-censorship (99), has also been read as a pur-poseful smashing of the Aristotelian construct, a challenge to the unifying conceptions and logical coherence of cultural imposition, and an attempt to transform language so that it cannot be used as a conditioning agent: "The fear of control and pattern is endemic to Burroughs' vision" (Tytell 132). The novel's pornographic violence, within this reading, becomes defiance of the tyrannical concept of "good taste," and a move to raise and confront "unsuitable" subject matter. If the relentless obsessiveness of Burroughs's fiction sometimes appalls, "his effort," writes John Tytell, "should be appreciated within the context of the tradition created by de Sade, Joyce, Lawrence, and Henry Miller, all writers who have tried to redeem our repressed fears and desires" (123). This tradition extends, in our own time, to the work of Dennis Cooper, whose novel *Frisk* I discuss in Chapter 5 of this study.

Burroughs's rejection of norms and paranoid fear of control help to explain his attitude to homosexuality, distaste for the concept of love, and sometimes rabid hostility to gay culture and politics. As commentators suggest,[17] his celebration of male aggression and anarchic sexuality, like John Rechy's, has its roots in a misogynistic terror of female influence and vaginal castration, as well as a rejection of "faggot" stereotyping. In *Naked Lunch,* these characteristics are on vigorous display in the savagely satirical episode that culminates in the love triumph of Brad and Jim, a section of the novel that reads like a vicious parody of a "gay romance" novelette (107–09). Here, Brad is the stereotype of the southern provincial who moves to New York and becomes a doyen(ne) of the gay scene. His susceptibility to the corrupting, emasculating power of women is indicated in his arrival from "Cunt Lick, Texas," as well as in his arty-crafty, "piss-elegant" skill at making costume jewelery to woo himself into the favors of rich elderly women (107). His fall from grace (after a gambling habit leads him to replace precious stones with cheap replicas) suggests that the story might end with his being liberated into a life of crime. But then "love sets in"; he meets Jim in jail, after which they settle down to a life of gay conformity and cozy domestic bliss: "The boys stand at the tenement window, their arms around each other, looking at the Brooklyn Bridge. A warm spring wind ruffles Jim's black curls and the fine hennaed hair of Brad" (108–09). The final tableau epitomizes Burroughs's loathing of gay coupledom, his hatred of "faggots" as the gelded playthings of "[old] moth-eaten tigress shit" (107) and poodles of the heterosexual establishment: "Dinner is Lady Bradshinkel's cunt saignant cooked in cotex papillon. The boys eat happily looking into each other's eyes. Blood runs down their chins" (109).

As my account of this episode shows, the paranoid bile of *Naked Lunch* is often expressed with scarifying wit and savage black humor. Indeed, critics are at pains to point out that Burroughs must be read as a comic writer, even if his sardonic laughter is not to everyone's taste. "Burroughs' mode is parody," writes John Tytell, adding as a later remark: "The carnival mood of [his] burlesque does balance the sense of violent terror in his work" (133). This is true, but it is also fair to say that the brutality of the humor, because it knows no bounds, also heightens our sense of Burroughs's universal transgressiveness. Thus his hatred and ridicule of all forms of social control, "whether they be left- or right-wing, female or male" (Woods, "Burroughs" 40) gives substance to the claim that he "never quite [fits] in anywhere, remaining an outsider figure to both straight and gay mainstream" (Manning 111).

I have discussed *Naked Lunch* here, even though, within the terms of the ideological opposition around which this study is structured, it belongs nowhere. Moreover, it would deny the very name of gay male fiction, a denial strengthened by its engagement with themes beyond the focus of this study. If all commentators agree that this is a nightmare vision of apocalypse, John Tytell concedes that there is room for doubt concerning the kind of apocalypse envisioned. Is it a nightmare of entropy and recidivism, of "matter returning to lower forms of organization . . . to some primitive feared state" (as the prevalence of insect imagery suggests), or a futuristic vision, equally nightmarish, of "cybernetic reality replacing human perspectives in the West" (138)? Whatever the case, there is no doubt (again the commentators agree) that *Naked Lunch* is death-haunted. For Stephen Adams, Burroughs, seeking "to release the entrapped spirit to some netherworld that lies, necessarily, beyond the scope of definition . . . to escape into a psychic nowhere" (104), offers only physical reductiveness and hopeless negation. For Gregory Woods, too, he "dramatizes a movement towards sterility and inhumanity" ("Burroughs" 42). Woods, like Adams, emphasizes the sense of exhaustion and loss in the writing: "His are books of the dead, books that look back to life, books that long for a return to life but acknowledge the fact that time—relativity notwithstanding—moves in only one direction. They are Pastorals" (42–43).

## SUMMARY

In this chapter I have traced the assimilative and radically transgressive impulses as revealed in representative examples from two distinct strains of gay male fiction of the pre-Stonewall era, in order to show the ancestry of the fiction discussed in my core chapters. However, all the novels examined here, as I point out at the start, are marked by internal tension, their general tendencies, whether assimilative or radically transgressive, never pure. In the assimilative strain, for instance, the general insistence on the normality of homosexuality is accompanied by a sometimes equally strong assertion of difference; while in the radically transgressive strain, the rejection of the concept of normality—the celebration of difference—is made in reaction to, and thus dependent on, the very norms it would defy. I return to these two strains of fiction, as represented in the post-Stonewall period, in Chapters 4 and 5, where they are treated separately. Meanwhile, the inner conflict revealed in the novels examined in this chapter is especially evident in gay male fiction of the 1970s, which is the focus of my next chapter.

# 3 "The Potency, Magnetism, and Promise of Gay Self-Disclosure"
Paradise Found?

> Gay liberation grew out of the progressive spirit of the 1960s—a strange and exhilarating blend of socialism, feminism and the human potential movement. Accordingly, what gay leaders in the late 1960s were anticipating was the emergence of the androgyne, but what they got was the superbutch stud; what they expected was a communal hippie freedom from possessions, but what has developed is the acme of capitalist consumerism. . . . Unfortunately, today this rampant and ubiquitous consumerism not only characterizes gay spending habits but also infects attitudes toward sexuality: gays rate each other quantitatively according to age, physical dimensions and income: and all too many gays consume and dispose of each other, as though the very act of possession brought about instant obsolescence.
>
> —Edmund White, "Paradise Found"

The riots at New York's Stonewall Inn in June 1969 gave birth to the modern gay movement. "From now on," in Neil Miller's words, "everything would be described as 'pre-Stonewall' or 'post-Stonewall'" (367). Edmund White, who took part in the riots, acknowledges the mythic significance of this moment in gay history in the final pages of *The Beautiful Room Is Empty* (1988), where it becomes the climax of the novel: "I stayed over at Lou's. We hugged each other in bed like brothers, but we were too excited to sleep. We rushed to buy the morning papers to see how the Stonewall Uprising had been described. 'It's really our Bastille Day,' Lou said. But we couldn't find a single mention in the press of the turning point of our lives" (184). White thus adds to the mythologizing process. This novel is the central volume of his autobiographical trilogy, a series that begins with *A Boy's Own Story* (1983) and concludes with *The Farewell Symphony* (1997). The placing of this event at this point in the narrative is thus part of the plot structure of the sequence as a whole: Stonewall becomes the curtain to the second act of the drama and the turning point not only of the hero-narrator's life but of the phase of gay history his life parallels.

Stonewall does not mark an absolutely clean break with the past, however, as many writers have remarked. Eve Kosofsky Sedgwick, for instance, argues that "the closet," or what she calls the regime of "the open secret," has been basic to lesbian and gay life for the last century, both before and after Stonewall. Nevertheless, she acknowledges that "the events of June, 1969, and later vitally reinvigorated many people's sense of the potency, magnetism, and promise of gay self-disclosure" (*Epistemology* 67). White's testimony would appear to endorse this. Seeking to define the significance of Stonewall, he considers the difference in his own life between his experience of group psychotherapy in the 1960s and his experience of group consciousness-raising in the early 1970s. He describes these as entirely separate experiences. Thus in the former he was attending group sessions with mostly heterosexual people and with a view to becoming "straight": "and always feeling that I was out of step, and that every action and every feeling was a symptom of my central neurosis, which was being gay" (Brookes 36).[1] In the latter, however, the aim was to allow the exclusively gay participants to give testimony to their experience with a view to changing society. One immediate and significant change resulting from these testimonies, as he points out, was that the American Psychiatric Association was forced in the early 1970s to redefine homosexuality as *not* a pathology, and indeed as part of a range of normal behavior.[2]

These changes, together with the success of gay rights legislation in parts of the United States and the passing of the 1967 Sexual Offences Act in Britain, created a space in which a modern gay movement and culture might grow. But this growth, and the freedom it implied, entailed a radical questioning of social forms, a rethinking of the kind of political and social arrangements that might express and accommodate the personal experience being discovered in group consciousness-raising. In short, what kind of gay movement, what kind of gay culture? According to White, the American gay movement in the early seventies was made up of people like himself—that is, of socialists. He is careful, however, to put a nuance on this word: his own brand of socialism is "more a sympathy than a program"; it does not subscribe "to the 'scientific' pretensions of Marxism"; it wishes to see "an end to racism, sexism, the exploitation of workers and other social inequalities so long as the means for eradicating them are consonant with nonviolence and democracy" (*States of Desire* 335). However, it is the collision between these ideals and the seductive reality of the dominant gay male culture of this period—largely that of New York and San Francisco—that is the source of the tension and unease in much of its fiction. In the case of White and Andrew Holleran (whose novel *Dancer from the Dance* is usually taken as sounding the keynote of this particular cultural moment) the tension is internal, since these writers are both charmed and repelled by the lifestyles they depict.

As White starkly reminds us, the new gay culture that emerged after Stonewall (with its attendant euphoria of sexual freedom and sense of "paradise found") was short-lived: "I thought that never had a group been placed on such a rapid cycle—oppressed in the fifties, freed in the sixties, exalted

in the seventies and wiped out in the eighties" (*Farewell Symphony* 494).
This much-quoted résumé pithily summarizes the meteoric path of gay history in White's lifetime, a half century that, to recall an earlier remark, has
seen the birth of modern gay culture, its brief flowering and near-extinction. And if the post-Stonewall period has seen an explosion of gay literature documenting these changes, the year 1978 is usually seen as marking
the arrival of this "modern gay literary movement," as some critics have
termed it. In this year a new generation of gay writers burst onto the literary scene with the almost simultaneous publication of several novels that
have since established themselves as gay literary landmarks: Andrew Holleran's *Dancer from the Dance*, Larry Kramer's *Faggots*, Edmund White's
*Nocturnes for the King of Naples*, and Armistead Maupin's *Tales of the
City*. These novels signaled the birth of a new kind of gay fiction. Indeed,
by the early 1980s, Holleran and White were meeting and reading their
work to each other as leading lights of The Violet Quill Club, that small
group of writers, based in New York, whose commitment was to writing
that was specifically and openly gay, and whose work, in David Bergman's
words, "has come to epitomize the dozen years of gay life between the outbreak of the Stonewall Riots—when everything seemed possible—and the
first reports of AIDS, a disease that has already killed four and infected a
fifth of the group's seven members" (Bergman, *Violet Quill Reader* xii).[3]
If Maupin's depiction of the West Coast scene, however, reminds us that
this new gay male culture was not exclusively an East Coast phenomenon,
Kramer's aggressively maverick novel—deliberately offensive, hortatory,
and controversial—suggests a writer whose principal concerns are political
rather than literary, an impression strengthened by his subsequent transformation into one of the leading AIDS activists of the 1980s.


**THE THEME ANNOUNCED**

But although the year 1978 looks like a convenient date from which to
begin an examination of gay male fiction since Stonewall, in fact the very
best point of entry is *Forgetting Elena*, Edmund White's first-published
novel, which appeared five years earlier in 1973. In a brief but aston-
ishingly prescient novel (a pre-echo of 1978), White brilliantly captures
the lurking zeitgeist of the decade. Like *Dancer* and *Faggots*, *Forgetting
Elena* is prophetic, undermining the period's superficial sense of euphoric
well-being and hinting at the underlying tensions of post-Stonewall gay
politics, tensions that will erupt in the era of AIDS. White's own remarks
on the novel throw light on its thematic relationship to the later literature
of the period:

> *Forgetting Elena* is, among other things, a fantasy novel about the
> charm—and repulsiveness—of a closed society that has allowed the

cult of beauty to replace genuine moral concerns. The denizens of my island kingdom, which sometimes resembles Fire Island, never stop to question if an act is good or bad so long as it is beautiful. (*Burning Library* 368)

While susceptible to the attractions of the new gay culture, then, White, like Holleran and Kramer, is disturbed by an underlying sense of unease about it, although, unlike them, he explores the theme obliquely through fantasy, in a novel that is not explicitly gay.

*Forgetting Elena*, as White suggests, is a covert investigation of the Fire Island gay scene. That Fire Island should be the setting for so much of this period's gay fiction (it is *Dancer*'s principal *mise-en-scène*, and the opening of the Fire Island season is the backdrop for the finale of *Faggots*) is hardly surprising, for in the 1970s this rich and fashionable beach resort off Long Island became the center of New York's glamorous, hedonistic gay male culture—the place where the dream of absolute sexual freedom that was fundamental to the new gay movement's ideology became reality. It was thus the obvious site to begin an investigation into the kind of society that might result from the realization of such a dream; and this is the problem with which *Elena, Dancer,* and *Faggots* are all, in their separate ways, centrally concerned. Indeed, as we might expect, what lies at the heart of the gay literature of this period is a passionate moral engagement with the ideals of the new gay movement and the values implicit in the new post-Stonewall social and sexual experiment.

Hence, the confused and morally ambivalent narrator of *Elena* is not only White's alter ego but also the perfect embodiment of the tensions humming beneath the outwardly exuberant Fire Island scene. This becomes clear when the novel is seen in context and with the benefit of hindsight. It is not obvious from a reading of the text alone, however, for *Elena* approaches its central problem indirectly, and its fantasy is White's means of keeping an anthropological distance between himself and the society he is investigating—or, in other words, of dramatizing his own split allegiances. This sense of detachment, of laboratory-like examination, is enhanced by the narrator's amnesia, a defamiliarizing device that compels him (and us) to discover the workings of the society he inhabits through analysis and close scrutiny. Thus obliquely disclosed, the island suggests a newly democratized country, whose old aristocratic order (the Old Code) has been replaced, theoretically at least, by an egalitarian one (the New Code). Theoretically, because, as the narrator's scrutiny reveals, the island's professed deregularization and egalitarianism is contradicted by its practice: "But my dear fellow, do as you like" and "We are all equals now" (13) are merely its glib refrains.

As White records in his essay "Fantasia on the Seventies," his enthusiasm for that decade is "not uninflected" (*Burning Library* 42). While welcoming some of its features—the new quality to gay life in New York, the growing self-acceptance—he is clearly disturbed by signs that suggest that the promise of the 1960s and of Stonewall has not been, and will not be, realized. Though the forces of sexual liberation have taken root and created very different and original sexual practices, this has resulted not in a new order, a new way of relating to each other, an end to the role-playing that feminism and gay liberation have promised. Instead, what has emerged is a way of life both shockingly different from the old one and yet depressingly the same: "Sexual permissiveness [has become] a form of numbness, as rigidly codified as the old morality. . . . Gay pride has come to mean the worship of machismo" (39–40). Moreover, the strong sense of gay solidarity felt at the Stonewall Uprising, and vividly re-created in White's writing from firsthand experience, now looks to be an illusion. Indeed his reading of the signs suggests to him that the gay movement is destined to fragment, as the rapport between lesbians and gay men inevitably collapses and gay liberation comes to seem like liberation for a few, already privileged, white middle-class males:

> Politically, the war will not take place. . . . I suspect individual gays will remain more loyal to their different social classes than to their sexual colleagues. . . . A general American rejection of the high stakes of shared social goals for the small change of personal life . . . has left the movement bankrupt. (42)

Central to White's work is a sense that he himself is implicated in this failure. As himself a privileged, white, middle-class male, with large ambitions and an attraction to wealth and success, White is acutely conscious of the contradictions within himself. In a passage of critical self-examination at the end of *States of Desire* he finds that "his most maddening fault . . . is a peculiar alternation between socialism and snobbism" (*States of Desire* 334). That a man of White's background and education, though "more inclined to side with the poor and with the Third World," finds himself, paradoxically, "more at home with rich whites" (335) might not surprise us, but White clearly detects in this paradox (a tension variously explored in his fiction) something deeper and more guilt-inducing. Betrayal, as White recognizes, is one of the deepest themes of his work, an insight that gives some clue to the impulse behind his full-length biographical study of Jean Genet:

> [If] betrayal is one of the deepest themes of my writing, and maybe of my life, it's so deep that I don't understand it. I know, for instance, that I made everybody laugh when I wrote that Genet is always talking about his three cardinal virtues being homosexuality, theft and betrayal. I thought: "Betrayal? I don't understand. Why would anybody want to do that?" But I had already written *A Boy's Own Story*, so clearly I had a blind spot to my own deepest compulsions. (Brookes 33)

Some of White's other remarks, too, seem relevant here. He has said, for instance, that although lost innocence is a great theme in American literature, he does not feel it to be a major theme in his own work, nor one that greatly interests him. He feels that his protagonists, like those of much nineteenth-century French fiction, are hungry for experience and gladly lose whatever innocence they have at an early stage in the narrative: "But I think that innocence, as such, doesn't interest me very much. It's a great American theme and I find it very annoying. I mean, in that way, I'm much closer to the French, who, if they should happen to have, say, a girl who loses her innocence, she loses her innocence on the first page so that she can get on with her life" (Brookes 33–34). This suggests that for White, as for his protagonists, innocence is less a virtue than a weakness and a hindrance. It suggests, too, that the moral system underpinning his fiction is based not on the simple binary opposition between innocence and experience (or between innocence/initiation, urbane/provincial, man/boy, to use some of the associated terms in Eve Sedgwick's analysis of the homo–hetero binary structure)[4] but precisely on a rejection of such essentialist categorization. It suggests, in fact, a belief in civilization and its constructionist possibilities, grounded on the assumption that, however susceptible to corruption it may be, civilization is not *inherently* corrupt or irredeemable.

The narrator of *Elena,* then, is engaged in a moral struggle and his amnesia seems to be a symptom of his ambiguity, suggesting a convenient and involuntary lapse of memory in response to moral uncertainties and divided loyalties. His character, which is a blend of innocence and cunning, is presented as in part the product of his social environment, as his means of survival in a corrupt and hypocritical culture that has "a surface democracy, but an actual hidden hierarchy" (Bonetti 102). In his need to learn the mores of the island community, to discover who has claims on him, to jockey for power, the narrator switches allegiances several times in the course of the novel. But although this progress may be seen as representative of any individual within any society, the society he inhabits is presented as a specific one: it is a society in which "morality has been replaced by esthetics" and where people are no longer "troubled about what [is] good, but only about what [is] beautiful," a society representative of "how a certain group of highly privileged gay men were living in the seventies" (Bonetti 102).

In *Elena,* homoerotic desire, as in the writings of Wilde and Firbank, is not directly addressed, but by a process of displacement articulated and explored through its metonymic associations with aestheticism and the cult of beauty. Thus what the novel evokes (again, as in the fantasy worlds of Wilde and Firbank) is a homosexual aesthete's dream of an island paradise of sophisticated decadence. But the island is *not* paradise: reality frequently intrudes on its artificiality and beneath the calm of its surface—as beneath the civilized banter of the Manor House, Woolton, and the spa resort of Valmouth—there is tension, suffering, and even tragedy. In this society, however, style is everything; and just as the elevated "camp" of the homosexual aesthete (the traditional source of so much gay writing) is a way of coping, of anesthetizing the pain, so the island community in *Elena* seeks to "forget" the suffering and tragedy in its own midst through its cult of beauty and hedonistic irresponsibility. Thus the sufferings of those representatives of the Old Code, burned out of their homes in the island's political conflict, are ignored, idealized, and sublimated into art by the representatives of the New Code, the island's new aesthetic order dedicated to freedom and democracy. Indeed the revelers on the yacht in the opening chapter of the novel are so insulated from reality that when the fire from a burning home lights up the sky over the island it immediately becomes subsumed within their narrow worldview as raw material for artistic creation:

> Never thinking for a moment that there might actually be a fire on the island, the messengers formed a semicircle around the girls performing the mirror dance, clapped and, their backs to the rouging sky, called out in a singsong fashion on every third and fourth beat, "Fire fire" . . . (22)

The narrator's progress in this milieu is accompanied by "a sense of ominous unease"—to use a phrase of A. Alvarez, noting one of Firbank's ingredients[5]—and suggests a process of corruption and moral decay. Thus, his "amnesia" allows him to keep an anthropological distance between himself and the islanders, so that, not knowing his relationship to those around him, he is able to retain his "innocence" even while using and betraying them. His reaction to the news of Elena's suicide, which has been caused, as her written account makes clear, by his neglect and desertion of her, reinforces this impression. Thus, when Herbert questions him about the cause of the rift between himself and Elena, he replies, "I don't know what to think" (122), a remark that suggests that he is using his "amnesia" as a convenient cover for his own moral failings.

The theme of betrayal becomes most explicit in the final pages of the novel, where the narrator both remembers who he is (the former prince of this newly democratized country) and forgets what he has done (caused the death of his beloved Elena). His discovery that he is not the outsider he thought he was, but, on the contrary, the ultimate insider of this sham democracy is significant: for if the movement described in the novel relates to the betrayal of ideals that White noted in his "Fantasia on the Seventies," in which the New Code simply repeats the old oppressive structures in disguised form, the discovery by the narrator that he is at the center of this movement suggests (paralleling, as it does, the theme of betrayal in White's self-avowedly autobiographical writing in *Nocturnes* and *A Boy's Own Story*) that White is presenting himself here as centrally implicated in this same betraying process.

*Forgetting Elena*, then, makes an ideal entry point for a study of post-Stonewall gay male fiction because it clearly announces the central theme not only of White's work but of post-Stonewall gay culture and politics in general: the problem of identity. White's examination of the Fire Island scene in this novel is essentially an engagement with what Eve Kosofsky Sedgwick calls "our chronic, now endemic crisis of homo/heterosexual definition" (*Epistemology* 1). Foucault identifies the moment, roughly contemporaneous with the creation of the medical category of homosexuality in the last third of the nineteenth century, when homosexuality becomes identified with a certain "sensibility" and the homosexual becomes a "species" (*History* 43)—a moment that, in Sedgwick's account, assigns to every given, already gendered person a further "binarized identity that [is] full of implications . . . for even the ostensibly least sexual aspects of personal existence" (*Epistemology* 2). In its concern with innocence/initiation, wholeness/decadence, nature/artifice, as with the whole range of connotations implicit in Sedgwick's analysis, *Elena* is an exploration of this binarism.[6]

In Sedgwick's analysis of the meanings and values implicit in the opposed identities of modern gay–straight definition, the qualities of depth, authenticity, and sincerity—of "naturalness"—fall on the dominant side of our essentially masculinist, and therefore heterosexist, culture. Wilde's attempt to subvert this structure, through his rejection of the depth model, his promotion of the artificial, his blurring of categories (trivial/serious, art/nature), and his focus on the insecurity of language, anticipates the work of modern deconstructive theory.[7] *Elena*, too, prefiguring the concerns of later gay fiction, reflects and engages with this discourse: its amnesiac narrator struggles with the fundamental existential question "Who am I?," while the focus of his anxieties is his lack of those qualities—depth, authenticity, sincerity—that fall on the "masculine" side of the homo–hetero divide. His "horrid adaptability" (to use the term that the narrator of *The Farewell Symphony* applies to himself [87]), the ease with which he becomes what others expect of him in this terminally sophisticated society, disturbs him. This reaction is dramatized in the opening scene of the novel, where, after registering a "natural" response to a spontaneous gesture from a boy singer, he is easily persuaded by Herbert to write a poem about it: "'Well, yes,' I said, not knowing what was in store for me but eager to oblige" (19). The ensuing contest reveals, as much in White as in this competitive, rule-bound society, a concern with identity, with (loss of) authenticity, with the relationship between art and nature, art and kitsch. Indeed, the narrator's desire to produce something "direct, modest and original" in contrast to the "strain" of Herbert's verse recalls the binary definitions of Sedgwick's analysis and suggests a relationship between poetry (viewed as an artificial construct) and the social construction (variously advanced in Foucauldian and Sedgwickian constructionist theory) of personality, gender, and sexuality.

In *Elena*, the ambivalent narrator is torn between the opposed attributes of Sedgwick's "binarized identity," a dilemma centrally dramatized in the tense triangular relationship that develops between himself and the characters who most clearly embody this opposition, Elena and Herbert. Herbert is quickly established as an authority (and surrogate father) figure in the opening scene of the novel. Appointed "regent" of the island by the narrator's actual father, he is the principal representative of its dominant political and cultural order, the New Code. Elena's Otherness, on the other hand, is suggested partly by her role as a woman in this male-dominated society and partly by the vagueness of her identity: for, unlike Herbert, who is named on the first page, throughout most of the novel she is referred to simply as "the woman."

Yet in other ways these two characters seem to represent the conventional attributes of the gender roles in reverse, since it is Elena who embodies the qualities of depth, authenticity, sincerity, and moral authority conventionally seen as "masculine." As regent of the island, on the other hand, Herbert exemplifies the values of the New Code, from which conventional moral concerns have been banished and replaced by a new aesthetic order, concerned only with appearances. He is thus situated at the center of an ideology dedicated to the pursuit of Wilde's dictum, "The first duty in life is to be as artificial as possible." Elena's opposition to the New Code is revealed both in what she says—"Are you laughing at me now? How can I know? We're so ironic, we never know when we're serious" (109)—and in her writing—"We saw how the island's cult of beauty was at the heart of its vapidity, and we tried to be as blunt and awkward as possible" (120). Herbert and Elena, then, challenge the narrator to make a moral choice, a challenge he initially ducks through his fugue into amnesia. Hence, when the choice he eventually makes leads to Elena's suicide, his memory responds selectively: he recalls his past life as prince of this vapid, style-conscious kingdom and conveniently, ceremoniously, in accord with the island's highly aestheticised burial ritual, "forgets" Elena (124–70).

The problem with which *Elena* is engaged, then, is one that has been absolutely central to homosexual culture since the birth of such culture, and explored in literature from Wilde to the present day—or for what Alan Sinfield calls "the Wilde century." Since homosexual men and women in Western societies have always been seen, even in sexually permissive times, as occupying a space outside the conventional moral code, they have attempted, through a radical questioning of that code, to create within their own space an alternative moral system. But cultural norms are not easily overthrown: we are all, whatever our sexuality, raised within them and molded by them. Hence the tendency for gay subcultures to define themselves *within the terms of* the dominant ideology: to create what Foucault calls a "reverse discourse," rather than develop an independent, truly alternative identity. Alan Sinfield neatly states the problem:

> Homosexuality and heterosexuality are mutually defining concepts; the one is stigmatized because it is not the other. That is why our [gay

political] strategies are bound, almost, to be reactive. . . . We have to invoke dominant structures to oppose them, and our dissidence, therefore, can always be discovered reinscribing that which it aspires to critique. (*Wilde Century* 203)

In *Elena*, the island's New Code is shown to be dependent on, as invoking and reinscribing, the still-dominant structures of the Old Code: for behind its "surface democracy" lurks "an actual hidden hierarchy," and behind its would-be insouciance lurks a nagging, rule-bound rigidity. Indeed, in its struggle to escape the past, the island is presented as having created not an alternative to the Old Code, but a mirror image of it. Thus it attempts to protect its ideological purity through exercise of power, to eliminate dissidence through acts of violent suppression. It is significant, too—and underlines this theme of reinscription—that Herbert, the chief representative of the New Code, is an authority figure set in place by the chief representative of the Old Code, the narrator's father and the old ruler of the island, and moreover that he and Doris (who, as a senior member of one of the island's old aristocratic families, the Valentines, also represents the Old Code) reconcile their differences during the course of the novel and thus form a sinister new alliance.

Elena is the dissident and renegade. Though by birth a Valentine, she shows allegiance to neither code. Her opposition to Herbert has been noted; and as Doris says, "Elena is not one of us" (110). In the novel's oppositional color scheme (the black of the Valentines, the white of the new prince) her association with the color gray is further indication of her outsidership: "Yes. There she is. Standing on a dune up ahead. She's still wearing gray, a gray cloak over a *feuille-morte* dress, a dress the colour of dead leaves" (94). Against the alliance of Herbert and Doris, hers is an independent voice, representing a possible alternative:

> I can imagine our going away. Or even staying here, but staying together. Becoming different people. Forgetting all codes, old and new. Walking out of a room in simple, natural fashion instead of *recessing*. No more arch comments. No more mystification. We all pass judgments on one another. We have to. It's the easiest way to be witty. But if we didn't? (109)

There is a hint of this alternative in the passage of Alan Sinfield I have cited above: "That is why our [gay political] strategies are bound, *almost*, to be reactive" [emphasis added]. In *Elena*, the island's culture and politics are an illustration of what Sinfield calls the "entrapment model" of ideology and power, whereby a political strategy designed "to challenge the system help[s] to maintain it" (*Faultlines* 39). Elena's dissidence is not reactive; it is more subtly subversive. She and her friends make up a small subcultural group, occupying a space outside the island's dominant cultural formation, in which New Code exists in mutually defining opposition to Old Code.

Their existence therefore challenges the dominant order by drawing attention to what Sinfield calls "faultlines" in the system.[8] Maria, for instance, as Harry Mathews points out, is apparently one of only two black persons to be seen on the island; Elena's choice of Maria as a companion is thus an embarrassment to the island community since it draws attention to what appears to be its white imperialist and possibly genocidal past ("A Valentine for Elena" 42).

## THE CENTRAL PROBLEM OF POST-STONEWALL GAY POLITICS

"So you will be changing, or adjusting to the New Code?"
"I don't like that word. It's silly. A New Order is what we have in
    mind, Herbert and I." (110)

From a gay political perspective, the new order that emerged after Stonewall was problematic from its very beginning. Its success, in Edmund White's view, was "strongly related to the rise of the gay market" ("Paradise Found" 148). Its politics were thus immediately compromised and called into question, since the beneficiaries of this new order—representatives of the "triumphant clone culture" (*Burning Library* 371)—were, as already noted, mainly white, middle-class, and male. Rampant gay consumerism, however, merely intensified a problem that, for gay politics, had been always already present. Foucault identifies this problem when he notes (in that passage quoted above) how nineteenth-century legal, medical, and sexological discourses on homosexuality provoked a "reverse" discourse, whereby homosexuality learned to speak "in its own behalf . . . in the same vocabulary, using the same categories by which it was . . . disqualified" (*History* 101): for the problem he recognizes here is that a reverse discourse is still dependent on tenets and vocabulary inherited from the dominant. As a reverse discourse, the gay liberation movement of the seventies, like the gay male culture it engendered, was, as Foucault saw, embedded in an ideology it wished to defy. "'Sexuality' may be an historical invention," Jeffrey Weeks writes, "but we are ensnared in its circle of meaning. We cannot escape it by an act of will" (*Against Nature* 166).

So what options are there? As a cultural materialist engaged in theorizing the scope for sexual dissidence, Alan Sinfield points out that Foucault is less drawn to the "entrapment model" of ideology and power than his writings initially suggest. Despite his assertion that there is "no single locus of great Refusal" and thus not much scope for a grand revolutionary gesture, Foucault nevertheless sees potential in "a plurality of resistances . . . spread over time and space at varying densities, at times mobilizing groups or individuals in a definitive way" (*History* 95–96). This is the idea underpinning Sinfield's own thinking about strategies for cultural change, although he also draws strongly on the work of Raymond Williams. Williams writes of the need to see ideology as a process, and one that is always precarious. Under pressure from diverse disturbances, it has always to be produced: "social orders and cultural orders must be seen as being actively made; actively and continuously, or they may quite quickly break down" (Williams 201). Thus, in proposing a strategic principle, Sinfield lays stress on diversity and cunning, flexibility, and surprise: "[W]e have to build a stronger subculture—more vigorous, intelligent and various" (*Wilde Century* 206). Straightforward reactive challenges to ideology, he implies, through invocation and reinscription of the very structures they seek to deny, are more easily contained. At all events, we must avoid replacing one form of oppression with another:

> [S]ubculture does not mean establishing a party line, but working questions out . . . We don't, we now realize, have to be clones . . . we have to recognize, dispute, negotiate each other's needs, elaborating ourselves across a range of discourses, some of them special to us, many of them in overlap and ongoing dialectic with other cultures. We need to be heterogeneous, contentious. (206)

This critique of the gay subculture is the central theme of post-Stonewall gay politics and culture, and is clearly announced in *Elena,* a novel published just four years after Stonewall. The island culture in *Elena* resembles not only the culture of the Fire Island scene but that of any society newly emerged from the shadow of an oppressive system: Harry Mathews suggests, for example, that of "an enlightened European principality in the wake of the French Revolution" (34). Within this culture, New and Old Codes become mutually defining concepts, and thus, through a process of reinscription, mutually supporting: "Under the New Code," says Elena, "the islanders, forbidden to ridicule people for their low birth or humble position, have resorted to rejecting their inferiors for some supposed insensitivity to beauty or for some social blunder" (120). Elena challenges the New Order (the alliance of New and Old Codes) through her loyalty to an ideal; and given the novel's context, this somewhat elusive ideal might be seen as emblematic of the new gay movement, described by White, in the passage quoted at the head of this chapter, as growing out of "the progressive movement of the 1960s" and characterized as "a strange and exhilarating blend of socialism, feminism and the human potential movement." Her idealism is opposed to the realism of the New Order—its fudge, compromise, and betrayal: "This is not the best of all possible worlds but we must live in it," says Doris (110); and Elena writes: "The odd thing was that Herbert had never converted to the New Code he had himself invented" (120).

As I have already hinted, *Elena* is a dramatization of ideas explored nonfictionally in White's journalism and in his *States of Desire: Travels in Gay America.* As these writings show, the "triumphant clone culture" of the seventies rapidly replaced a long-established stereotype, derived from the Wilde model, of gay men as effeminates and losers in a dominant male culture with a new one constructed from the imagery of machismo, in which gay men figure as confident winners precisely at the center of this male culture. For White, this development, though a welcome demonstration of gay ingenuity and resilience, is profoundly unsettling, not only because, in its materialism, sexism, and racism, it offends his socialist principles, but also because its very success appears to vindicate that Foucauldian and constructionist view of human nature in which stable notions of personality, gender, and sexuality dissolve. Yet simultaneously and paradoxically, this instability, this dissolving of fixed notions of identity, is powerfully attractive to him, for under the impact of such theory and its resulting social change, Sedgwick's "crisis of homo/heterosexual definition," which traps gay men within a minority identity—a "minoritizing" construction that devalues "one of the two nominally symmetrical forms of choice" (*Epistemology* 9)—seems weakened, vulnerable, less oppressive.

In his interview for the *Paris Review* White says that, although as a novelist he must proceed in the belief that each individual is distinctive, in a philosophical sense he is convinced that "the self" is an illusion and that the way to enlightenment is, as the Buddhists teach, "to dissolve the illusion of unity and return all these elements [of association and memory] to their original constituents, thereby ridding oneself of the notion of identity" (*Burning Library* 266). Likewise, the narrator of White's novel *The Beautiful Room Is Empty*, expanding on this theme, sees a link between his attraction to the Buddhist doctrine of the nonsoul and his hatred of his homosexuality. This doctrine, the *anattā*,

> suggested I was potentially everything and actually nothing. I could wake up one morning gay or straight—or as nothing, since Buddhism seemed to annihilate such essences. I was afraid to make a choice of any kind. (66)

He is attracted to Buddhist doctrine, then, because it eliminates the need for self-definition within the defining terms of an oppressive, minoritizing system. And here White is addressing a central paradox in modern gay politics, a paradox that is bound up with his ambivalence to certain aspects of post-Stonewall gay culture: namely, that it is only through self-definition within this minoritizing system that homosexuality can become universalized, to use Sedgwick's terminology—that is, seen "as an issue of continuing, determinative importance in the lives of people across the spectrum of sexualities" (*Epistemology* 1). Just as the tenets of structuralism are revised and developed by deconstructive analysis (and Sedgwick's is essentially a deconstructive exercise) so a minoritizing view of homo–heterosexual definition can only proceed to a universalizing view through an initial assertion of gay identity. Gay identity, in other words, must first be asserted before it can be deconstructed; and since the 1980s, in a period when gay identity has been severely threatened from the impact of AIDS and general cultural change, this paradox has been all the more keenly felt.

## THE THEME PURSUED

As David Bergman writes, the twelve-year span between the outbreak of the Stonewall Riots and the first reports of AIDS "has been execrated for all that is worst in gay life—its shallow hedonism, its mindless trendiness, its self-indulgent irresponsibility, its empty narcissism," and yet also celebrated "as a period of rare freedom, intense communion, unsurpassed energy and creativity" (*Violet Quill Reader* xii). These opposed views of the period are represented in its fiction, and indeed, as *Elena* demonstrates, sometimes within the same work. In White's stark summary of recent gay history ("oppressed in the fifties, freed in the sixties, exalted in the seventies and wiped out in the eighties"), the seventies figure as the high point. Yet, as we have seen and he himself notes, White's attitude to the period is actually deeply ambivalent: "I was attracted to both gay politics and the gay sensibility, two very different entities; the tension humming under every page of *Forgetting Elena* was born out of this conflict" (*Burning Library* 368).

The decade is famed then for its feelings of gay exaltation, yet the best-known novels of the period—White's *Forgetting Elena* and *Nocturnes for the King of Naples,* Holleran's *Dancer from the Dance* and Kramer's *Faggots*—are all driven by the same sense of moral unease and thematically linked by their critique of the gay subculture. This critique, however, as we might expect from three such varied writers, comes in diverse forms. White and Kramer, for instance, have quite different perspectives: White is ambivalent; Kramer is openly hostile. But if the outbreak of the Stonewall Riots was a moment "when everything seemed possible," as Bergman puts it (*Violet Quill Reader* xii), what links the critique of these two writers is the idea of possibilities unfulfilled. For Holleran, on the other hand, politics seem beside the point, and his celebration of the seventies is undercut by a sense of guilt, alienation, and melancholic fatalism.

I should make clear that the writings of White, Holleran, and Kramer do not make up the whole of gay male fiction in this decade. Fiction in the popular tradition of the coming-out novel, or offering a more positive view of gay experience, also began to appear, of which Daniel Curzon's *Something You Do in the Dark* (1971) and Sanford Friedman's *Still Life* (1975) are early, notable examples. It is White, Holleran, and Kramer who provide the dominant theme, however, even if this is clearly more complex than the epigraph to this chapter suggests. In that passage, White finds the progressive spirit of the sixties obliterated during the seventies by the rise of the pink economy and the commercialization of the gay scene. His critique of the gay subculture is thus founded, like Holleran's and Kramer's, on a sense of ideals betrayed: ideals rooted in socialism, feminism, and the gay liberation movement. But I want to avoid overemphasis: the theme of betrayal in gay male writing of the seventies has many strands and the critique of these three writers is wider, more contradictory, less clear-cut than this account suggests.

*Dancer from the Dance* and *Faggots* have at least this in common, that, unlike *Forgetting Elena,* they are open depictions of the new post-Stonewall urban gay male culture, as well as best-sellers. They therefore mark the emergence of the new gay fiction more obviously than White's novel. But if they are often bracketed together, it is *Dancer* that is widely seen as the defining novel of the decade. This is not just a matter of literary judgment: it results in large part from the virulence of Kramer's hostility to the gay scene and the controversy his portrayal of it has aroused. I therefore intend to examine these two novels separately—although I shall start by considering them (briefly) together, focusing in particular on what kinds of innovation, what qualities of newness, they bring to fiction.

In his essay "Out of the Closet, on to the Bookshelf," Edmund White finds that most gay novels written before the 1970s render gay life as "exotic, marginal, even monstrous," although he mentions the notable exception of Isherwood's *A Single Man.* He tells of how, as a teenager desperately seeking confirmation of his identity, he was relieved to find that George, Isherwood's protagonist, is not presented as damned "in ways supposedly peculiar to homosexuals" (*Burning Library* 275). In contrast, what both *Dancer* and *Faggots* bring to literature is a sense of gay community—a picture of gay men relating to each other in a broadly realistic social context, and not just as lovers but also as friends. Like *Elena,* they focus on the New York/Fire Island scene, but whereas *Elena* disguises its subject, viewing it from what might be called a closeted position, *Dancer* and *Faggots,* with their open depiction of the new urban gay male culture, are arguably the first truly *gay* novels (to use the term "gay" here in its culturally specific sense).

To call *Faggots* a gay novel is to invite controversy, however. For many gay critics and readers, this is essentially an antigay novel—a spewing-out of internalized homophobia. Moreover, the term is equally problematic when applied to *Dancer.* Often described as the celebrant of Fire Island, Holleran, as we noted, is in fact, like White, deeply ambivalent about it, intimating that its cult of physical beauty is narrow, addictive, and ultimately self-destructive—a form of spiritual death:

> And even so, do you realize what a tiny fraction of the mass of ho-mosexuals we were? That day we marched to Central Park and found ourselves in a sea of humanity, how stunned I was to recognize no more than four or five faces? (Of course our friends were all on the beach, darling; they couldn't be bothered to come in and make a politi-cal statement.) I used to say there were only seventeen homosexuals in New York, and we knew every one of them; but there were tons of men

in that city who weren't on the circuit, who didn't dance, didn't cruise, didn't fall in love with Malone, who stayed at home and went to the country in the summer. We never saw them. We were addicted to something else; something I lived with so long it had become a technique, a routine. That was the real sin. I was too smart, I built a wall around myself. I might as well have been living in the desert, where the air is, after all, cleaner. (243)

Hence these two novels are more than just records of seventies urban gay male culture. Like *Elena*, they seem prophetic—presciently aware that the lifestyles they depict are transient.

However, I want to argue in this section that Holleran's fiction is based not so much on a critique of the gay subculture as on a critique of life. *Dancer* is the principal focus of my attention here, but since this novel and its successor, *Nights in Aruba* (1983), in many ways form a single text (as Gregory Bredbeck remarks [198]), I want to draw evidence for my argument to some extent from this latter novel too. In an interview granted to *Publisher's Weekly*, Holleran describes *Aruba* as being loosely based on the general facts of his own life and implies a strong autobiographical link between this novel and the earlier one: "[I] drew on the material that is now in the first person in *Aruba* for Malone's life in *Dancer,* even though they are certainly not the same person at all" (quoted in Bredbeck 198). In fact, the narrower, more personal experience recorded in *Aruba* suggests an attempt to bring focus to the kaleidoscopic impressionism of the earlier text, although both novels show a tendency to see the lives they examine in universal terms. In the case of *Dancer*, this tendency has been seen as an area where the writing fails; but I prefer to postpone discussion of this issue for the moment.

*Dancer* consciously rewrites *The Great Gatsby* for the seventies, echoing its themes in a gay context: the lure of glamour; the chimera of happiness; the need for stoicism; the sense of hollowness and guilt beneath American plenitude. Indeed, it suggests, again echoing *Gatsby*, the death of the American (gay) dream. Its central theme, however, exactly parallels that of *Forgetting Elena:* in their pursuit of freedom and happiness, the characters in *Dancer*, like those in *Elena*, have replaced one form of oppression with another, their cult of beauty being an enslavement to style and custom. Exclusion from heterosexual society leads not to an overthrow of its oppressive structures, but to a systematic and culpable re-creation of its worst features. The frenzied pleasure seeking in Holleran's Twelfth Floor disco cannot disguise the suffering of its denizens, the sense of emptiness in their lives:

They seldom looked happy. They passed one another with out a word in the elevator, like silent shades in hell, hell-bent on their next look from a handsome stranger. Their next rush from a popper. (30)

Indeed Holleran's portrayal of the gay ghetto bears an uncanny resemblance to Auden's description of an earlier New York scene in "September 1, 1939," which may account for the fact that this poem supplied Larry Kramer (another dissector of the gay ghetto) with both the epigraph and title for *The Normal Heart*, his play about the early years of the AIDS crisis. As Holleran portrays it, the seventies, from a gay perspective, is "a low, dishonest decade," and, like Auden, he knows what "has driven a culture mad." The delirious disco dancers in Holleran's novel live in "an euphoric dream" and crave "Not universal love / But to be loved alone." Their ghetto is a fortress, sealing them off from the wider world and postponing any facing up to the hard "truths" and responsibilities of life:

> Faces along the bar
> Cling to their average day:
> The lights must never go out,
> The music must always play,
> All the conventions conspire
> To make this fort assume
> The furniture of home;
> Lest we should see who we are,
> Lost in a haunted wood,
> Children afraid of the night
> Who have never been happy or good.[9]

In *Dancer*, Malone's naivety and romantic idealism—his search for, and belief in, an ideal love relationship—is an echo of Gatsby's, and makes him, like Gatsby, an archetypal figure: "I had no idea who he was, he was just a face I saw in a discotheque one winter; but he was for me the central symbol on which all of it rested" (48). As the central symbol of the novel, Malone represents the spiritual heart of the community and way of life—the romance and decadence of seventies urban gay male culture—that the novel evokes: a community and way of life still emerging from the preliberation era and still redolent of the "madness, the despair, of the old-time queens," who, unlike the coming generation, still consider themselves "doomed" (7). The romantic strain in *Dancer*, then, as Mark Lilly points out, is accompanied by an austere, Chekhovian stance, which lays stress on stoicism, on deferred happiness, on the need for hope even in the knowledge of life's inevitable disappointment (191–93).[10]

But the central question, it seems to me, is this: does Malone stand for something more than the community he represents? Does he, in other words, have some greater symbolic weight invested in him? And the answer, I think, is both yes and no, since the evidence of the novel suggests that Holleran's attitude to Malone is confused. Moreover, his confusion here is a reflection of his ambivalence not only to the whole New York/Fire

Island scene but also to life in general. Like Gatsby, Malone is the focus of his creator's conflicting romantic–antiromantic attitudes—conflicting attitudes so strong that they split the character in two, Malone becoming Malone/Sutherland. Like any comic duo, any romantic hero and his comic foil, Malone and Sutherland endlessly perform an act in which romantic illusion, doomed to perpetual disappointment, is constantly undercut by cynical disillusion. They are two sides of the same coin: hence their closeness, mutual sympathy, and spiritual understanding of each other. Malone/ Sutherland, then, is the double-guise through which Holleran projects the poles of his split personality.

Thus, on the one hand, Malone is the lone, romantic, Yeatsian figure suggested by the title of the novel: a figure representative of the questing, questioning, aspiring human spirit, stranded between romantic illusion and disillusion, evoked in the epigraph:

> O chestnut tree, great rooted blossomer,
> Are you the leaf, the blossom or the bole?
> O body swayed to music, O brightening glance,
> How can we know the dancer from the dance?[11]

From this standpoint, the novel becomes a critique of life and Malone a representative of the universal human condition. But just as in Yeats's poem, the human spirit vacillates between "beauty" and "despair," so the novel questions (in a way similar to *Gatsby*'s probing of *its* protagonist) whether Malone can bear the symbolic weight invested in him. Significantly, *Dancer* begins and ends with a series of letters between two unidentified gay men, one of whom is writing a novel about Malone. As the core of the text, then, Malone's story appears in the guise of a manuscript that passes between them as part of their correspondence. This framing device changes our perception of the novel, seeming to confine, limit, periodize it. It places the self-contained world of Malone and his friends in a wider context, a context that recognizes that world as "a tiny fraction of the mass of homosexuals" (243), as mere part of a much larger scene, which now includes "activists" and "young queens . . . utterly indistinguishable from straight boys" (7). So the ambivalence remains: does Malone's story speak of universal experience or of something much smaller? Thus, as one of the correspondents writes: "Let us not, after all, dignify Malone too much: He was in the end a circuit queen" (243). Or as Sutherland more tartly puts it: "Do you think the reason Americans are boring . . . is that they believe in happiness on earth?" (203).

But despite doubts about its own powers of transcendence, *Dancer* clearly *aims* at a critique of life. Malone is presented not only as the spiritual heart of the community he inhabits, but as symbolic of human aspiration in general. Moreover, the delirium of the dancers at the Twelfth Floor disco, of which Malone is the central symbol, figures as a merely heightened expression of the euphoric dream that grips all humanity, just as the Twelfth Floor disco itself becomes a metaphor not just for their world but for *the* world. This symbolic suggestion is reinforced by *Dancer*'s (and *Aruba*'s) depiction of life outside the gay ghetto, where the principal focus is family life. These novels, as David Bergman has demonstrated, are thoroughly imbued with the belief that gay life and family life are mutually exclusive and irreconcilable.[12] Yet paradoxically, they also suggest that Holleran sees the two as simply different aspects of the same condition. The inhabitants of Sayville, the suburban residential district of Long Island through which Malone and his friends pass on their way to Fire Island, live in "big white houses" with "friendly front yards . . . picket fences and climbing roses" (16). But the novel presents Malone's lingering regret for what he takes to be their suburban security ironically: it is sentimental, part of his romantic illusion, a sentimentality and romantic illusion he shares with the inhabitants of Sayville, who, like him, hide their fear of death, life's meaninglessness, and seemingly limitless personal freedom ("the multiple choices offered by a modern capitalist 'democracy'" [Lilly 191]) behind white walls, picket fences and climbing roses. The suggestion in the novel, then, is that the gay ghetto, where the lights must never go out, the music must always play, is no different from a bar on Fifty-Second Street or a house in Sayville. We are *all* children afraid of the night.

I remarked earlier that Holleran's attempt to universalize the theme of *Dancer* has been seen as a weakness in the writing. Rodney Marshall feels that *Dancer* fails from a sociohistorical point of view precisely because it attempts to universalize "a specific time in a specific sub/culture" (Marshall 103). He suggests that the novel lacks historical context: that the characters appear to be "everywhere" and "nowhere" (103). But this, it seems to me, is to conflate two arguments. Is Marshall criticizing *Dancer*'s attempt to transcend a specific time in a specific subculture, or its failure to evoke that specific time and subculture? If the latter, then I must disagree: *Dancer* is surely a haunting and precise evocation, impressionistic rather than historically accurate, of the small world it depicts.[13] But if the former, then the complaint seems subsumed within, and disarmed by, the novel's own self-critical irony.

Whatever our response to this criticism, the sense we get from *Dancer* that what is being attempted is a critique of life is reinforced by a reading of its companion piece. Thus, in *Aruba*, Mr Friel's reply to Vittorio's suggestion that people buy encyclopedias from him out of a need to break the monumental boredom of their lives encapsulates the universal principle that informs Holleran's fiction generally: "It only confirms Schopenhauer's dictum that once a man is free of his material needs, he is only confronted with the consciousness of life's essential emptiness" (95). Although the closeted narrator complains that the split between his gay life in New York and his domestic life in Jasper "left an odd void . . . where a life should have been" (161), the novel goes on to suggest that this sense of void is not specific to closeted gay men, but universal: that we all, gay or straight, structure our lives around meaningless rituals as a way of filling the void. Thus Holleran's gently mocking description of church attendance carries with it the implication that people (in the form of congregations) are less concerned with spiritual experience than with the performance of comforting, inane routines. In Jasper, for instance, where church services are the "only social event" (167), the congregation are asked to shake hands with each other during Mass and murmur, "Peace be with you," while the narrator and Vittorio appear to attend church principally for the pleasure of eyeing up the altar boys (168). Nor is Mr. Friel an exception: he quietly fulminates against his priest's faulty syntax and deplores the loss of the "full splendor of the Catholic Church" (140), but his critical stance here, Holleran implies, is mere elevation of form over substance and no more spiritual than the popular, supposedly debased, style of church service he condemns.

For David Bergman, Holleran is the gay novelist "most dependent on heterosexist values" and hence one of the few "to have found recognition in the straight press" (*Gaiety* 192). This is probably true of Holleran's work as a whole, though it is less easily concluded from a reading of *Dancer* alone, where the careful ambiguity of the writing leaves room for doubt. In *Dancer*, Holleran places himself at a distance from his text through the framing device of the letters, within which the novel becomes a "missive" between one unidentified gay man and another (Bredbeck 198). The authorial voice is thus disguised: buried within the writing, yet also above and beyond it. This pervasive irony also denies any sense of closure; as the narrator of *Nights in Aruba* remarks: "I was certain that even death would provide no illumination—that we died ignorant, confused, like novelists who cannot bring an aesthetic shape to their material" (239). *Dancer* balances one way of life against another, one view of life against another, and cannot answer its own questions. Maybe gay is good—but isn't it also, in common with other ways of life—dare one suggest—sometimes sad? And are straights any less deluded if they believe "that to be happy you must have a two-story house in the suburbs . . . a station wagon and a big dog and an elm tree with a tire hanging from it on a rope" (7)? Thus Holleran is less interested in what makes gays different than in what links them to the rest of humanity. In *Dancer* the gay ghetto is both particularized and universalized: it becomes a paradigm of life itself, viewed from the vacillating insecurity, the ecstasy and despair, of Yeatsian-Keatsian romantic idealism. For Holleran, life is split between gain and loss, and involves both "glamour and squalor" (Lilly 197); and this, though intensified by "the split inherent in a closeted identity" (Bredbeck 200), is a universal principle.

## ART VERSUS ACTION

*Dancer* is a reflection on human experience, intended primarily for gay men, but also offered, if somewhat diffidently, to the general reader. Hence,

"Canons of taste must be observed, darling. People are tired of hearing about sex, anyway. And the story of a boy's love for a boy will never capture the world's heart as the story of a boy's love for a girl" (6–7). *Faggots,* in contrast, is a rhetorical call to action, directed exclusively at gay men, especially those within the ghetto, whose behavior it seeks to change. Kramer has written:

> I don't consider myself an artist. I consider myself a very opinionated man who uses words as fighting tools. I perceive certain wrongs that make me very angry, and somehow I hope that if I string my words together with enough skill, people will hear them and respond. (*Reports* 145)

This of course raises the question of what art is. I prefer to see Kramer as an artist, albeit an artist of a certain kind, and admittedly of a very different kind from Holleran. However, rather than discuss what kind of artist he is, what I want to examine here are the ideas that inform his writing (the opinions of this "very opinionated man") and how they relate to the conflict explored in this study.

Coming to *Faggots* after *Dancer,* the first thing that strikes the reader is the change in tone, a difference already suggested in their titles, where poetic allusion is replaced by contemptuous expletive—or what the novelist Christopher Bram, speaking on the television arts program *Arena,* calls "a slap in the face." What Kramer is attempting here is a harsh satirical exposé, attacking the whole New York/Fire Island scene for its shallowness, priapism, and general excess. The precise target of his attack, however, seems to be the alleged pursuit by gay men of individual self-gratification at the expense of any sense of collective responsibility. In fact, the critical stance of *Faggots* is, as I have already hinted, close to that of Auden's in "September 1, 1939." Like Auden, Kramer censures his characters for craving "not universal love / But to be loved alone." Where Holleran, the romantic idealist, is seduced by both the glamour and the squalor, the one being simply the reverse of the other, Kramer, the realist, resolutely resists seduction and keeps his eyes firmly on the squalor. *Faggots* angrily rejects the Malone/Sutherland opposition, together with the optimistic/nihilistic ecstasy/despair that pervades Holleran's novel generally, whether psychically caused or drug induced. In Kramer's novel, Malone *and* Sutherland stand accused of moral cowardice and abuse of sexual freedom:

> I purposely made the chief characters in my book intelligent, educated, and affluent men who should be role-models for the rest of us. Instead they're cowardly and self-pitying persons who retreat into their own ghetto because they feel the world doesn't want them. . . . It just seems that we should be angry at our own cowardice instead of the world's cruelty. (quoted in Shatzky 245)

In *Faggots*, Kramer, with admonishing tone and righteous zeal, sets out to hold up a mirror to the New York's self-imposed gay ghetto. His aim is to cause fertile controversy and give salutary offense: to make his readers (and his novel directly addresses the gay men who are the targets of his satire) "hear" and "respond." Thus, with bold recklessness, he launches a ferocious assault on that holiest sacred cow of the early gay liberationists: sexual freedom. Intent on exposing the squalor beneath the glamour, his method is to tear away what he sees as the veils of gay self-deception. He becomes Hamlet in his mother's bedchamber. Thrusting a mirror in his reader's face, where "you may see the inmost part of you," he protests that he must be cruel only to be kind. For Kramer, the flattering unction that gays apply to their souls (with the arrogant irresponsibility of bohemian artists, though without the compensating genius) is that their sensibility and love of beauty place them above the common herd and beyond ordinary morality. Hence their tendency to recite ever-expanding lists of Great Artists (presumed, in gay mythology, to be homosexual) in an attempt to put themselves among exalted company. *Faggots* contains a parody of such a list, which, in its concluding passage, makes its satirical purpose abundantly clear:

> Thanks a lot, gang. . . . You've made it so much easier for us to tell the world we're here . . . and we shall make our presence *known!, felt!, respected!, admired!, loved!* (118 emphasis in original)

In *Elena*, as we saw, White, metaphorically alluding to homosexual desire, writes about a closed society that has allowed the cult of beauty to replace genuine moral concerns. Like Kramer, he sees the squalor beneath the glamour, but being ambivalent, he equivocates. Seduced by a privileged way of life, even as he lays bare the moral bankruptcy of a corrupt society, he swooningly invokes the rare beauty of the island, its light on water, its sand, surf, and sky:

> Gilt clouds tumble like dwarfs along the horizon. Ahead of us sandpipers evade the surf . . . Bubbles topping one shred of foam glower red and green in the late afternoon sunlight and then break, one after another, like small eyes winking shut. (39)

But in *Faggots* there is no equivocation; a spade is called a spade. Kramer's style here reflects the man and his purpose: it is direct, blunt, rude, crude, and rebarbative. This makes it, together with the coarseness of the humor, not a comfortable or easy novel to read. However, Kramer wants to disturb rather than give aesthetic pleasure, and the bluntness seems to be offered as a signifier or guarantee of sincerity, asserted in opposition to the corrupting concealments of sophistication. It recalls *Elena*'s engagement with this theme, summed up in the line from Elena's diary: "We saw how the island's cult of beauty was at the heart of its vapidity, and we tried to be as blunt and awkward as possible" (119–20). In *Faggots,* moreover, form is appropriate to content; hence the circularity, repetitiousness, and episodic structure. These are mimetic: they reflect the inconsequentiality and meaninglessness of the lives depicted. Nor is it fair to fault Kramer here for his paper-thin character drawing. This too is part of his purpose; he deliberately overpopulates his novel, fills his canvas with cartoon stereotypes, in order to convey the shallowness of the world his creatures inhabit, with its narrow, kaleidoscopic round of party going. Except for Fred Lemish, who keeps himself aloof from the scene and finally breaks with it, the characters in *Faggots* are not social beings at all, but sex-obsessives; and Kramer denies them an inner life as a way of suggesting that they have none.

*Faggots* created a storm of controversy when it first appeared in 1978, and has been in print ever since. Controversy still surrounds it. Is it a successful satire, "written, like all good ones, from the inside" (McCracken 23); or "a plastic, trashy artifact of the worst aspects of a scene to which it high-mindedly condescends" (Duberman, Review of *Faggots* 31)? Admirers of the novel claim that it administers a much-needed corrective to the post-Stonewall gay self-image, a necessary puncturing of its air of smugness and self-congratulation; and they argue, with help from some of Kramer's own comments, that the book intends to be curative and compassionate, rather than negative and spiteful. Detractors, on the other hand, accuse the novel of being regressive and pitifully reliant on heterosexist attitudes. They see its lofty censoriousness as a colossal overstatement, largely rooted in Kramer's personal sexual problems.[14] However, that *Faggots* is still in print and still provokes controversy suggests that it touches a raw nerve—indeed, that Kramer has identified (in a particular circle of gay men, in a particular time and place, though with far-reaching implications) an appropriate target for satire and that his shafts are not all wide of the mark.

Like White in *Elena* and Holleran in *Dancer,* what Kramer is addressing in this novel (although *his* approach is direct where theirs is oblique) is an issue central to the movements for sexual liberation that arose in the 1960s: namely, the conflict between duty and desire. As Jeffrey Weeks has written: "Any progressive approach to the question of sexuality must balance the autonomy of individuals against the necessity of collective endeavour and common cause" (*Discontents* 241). But this balance, as Weeks admits, is difficult to achieve, and the radical pluralist approach he advocates begins with the recognition that perhaps certain conflicts can never be resolved. On the one hand, the kind of libertarianism that takes an absolutist attitude to the fulfillment of individual desires means that sexual liberation "becomes merely a synonym for individual self-expression, with scarcely a thought for the social relations in which all action must be embodied" (242). Such egocentricity, Kramer suggests, leads ultimately to the preening narcissism and retreat into privacy that is the prime target of his satirical attack in *Faggots*. Yet, on the other hand, the difficulty of mobilizing individuals to belief in collective endeavor and to recognition of common cause (and, as we have seen, there is a particular difficulty in forging a sense of collective identity around issues of sexuality) can lead, in the search for new absolutes, to the imposition of unifying norms just as oppressive as the ones liberationist movements seek to overthrow.

The controversy surrounding *Faggots* is essentially the controversy surrounding this issue, and Kramer weighs into the fray with the clear intention of reversing the trend of the argument. What moves him is the belief that the debate has become dangerously unbalanced, too heavily weighted in favor of individual autonomy: autonomy that, without a restorative sense of social responsibility, quickly slides into pathological self-indulgence. Thus he proceeds with single-minded vision and purpose, screening out anything that might appear at the edge of his vision to muddy his purpose, challenging enormity with enormity, matching excess with excess. It therefore seems inappropriate to complain about the novel's lack of a balanced viewpoint: what concerns Kramer is not balance, but change. *Faggots* makes no pretense to fairness, and presents a particular gay moment in a particular gay setting as if it reflected the behavior of a whole sexual group. But again, this is part of its strategy: fairness would complicate its message. In this respect, it makes an interesting contrast with *Dancer,* which, as we have seen, appears to recognize the particularity of its time and place, even as it seeks to universalize its theme.

Nevertheless, the message of even a self-styled "message queen" must still be examined. In *Faggots,* Kramer castigates his characters for their failure to distinguish between love and sex. He presents Fred Lemish, his protagonist and alter ego, as a man looking for love in a loveless milieu: in a society that continually speaks of love with no understanding of what the word means. This is made clear in the concluding scene of the novel, where the disillusioned Fred, the scales having fallen from his eyes, makes his final break with Fire Island and, looking back, sees the vast gathering of gay men sitting in circles on the white sand, all murmuring "I love you": "There are hundreds, thousands, passing the message of love from body to body . . . celebrating this morning and this summer's love" (382–83). What these gay men want, the novel suggests, is a long-term relationship based on the model of heterosexual marriage. Sometimes they acknowledge this: "I believe in old-fashioned marriage," says Dinky, "where people make commitments and out of respect the love just grew and grew" (32–33). But what hinders them is weakness of character, an inability to resist sensation and immediate self-gratification. This makes them self-deceived, so that they confuse sex with love.

*Faggots* as a whole, however, suggests that Kramer is himself confused, an impression reinforced by a consideration of his novel alongside his other writings and pronouncements. His confusion reveals itself in his contradictoriness, since he appears to uphold certain values while simultaneously recognizing those values as hollow. Thus the main representatives in the novel of long-term commitment, old-fashioned marriage, and family are Fred's parents, Lester and Algonqua. Yet their marriage is revealed as a loveless sham, founded on appearances. Lester, moreover, is excoriated as a miserable failure whose inability "to kiss and hug . . . [and] offer love" deprives his son of a role model: "Wasn't it Lester who was terrified of life and sex and life and family and life and Algonqua?" (70). Here, Kramer's vituperation, whether it has its roots in personal experience or in a desire to satirize the strong mother–weak father theory of homosexuality, thoroughly undermines the thrust of his own argument.

Indeed, Kramer appears to value long-term commitment, on the model of heterosexual marriage, not for any inherent quality it might have but for its standing in the heterosexual population: for the possibility that it will win for gay men, if they follow it, the respect of that population. The guilt the characters in his novel experience arises largely from a missing sense of self-determination and sufficiency: they carry with them an ideological baggage inherited from family (the very "family values" by which they were raised and by which they have become discredited) and are constantly viewing their own behavior through its eyes, as if one or other member of their family were looking over their shoulder. Thus Fred lives in the shadow of his parents, Richie Bronstein of his father, and Laverne of his sister-in-law: "My sister-in-law does not speak to me, not because I'm a faggot . . . but because she says I'm a coward . . . I'm not proving to the world or myself that I know what to do with this freedom" (43).

Again, Tim Purvis's history is recounted as a kind of cautionary tale or rake's progress. Tim breaks with family, embarks on a life of debauchery, and ends up a figure of monumental narcissism, as remote and frigid as Turandot: "I just want to be seen. And to be worshipped for my beauty" (352). But Kramer's outward disapproval of Tim's hard, go-getting ambition seems mixed with secret admiration for his energy, wit, and sparkle, his determination to escape the oppressive conservatism of his Maryland background and reinvent himself in New York. Kramer writes nothing to suggest that he sees Tim's prospects in Maryland as other than the death-in-life that Tim himself perceives it to be: "I don't want to be like these people . . . Imagine complaining about the price of food and getting up at 6:30 every morning to go to work" (106). In short, for all Kramer's moral strictures, Tim looks more attractive, even in his final apotheosis, than the dull-but-solid family values he has left behind.

The message of *Faggots*, then, is loud, direct, and yet unclear because shot through with contradiction. Thus Kramer rebukes his characters on the one hand for their pathological enslavement to sex, while ridiculing them on the other for holding a sentimental and chimerical concept of idealized love. This is well exemplified in the scene where Fred, in the middle of sexual congress with Dinky, fantasizes about their future life together:

Dinky and Fred! get the embroidered towels ready! order them now! find that spot in the country! sign the lease! Dinky will remodel! happily ever after is beginning right this very Now. (34)

Does Kramer see a connection here? Is he drawing attention to the link between promiscuity and the pursuit of an impossible ideal? Perhaps; although elsewhere the evidence of the text suggests otherwise. As David Bergman writes: "Kramer never quite sees that promiscuity may result as much from searching for a pseudo-spouse as from avoiding the commitment of a relationship" (*Gaiety* 135). Actually, what the novel as a whole suggests is that the concept of love Kramer is satirizing here is in fact his own, and indeed the very ideal he is urging his readers to adopt. Thus it is Fred, Kramer's alter ego, who embodies the confusion at the heart of the novel. Fred is Kramer's means of satirizing himself; yet he is also, we are asked to believe, the bearer of the novel's serious message. In Fred, Kramer seems to acknowledge the absurdity of his position, even while insisting on its validity.[15]

Yet, as we have seen and as commentators observe, *Faggots*, whatever its faults, does address an issue of genuine moral concern, and sometimes with acuity and insight. Even Martin Duberman, who clearly dislikes the book intensely, concedes that what *Faggots* sets out to do would be well worth doing, if only it were better done: "a serious dissection of the self-absorbed frivolity of this subculture within a subculture would be well worth having" (quoted in Shatzky 246). *Faggots* is at its strongest, Rodney Marshall feels, in its satirical attack on the "pink economy," in its depiction of "the growing commercialization of sexuality in general, and male homosexuality in particular" (98). This seems true to me; and in this respect it is interesting to compare Kramer's novel with White's and Holleran's.

*Elena*, of course, does not refer directly to money; it refers instead to "the cult of beauty." Yet in its depiction of a leisured, affluent society there is a clear and disturbing suggestion of the rich man's sexual playground that Fire Island had become: disturbing, that is, for writers like White, Kramer, and Holleran, raised on the gay liberation ethic of the early seventies. The novel thus shows White wrestling with his social conscience and sense of guilt. Likewise, the Twelfth Floor disco in *Dancer* reflects Holleran's very personal, glamorized response to New York's newly commercialized gay scene. The Twelfth Floor is clearly related to the string of mushrooming gay venues in *Faggots*—The Ice Palace, Balalaika, The Toilet Bowl—that are part of Kramer's exposure of the phenomenon. But Holleran's romantic idealism blunts his critical edge; like White, he is half in love with the thing he would expose, and in *Dancer* the evils of commercial exploitation all but vanish, veiled in the mists of his poetic prose. Both White and Holleran are caught up in the war between flesh and spirit, and their attitude as they confront their personal demons is reminiscent of St. Augustine: "Give me chastity and social responsibility—but not yet!"

In contrast, Kramer confronts the commercialization issue head-on. Relentlessly exposing the growing consumer culture of New York's burgeoning gay scene, he shows all values giving way to the profit motive. Thus, in *Faggots,* new gay clubs and discos, with no regard for safety standards or the lives of clients, spring up overnight and vie for custom. Kramer is scathing in his condemnation of these dangerous, cramped, and overcrowded dives, but at the same time quite as scathing in his condemnation of the gay men who give such places their patronage. Where, he asks, is their self-esteem? Kramer's attack here is delivered with ferocious black humor and nowhere more so than in his account of the fire at the Everhard Baths. In this scene, the clients of the Baths are so preoccupied with sexual activity they only belatedly perceive the smoke enveloping them: "Seven brothers perished in the famous Everhard fire" (194). Later, the humor becomes even more savage, with the suggestion that for some of the clients fire, together with the proximity of danger and even death, is a sexual turn-on: "The Pits, he'd heard about the infamous Pits, why end this evening on such a charred note, let's head for the Pits and more!" (198). There is surely a link between this episode and the scene in the opening chapter of *Elena* where the revelers on the yacht become aesthetically excited by the sight of a fire destroying someone's home. In both instances the image of fire seems to be used to suggest the destructiveness of all-consuming passions, whether aesthetic or sexual, and hence to shock the reader with a sense of the callousness and moral blankness that can result from such surrender.

In confronting the commercialization of sex as an issue, Kramer makes the connection between sex and money perhaps most explicit in the story of Richie Bronstein's attempt to extort a ransom from his multimillionaire father. Thus the significance of Richie's "self-inflicted kidnapping" (34) is that it underlines his willingness to betray his sexuality in pursuit of gain. Indeed, it suggests, since his imprisonment is self-imposed, a kind of self-victimization. Richie's story reaches its climax in the final pages of the novel when his father, bearing his ransom, comes to rescue him from the place on Fire Island where he is supposedly held prisoner. Richie's father discovers his son in a pit, a pit Richie has dug for himself (with obvious symbolic meaning) as his place of self-imposed captivity. But it is the gala opening night of the Fire Island season, and the pit has been mistaken for a cesspit by some of the other revelers on the island. Richie's father thus discovers his son in a state of utmost degradation and at a moment of total abjection. This episode, then, seems to carry the novel's culminating statement.

However, it also seems like the expression of a private nightmare; and it is this private-nightmare aspect of Kramer's writing that undermines the plausibility and effectiveness of his general critique. Once again we see how Kramer's viewpoint depends on a collision with family. Richie Bronstein's final humiliation, for instance, is viewed through the eyes of his father, whose moral authority is never directly questioned. Abe Bronstein, after all, is presented as an old-fashioned patriarchal figure, an obsessive money

maker and compulsive womanizer, bristling with every kind of heterosexist prejudice. About to divorce for the fourth time, he is no advertisement
for fidelity. Deserted by Peetra, he moves back in with Ephra, using her as
a convenient interim measure "before setting forth to seek another poop-
sie to brighten his declining years" (47). The neglected Ephra, of course,
eventually finds fulfillment in the arms of another woman: "Out here, on
this tiny island, her heart had been touched, and someone, at last, had
said: I care" (303). Thus the terror at the center of the private nightmare
that haunts Kramer's novel is fear of failure: the failure of Kramer and
friends to live up to a set of values that the novel seems simultaneously to
recognize as hollow.

## SUMMARY

In *Elena, Dancer,* and *Faggots,* gay male fiction of the seventies immediately engages with the central theme of post-Stonewall gay politics and
culture, fully exemplifying and exposing the tensions that are the focus of
this study. In these novels, as in the decade generally, the conflict between
assimilationism and radicalism is grounded in the clash between the revolutionary socialist ideals of the early gay liberationists and the extraordinarily
rapid growth of gay consumerism. Indeed it may not be too extravagant to
see this clash as at the root of all post-Stonewall debates, for these are all
related and revolve around the same point of conflict.

In the debate between essentialists and constructionists, for instance,
there is a clear link between the constructionist position and the ideals
of the early gay movement, because that movement was a movement for
change. It therefore laid stress on sexuality as a social construct, since social
constructs, as well as being instruments of change, are themselves subject
to change. As a socialist movement, too, it tended to see sexual taxonomies
as both artificial and socially divisive, and hence it sought to dissolve differences by laying emphasis on the fluid, binding, and universalizing aspects
of sexuality: on sexuality as a continuum. Likewise, there is a clear link
between the essentialist position and the stress on individual autonomy and
difference that characterizes consumerist, free-market economies. If essentialism resists change through its belief in inherited, inborn difference, the
free market thrives on the preservation of a similar sense of difference: the
difference that reveals itself in the "natural" social hierarchy (the status
quo that feels "natural" simply by being the social order within which we
live); the difference that demands an endless array of commodities to meet
individual needs; the difference that gives rise to individual will, enterprise,
competitiveness, and ambition.

Again, our current use of the terms "gay" and "queer" can be seen to spring
from this same point of conflict. For "queer," as we have seen, is emphatically
not just the latest in a historical series of terms denoting same-sex desire: in

its current political and academic appropriation, it marks a distinct change of focus and emphasis. Opposed to the view that sees sexuality wholly in terms of the homo–hetero dyad and fixed categories, contemporary queer theory is firmly committed to the reconceptualizations that have arisen from the constructionist account. Its questioning of identity challenges the politics that have characterized gay campaigning since Stonewall. It therefore reconnects with the radicalism of the early seventies. *Gay*, on the other hand, with its subsequent emphasis on fixed identity, has come to suggest resistance to change, and hence assimilationism to the dominant ideology: that is, to the prevailing view of homosexuality as the defining characteristic of a minority, and to the consumerist ethos of the free market.

The tensions humming beneath the surface of *Elena, Dancer,* and *Faggots* thus turn out to be the same as those that animate our current debates. These tensions, as we have seen, are more explicitly explored in some of White's nonfiction writing. For example, in "Fantasia on the Seventies," in "Paradise Found," and especially in *States of Desire*, a major theme is the way that the rise of the gay market has blunted the radicalism of the gay movement. The problem was there, White contends, right from the start:

> From the perspective of the present, we can now look back at the beginning of gay liberation and observe that it flowered exactly at the moment when gays became identified, by themselves and by the market, as a distinct group of affluent and avid consumers. (*Burning Library* 148)

Through the gay market, White implies, gays are co-opted and assimilated into mainstream conformity. For adopting consumerism as a way of life means adopting a set of principles and attitudes to which that way of life is indissolubly bound: principles and attitudes based on heterosexist notions of hierarchy and competitiveness. In short, consumerism comes as part of a package, and gays cannot take the one without the other.

If the tensions of post-Stonewall gay culture and politics can all be traced back to this central conflict, however, the conflict itself (as my examination of *Elena, Dancer,* and *Faggots* shows) is clearly more complicated than it at first appears. From a queer perspective, the problem with gay identity is that it gives support to a view of sexuality based on the simple notion of a binary. Hence, from this viewpoint, it is assimilationist, in that it assimilates to the view of sexuality that prevails in society generally. From the other side of the debate, however, it is the queer program that looks assimilationist. Gay identity, it is argued, is independent and assertive, whereas the term "queer," through its dissolution of difference, erases the resisting subject and threatens the gay presence with absence: "almost as if homosexuality were nothing but a reaction, the responses of a social group to its own invention" (Bersani, *Homos* 33).

The complications, confusions, and contradictions of this central conflict are all revealed in the fiction examined in this chapter. For here the

New York/Fire Island gay scene is censured both for its numbing conformism (its imposition of a set of regulatory practices "as rigidly codified as the old morality") and for its waywardness and perversity (its *refusal* to conform). Condemned on the one hand for its surrender to consumerism and hence for its assimilation into the American mainstream way of life (gays have sold out, swallowed the whole package; they even "consume" each other), it is yet condemned on the other for its ghetto mentality, for its *failure* to assimilate: in short, for its rejection of that set of values—patriarchal, heterosexist, family oriented—traditionally seen as installed at the heart of that way of life.

In *Dancer* and *Faggots* the central characters pursue an ideal of love—indeed, that same ideal of love, founded on the notion of lifelong fidelity, that is enshrined in Western culture. Moreover, in *Elena,* the narrator is haunted by his betrayal of this romantic archetype. Hence, in their endorsement of this ideal, as in their critique of the gay subculture for its rejection of it, these novels ally themselves to the values of the dominant culture. Yet at the same time they attack those values through their presentation of a subculture that, through its enslavement to this model, its imitation of the dominant culture, and its consequent pursuit of individual self-gratification and fulfillment, ignores the demands of social responsibility and justice. *Dancer* and *Faggots,* after all, present the gay subculture as largely made up of self-seeking individuals, whose narcissism and callous indifference to others is fundamentally driven by a notion of idealized love; and this is also true of *Elena,* although here the ideal, as we saw, is metaphorically transformed into an aesthetic one. Thus, in clinging to the values of the dominant culture even while working to deny them, these novels are idealist and anti-idealist, assimilationist and antiassimilationist. Indeed, the conflict that they embody, as I have proposed throughout this chapter, is the central theme and struggle of gay male fiction since Stonewall.

In the following two chapters, I pursue this argument by looking separately at the opposing strains of this fiction. Chapter 4 looks at novels that show a strong assimilative tendency, while Chapter 5 examines novels in which the drive is clearly antiassimilative.

# 4 Centripetal Tendencies
## Gays, Heterosexuality, and the Family

> It's finally spring down here on the Chattahoochee—the azaleas are
> in bloom, and everyone is dying of cancer.
>
> —Andrew Holleran, *Dancer from the Dance*

> Yeah. It tells me something. It tells me no relationship in the world
> could survive the shit we lay on it. It tells me we're not looking at the
> reasons why we're doing the things we're doing. It tells me we've got a
> lot of work to do. A lot of looking to do. It tells me that, if those happy
> couples are there, they better come out of the woodwork fast and show
> themselves pronto so we can have a few examples for unbelieving hea-
> thens like you that it's possible. Before you fuck yourself to death.
>
> —Larry Kramer, *Faggots*

In 1981, just three years after these passages appeared in print, a gay man,
suffering from a serious fungal infection of the throat, was admitted to a
medical center in Los Angeles. Within two weeks he had developed *Pneu-
mocystis carinii* pneumonia, a lung infection previously seen almost exclusively in cancer or transplant patients. At almost the same time, several gay
men in New York and San Francisco were diagnosed as having Kaposi's
sarcoma, a rare form of skin cancer found usually in older men of Mediter-
ranean origin. Physicians were puzzled: all these symptoms suggested an
unexplained lowering of immune function. Here, then, were the first indications of the AIDS epidemic, and they presaged a new era in gay history.

This change, moreover, was given added force by an accompanying development: namely, the dissemination and discussion of the ideas contained in
Volume 1 of Foucault's *History of Sexuality,* first published in English in 1979.
Foucault's groundbreaking study is in large measure an attack on that central,
mobilizing concept of the gay movement: gay identity. As much as AIDS,
therefore, it struck at the very foundations of those gay cultural forms that
had emerged since Stonewall in New York, in San Francisco, and across the
Western world. Those forms, as we have seen, were based on a fundamentally
essentialist view of human nature and sexuality. The early gay liberationists,

to be sure, argued from a constructionist position; but this viewpoint does not in the end appeal to a mass movement. Constructionism questions received ideas, contradicts "common sense," and challenges the innate conservatism of people through concepts that are difficult to grasp. Most important, however, it lacks the rallying power of that most naturalized of cultural categories: the concept of "self." Foucault's book, on the other hand, leant great weight to the constructionist position, making it for many people irresistible. To be sure, the debate between essentialists and contructionists still rages,[1] but since the mid-1980s the balance of the argument, at least among academics and intellectuals, has fallen strongly on the constructionist side. Hence, the dominant process of thought about sexuality of the past two decades is frequently traced back to the work of this French philosopher. Historically, this comprises the deconstruction of the concept of "gay identity" in the 1980s and its partial replacement in the early 1990s by the political and academic appropriation of the term "queer."[2]

Queer, as we noted, is a term that, almost by definition, defies definition. This is because its roots are in the linguistic theory associated with post-structuralist thought, which emphasizes that meaning in language is always dependent on those who use and interpret it. Queer is thus opposed to the sense of fixed sexual identity implied in the term "gay," and indeed suggests a questioning of the very idea of sexual identity. But the general elusiveness of the term is in large part the cause of the controversy surrounding it. Joseph Bristow and Angelia Wilson, on the other hand, have made some attempt to clarify. In distinguishing the Gay Liberation Front from Queer Nation, for instance, they consider it definitionally significant that "an erstwhile politics of identity has largely been superseded by a politics of difference" (Bristow and Wilson, 1–2). This suggests that the movement from "gay" to "queer" is a shift away from an assimilationist emphasis on similarity between people and groups to one that lays stress on "identity" as a mythical construct: as part of a rationalizing process that disguises difference.

Queer, then, has to be seen as part of the conceptual shift that characterizes poststructuralism and late twentieth-century Western thought in general. It relates, in fact, to similar shifts in both feminist and postcolonial theory and practice, and emerges from a context that includes the theories not only of Foucault but also of Althusser, Freud, Lacan, and Saussure. Thus Donald Morton writes:

> Rather than as a local effect, the return of queer has to be understood as the result, in the domain of sexuality, of the (post)modern encounter with—and rejection of—Enlightenment views concerning the role of the conceptual, rational, systematic, structural, normative, progressive, liberatory, revolutionary, and so forth, in social change. (Morton 370)

It also has to be understood as an encounter with—and rejection of—the Enlightenment concept of "the self": that is, with that concept of "the self" that sees it as the final repository of "reality" or "truth." Queer, in other words, has arisen in a theoretical climate that has seen, in Stuart Hall's words, "the final de-centring of the Cartesian subject" (Hall 120). In this climate, "identity" is perceived as a provisional and contingent product of history: a social construct that has become naturalized through cultural establishment and familiarity.

The word *familiarity* prompts the thought that the institution that best transmits—and within which we most obviously come to—a sense of social and cultural identity is indeed the family. This may help to explain why so much gay literature since Stonewall explores the concept of identity through an exploration of the conflict between gay life and family life. Both John D'Emilio and Jeffrey Weeks, taking a Marxist approach, see the emergence of gay identity as dependent on the historical development of capitalism and the free-labor system. D'Emilio writes:

> Only when individuals began to make their living through wage labor, instead of as parts of an interdependent family unit, was it possible for homosexual desire to coalesce into personal identity—an identity based on the ability to remain outside the heterosexual family and to construct a personal life based on attraction to one's own sex. (*Making Trouble* 8)

For these writers, then, it is the urbanized, industrialized countries of the developed world that provide the necessary background for the emergence of gay identity and lifestyle, for it is only in advanced capitalist countries that people acquire sufficient economic independence to break free from traditional social structures.

Hence, gay life and family life, representing the poles of the homo–heterosexual divide, are often seen as essentially irreconcilable, and the conflict between them was perhaps most visible during the 1970s, when sexual freedom became an axiom of gay liberation ideology. As Edmund White (to recall an earlier quotation) remarks: "Young people now think that if people were promiscuous in the seventies it was because they were sexual libertines. They have no idea that it was actually a form of idealism, that we wanted to find new ways of relating" (Brookes 37). But the AIDS epidemic brought with it a new moralism that laid stress on the value of long-term, monogamous relationships and encouraged a style of living based on the heterosexual model. Meanwhile, this assimilationism was assisted (it has been argued) by the Foucauldian deconstructive analysis of gay identity, which, in a parallel development, effected a weakening of the belief in fixed sexual categories.[3]

These changes, however, merely altered the balance of a conflict that, as I argue throughout this study, has been central to gay culture and politics since the late nineteenth century. But if the key gay novels of the 1970s reflect this conflict as an inner tension, in the AIDS-conscious world of the 1980s and 1990s the conflict is reflected more evidently in two distinct strains of gay fiction. These correspond to those tendencies we examined in the last chapter, even if the strains are also impure because similarly self-conflicted. Thus on one side of this opposition is a strain of fiction that could be broadly classified as assimilationist. This term is often used pejoratively, as if to suggest that what a certain kind of fiction offers is a form of bland accommodationism. However, viewed from another angle, this fiction looks radical, offering an approach that has adapted to the reality of a changed world: a post-AIDS world that requires a change in personal and sexual relations; and a poststructuralist world, in which a politics of difference has begun to supplant a politics of identity.

This strain of writing is perhaps best represented by the fiction of David Leavitt. In a clear account of his own position, as well as of the conflict at the center of contemporary gay/queer antagonisms, Leavitt writes:

> I flinched at the notion that coming out somehow meant that I would not only have to reimagine myself totally but to cut off my ties to my family, my heterosexual friends—indeed, the totality of the world I'd grown up in. To do so, it seemed to me, was to risk doing myself real psychic violence. Yes, I was gay, but I was also Jewish, a Leavitt, a writer: so many other things! Why should my sexual identity subsume all my other identities? I wondered. And then I saw the answer: because the world, the "normal" world, upon learning I was gay, would see me only as gay; because ghettos are invented not by the people who live in them but by the people who don't live in them. A new level of liberation needed to be achieved, I decided then: one that would allow gay men and lesbians to celebrate their identities without having to move into a gulag. (*Penguin Book of Gay Short Stories* xxii)

Leavitt, then, is an assimilationist, and assimilationism is generally associated with an ideologically and politically conservative position, deriving from essentialist notions of fixed sexual categories and identities. But is this fair? Leavitt's position, in the account he gives of it here, does not obviously derive from an essentialist viewpoint. Indeed it suggests quite the opposite. His quarrel with gay identity, on the grounds of its tendency to subsume all other identities, is clearly related to Foucault's constructionist line of argument and sounds in fact very close to the following: "Nothing that went into his [the homosexual's] total composition was unaffected by his sexuality" (*History* 43). It also echoes later refigurings of Foucault's idea: for instance, Eve Sedgwick's complaint against nineteenth-century sexological categorization that it assigned "to every given person . . . a binarized identity that was full of implications, however confusing, for even the ostensibly least sexual aspects of personal existence" (*Epistemology* 2). Clearly, Leavitt does not reject the notion of gay identity altogether: he acknowledges it, and indeed wants to celebrate it. But equally clearly, he *does* reject it as an all-consuming passion, a monomaniac obsession, an all-embracing self-definition.

Accordingly, Leavitt writes about homosexuality, but not as the only focus of his concern. Thus his gay characters are subsumed within a larger social group and placed within the wider social scene. In this respect, as I have already indicated, his work seems representative of that strain of gay writing since Stonewall that includes, for example, the fiction of Michael Cunningham and Armistead Maupin. In its attempt to see homosexuality as merely one aspect of life among many, to treat it as simply a fact and not as an issue—in short, to present rather than explain it—this writing relates back to the work of Forster and Isherwood. But to write about homosexuality in this way is not easy, as Leavitt himself acknowledges:

> Because heterosexuality is the norm, writers have permission to explore its nuances without raising any eyebrows. To write about gay characters, by contrast, is always, necessarily, to make some sort of "statement" about the fact of being gay. Stories in which a character's homosexuality is, as it were, "beside the point" confuse us: why bring it up? asks the writing teacher in our heads. (*Penguin Book of Gay Short Stories* xxvii)

Here, Leavitt is addressing a problem that is inherent in an assimilationist approach and that many see as good reason to reject such an approach. This problem, which is as much cultural and political as literary, is closely related to the question that I raised earlier: that is, are homosexuality and heterosexuality—given the latter's concomitant "family life"—incompatible? Leavitt's remarks, in the passage quoted above, suggest that a character's homosexuality is never "beside the point" for readers of fiction, whatever the author's intentions, because in a predominantly heterosexual society homosexuality is always problematized, always an "issue." For Leavitt, it seems, the problem arises not from an unwillingness to assimilate on the part of lesbians and gay men, but from an unwillingness on the part of the wider heterosexual population to allow them to assimilate: "ghettos," we recall, "are invented . . . by people who don't live in them."

Leavitt's remarks suggest that his response to the problem is to behave as if it does not exist. His approach, in life as in fiction, is to seek what people have in common rather than what separates them. This is a response that some would censure as a form of self-deception and evasion: a means of escaping the ghetto by refusing to identify as an inmate. The response and the censure thus relate to that central conflict we have been tracing in post-Stonewall gay writing generally, for Leavitt's uneasiness with gay identity and his partial rejection of it originate, as we have seen, from a fundamentally antiessentialist viewpoint:

> To envision homosexuality . . . as an ethnic identity is to risk forgetting that sexuality is an extremely individualistic business; that each

gay man and lesbian is gay or lesbian is his or her own way. Literature confronts the perversity of individual experience. (*Penguin Book of Gay Short Stories* xxvi)

But if Leavitt's preference for difference over identity in this passage hints at a "queer" theoretical perspective, it also highlights the contradictions within that perspective: for Leavitt seeks to assimilate his gay characters by concentrating on the differences between people. This is to suggest, to put it another way, that what people have in common is their lack of common experience.

Hence the criticism that is often leveled at Leavitt is the same as that which is directed at the constructionist approach to sexuality in general: that it seeks to dissolve difference and at the same time to retain it—criticism that goes, in fact, to the heart of our contemporary debate about sexuality. Christopher Lane, for example, puts his finger on this particular tension when he writes:

Contemporary Queer Theory is ambivalent about Foucault's preference for "acts" rather than "identities," however, since it wants to celebrate "perverse" visibility without the constraints of identity politics. All the same, Queer Theory at crucial points rebels against its push for sexual diffusion, seeing the side effects of its arguments as coercive bids to repress or absorb homosexuality's radicalism. (168–69)

There are echoes of Leavitt here. For instance, Leavitt, feeling the constraints of homosexuality as an ethnic identity, wants to confront the "perversity of individual experience"—or, as Lane puts it, to "push for sexual diffusion." Yet his call for a "new level of liberation . . . one that would allow gay men and lesbians to celebrate their identities without having to move into a gulag" hints at an anxiety about loss of identity—and, with it, loss of radical edge, loss of power to effect change.

## DISSECTING THE FAMILY

Leavitt's assimilationism, then, is much more subtle, complex, and finely balanced than many critics allow. Thus his fiction, while eschewing the uncompromising militancy and separatism that sees all heterosexual institutions and practices as totally alien, is in no way apologetic or fearful of disturbing heterosexual sensibilities. This complexity is well-illustrated in his novel *The Lost Language of Cranes*, which is primarily an examination of the relationship between Philip, the novel's young gay protagonist, and his parents, Rose and Owen. In the sense that he proceeds on the assumption that homosexuality and heterosexuality *are* compatible, Philip is Leavitt's alter ego. Like Leavitt himself, Philip sees the process of coming out not in terms of cutting himself off from his roots but of strengthening his ties to family, heterosexual friends, and the world he has grown up in. Indeed he seems motivated by a strong determination to resist pressure to cut himself off from the dominant culture and "reimagine [himself] totally" within a subcultural gulag. At the same time, the novel is in no way dependent on the values of the heterosexual mainstream. In fact, to a large extent, it acts as a critique of them. Thus Philip's gay relationships are presented in significant contrast to the apparently staid and conventional relationship of his parents, the main contrast being that the former are more relaxed and egalitarian, and characterized by a greater degree of honesty. Indeed, in some respects, the novel looks like an illustration of Alan Sinfield's contention that, before the AIDS pandemic came along to undercut gay advantage, gay relationships were beginning to appear more satisfactory and viable than straight ones:

> The idea was that we were doing better with the sex-and-love questions. Gay men had organized genial ways of meeting for casual sex, as well as loving couples that might manage, even, to evade gendered roles. We knew how to see other men without falling out with our partners; how to go to bed with friends, how to remain on close terms with former lovers, how to handle age and class differences. (*Wilde Century* 185)

For at the heart of the novel's critical examination of relationships, gay or straight, is the question of honesty. This is what makes the scene in which Philip comes out to his parents so crucial—in fact, *the* central scene of the novel. The almost inevitable pain involved in the process of coming out to parents is vividly caught in the writing here; but what makes the scene especially shattering for Rose and Owen (as for the reader, who, experiencing it as theater, is also subject to the full impact of its dramatic irony) is that it exposes the fundamental dishonesty of their own relationship. For, as we already know and Rose is soon to learn, Owen is himself gay and has sought cover for his homosexuality in marriage to Rose. But Rose is not shown as blameless. Rather, she is shown as complicit in the deceit, as someone who has settled for an unsatisfactory marriage and a life based on appearances in return for the comfort and security to be found within the conventions of an affluent, middle-class way of life. The meagerness of the life she has settled for is implied in her devotion to television, and in particular to the serial dramas we call soap operas, or soaps. These, the novel implies, as well as supplying her with a substitute life, a replacement for the human drama and emotional involvement her own life lacks, also provide her with an escape from those aspects of her own life she would rather not think about.[4]

Indeed this scene, through the revelation of Owen's sexuality, breaks the mold of the coming-out scene in gay novels and clearly exemplifies Leavitt's assimilationist approach. Usually, in such scenarios, gay children and their parents stand on opposite sides of a clear-cut ethnic divide. This us-and-them polarity turns the encounter into a contest, in which the gay children, as protagonists, become the heroes and their parents the enemy. The effect here, however, is to dissolve such differences: to shatter the illusion of fixed (sexual) identities, indeed to draw attention to the constructedness of social frameworks based on the supposition of such categories. In unpacking the tidy Rose-Owen-Philip family unit, the novel denaturalizes it: reveals it as an assemblage of parts not naturally adapted to the constraining social form that holds it together. Leavitt's assimilationism, then, is clearly not based on belief in accommodation to existing arrangements, on deference to the status quo; and hence, in this sense, it could be considered challenging, even radical.

This impression is reinforced in a parallel narrative strand of the novel: the story of Jerene, Eliot's black lesbian roommate. Jerene's parents by adoption are a black couple, whose strong impulse to become part of mainstream American life (and consequent espousal of mainstream American values) is exactly the form of assimilationism that is critiqued and rejected by the novel. However, the line of assimilation the novel does pursue is revealed in its attempt to link the experience of black and gay people through an examination of the pressures exerted on both groups to conform to the values of mainstream society: by showing homophobia and racism as the source of a similar need to become accepted. The novel therefore treats Jerene's parents sympathetically, seeking to understand their behavior and discover the roots of their homophobic prejudice: in short, to find common ground with them. But at the same time it maintains its critical distance, asserting its own individual viewpoint and sense of gay identity. Thus the novel shows the dilemma of Jerene's parents as one they share with lesbians and gays: namely, whether to endure life on the margins, with one's sense of personal and political identity intact, or enjoy life in the mainstream, with the attendant compromise and possible loss of integrity.

In respect of Jerene's parents, then, the novel on the one hand recognizes their problem and identifies with their dilemma, while on the other rejecting their solution. In other words, its assimilationist approach, its tendency to seek understanding and common ground, never gives way to wholesale compromise. Indeed, in its maintenance of certain bedrock values, it could be said that the novel's ultimate statement is about the need to *assert* one's sense of identity and personal integrity. Jerene's parents, in their pursuit of respectability, are shown as turning a blind eye to—and even colluding with—those forces of racist prejudice that oppress them and seek to deny their existence. Jerene's father, for instance, is a rich and successful lawyer, who becomes a delegate for Richard Nixon at the Republican Party convention of 1968 and appears on television in a clear case of tokenist support for black civil rights. When the interviewer questions his support for Republicanism, his reply—"I fully believe that Richard Nixon is what our country and our economy needs now" (61)—makes him sweat and look uncomfortable. It also calls forth a gasp of protest from Jerene, although his wife seems merely pleased that a black face—and particularly her husband's face—has been allowed to appear on television.

The novel thus firmly rejects that form of assimilationism that seeks acceptance at any price, and specifically at the price of denying one's own identity and that of others. The violently homophobic response of Jerene's parents when she tells them of her lesbianism is shown as horror of scandal, of tainted reputation. Blacks, in their pursuit of respectability, must be—or be seen to be—whiter than white. In contrast, Jerene is shown as striving to achieve that degree of balance the novel approves. Her assertion of lesbian identity is accompanied by an attempt to keep open the lines of communication between herself and her parents. Moreover, her doctoral dissertation on the phenomenon of language, which has occupied her for seven years, suggests a process of self-discovery—an attempt to ascertain the truth of our being: "For each, in his own way, she believed, finds what it is he must love, and loves it; the window becomes a mirror; whatever it is that we love, that is who we are" (183). At the same time, in its concern with the limits and possibilities of communication, it reveals the potential of language to frustrate as well as empower: to divide people, as well as bring them together. Ultimately, however, the novel sides with Jerene in suggesting that the attempt to build bridges, whatever the outcome, *must* be made.

But this central tension of the novel—how to assert one's gay identity without cutting oneself off from family and heterosexual friends—is principally embodied in Philip. In keeping with the novel's assimilationist approach, Philip is portrayed in a balanced way, for Leavitt clearly identifies with his protagonist, while at the same time viewing him with some degree of detachment and irony. He is thus shown as too dependent on the approval of his parents, the presentation of whose marriage becomes emblematic of the novel's critique of heterosexual relations and values as a whole. The Rose–Owen marriage is shown as doomed to failure, and not just because of Owen's homosexuality but also through subscription to an unattainable ideal based on the concept of lifelong love and fidelity. It thus becomes mired in dishonesty: Owen makes love to Rose while fantasizing about making love to a man; Rose keeps secret her sexual liaison with Karl Mutter and her affair with Nick at the office.

Philip's relationship with Eliot is more open than that of his parents, but the novel suggests that its failure is caused in part through pursuit of a similar ideal. From the moment he and Eliot appear together, Philip is shown as a man romantically "in love." Indeed the opening words of the scene—"Philip was in love" (25)—sound ironic, as if secretly placed within quotation marks; and the scene ends with a line that suggests an understanding of human relations gathered from Hollywood cliché: "Then—in a voice he had never heard before, a voice that belonged to Greta Garbo—he said to Eliot, 'I am yours'" (27). Moreover, the novel suggests that the relationship begins to go wrong as a result of Philip's inability to accept it for what it is, and his urge to make it conform to his romantic ideal. Eliot nails the problem nicely: "I've been an emblem of the sort of person you could imagine loving, not a person you loved" (163). The difficulties of the relationship, Leavitt suggests in an implied endorsement of Eliot's remark, spring from Philip's anxiety to win approval from his parents. This is reinforced a few pages later when, trying to explain to Rose and Owen why he has kept his homosexuality concealed from them for so long, he says: "I guess I've been scared of disappointing you. I wanted to wait until my life was good enough so that I could show it to you and not be ashamed. I wanted to wait until I could show you that a homosexual life could be a good thing" (169).[5]

Thus, even as it engages with the heterosexual mainstream in a search for common ground, the novel asserts the need for an independent and self-created gay identity. This becomes especially evident in the final scene, where Owen—distraught, unstable, his life and marriage in disarray—has clearly lost all credibility as a role model for Philip. Indeed, in a reversal of roles, it is he who turns to Philip for help and guidance. At the same time, Philip himself is starting to look more confident and independent. Following the collapse of his relationship with Eliot, his friendship with Brad seems set on a firmer foundation, since, in contrast to the earlier relationship, it has arisen naturally and almost inadvertently, the two men scarcely aware of their feelings for each other until unable to ignore them. It is significant that both Philip and Brad have been pursuing an ideal of love and discover each other only by accident, the ideal having proved chimerical. Theirs is a relaxed friendship, affectionate but not driven by sexual passion; and Philip seems to have given up worrying about appearances—such as whether Brad is a suitable boyfriend to introduce to his parents, for instance.

## POSTMODERNIST PERSPECTIVES

As I have already remarked, theorists often assert that, whereas gay is part of the legitimating metanarratives that characterize Enlightenment thinking, queer is postmodern. Postmodernism, according to Jean-Francois Lyotard, imposes "a severe reexamination on the thought of the Enlightenment, on the idea of a unitary end of history and of a subject" (73). This unitary end of history includes, Judith Roof suggests, heterosexualized notions of production/reproduction that have excluded homosexualities as "degenerescence" (to use Foucault's word); and thus postmodernity can be seen as having liberated certain subjects from the tyranny of such thinking (177). But the central feature of postmodernism, in Lyotard's account, is its challenge to the totalizing claims of reason: its questioning of the truth claims of knowledge and science. These claims, he argues, are an attempt to cope with the chaotic flux and bewildering complexity of human experience through the imposition of closed, self-referential systems; and he suggests that what is needed is a more experimental attitude, a greater openness to what is new and unknown.

As we have seen, despite inner tensions and contradictions, Leavitt's personal ideology in many ways suggests an approach informed by such queer challenges. Furthermore, in *The Lost Language of Cranes*, there is a clear engagement with some of the ideas raised in Lyotard's analysis of our postmodern condition. Avoiding a linear narrative, for instance, the novel moves backward and forward in time, replacing numbered chapters with a division into four very unequal parts. Thus, without resorting to a stream-of-consciousness technique, it attempts to convey the untidiness of human experience: its flux, its ebb and flow, its oscillation between the immediate present and the remembered past. In this way, its fragmented eclecticism chimes with the postmodernist refusal to impose unitary design on intractable material, an impression reinforced by its open-endedness, lack of closure.

Moreover, it could be said that a postmodernist questioning of legitimating metanarratives—of closed, self-referential systems of thought—supplies the novel's central trope. Lyotard argues, for instance, that the criteria regulating the truth claims of knowledge derive from discrete, context-dependent language games, not absolute rules or standards. It is thus significant that both Rose and Jerene are much concerned with language, and in particular with language as a closed, self-referential system or game. The novel lays great stress on the way Rose, both as proofreader and crossword puzzle addict, uses language to impose order on what she perceives as an increasingly chaotic and disordered world. Seeing life, symbolically represented in the novel by the teeming maelstrom of New York, as a threat rather than a challenge, she seeks security in the rule-bound world of language, and particularly that of crosswords. Language, in fact, becomes her means of withdrawal. Likewise, in her investigation into the phenomenon of language for her doctoral dissertation, Jerene becomes interested in the existence of private—or "lost"—languages. The story of the crane-child, from which the novel takes its title, suggests that the individual oddity of human experience remains largely outside the scope of our common linguistic inheritance—the totalizing claims of our metanarratives—and is thus destined to remain forever hidden or "lost." These ideas, as well as recalling Leavitt's above-quoted comment that literature "confronts the perversity of individual experience," bring to mind those theories of language that are at the root of poststructuralism and postmodernist thinking. My point here is that Rose, through her interest in crosswords, and Jerene, through her fascination with lost language, seem deeply bound up with, and to reflect the concerns of, our logocentric culture. In other words, a major strand of the motivation of these characters seems "organised around the belief or hope that there is meaning in language, and even some ultimate final meaning, such as God or Truth, rather than the endless play of *différance*" (Gray 164).[6]

In this respect, as in many others, there is a strong resemblance between *The Lost Language of Cranes* and Michael Cunningham's second novel, *A Home at the End of the World*. Cunningham's title is of course richly suggestive. Among other things, its tone of beleaguered nostalgia seems to look back not only to a pre-AIDS era of gay solidarity and progressivism but to a vanished view of the world based on the Enlightenment concept of "a unitary end of history and a subject." It is also significant that the "home" of the title—the home that Bobby, Clare, and Jonathan create for themselves—becomes finally and symbolically established at Woodstock, the site of the 1968 rock festival: for the symbolic significance of Woodstock, it could be argued from a postmodernist viewpoint, lies in its accent on the concepts of "community," "global identity," and "the human family" and hence in its subscription to the rationalism and progressivism of Enlightenment metanarrative thinking. The "home" of the title is an attempt to find refuge in a wrecked world: to reconstruct from a deconstructed mental landscape. Like the characters in Leavitt's novel—Rose, with her soaps and crosswords; Owen, scared and broken; Philip, tentative and insecure—Bobby, Clare, and Jonathan are troubled and confused. Indeed, in the Leavitt sense, they are "lost."

As we have seen, the central trope of Leavitt's novel alludes to the question of difference: to our human sense of personal uniqueness. In other words, the story of the crane-child is Leavitt's way of confronting what he calls "the perversity of individual experience." The singularity of the crane-child's knowledge of the world becomes lost through the loss of a uniquely personal language; and the novel suggests that Leavitt is using the story symbolically, as a metaphor for human experience in general. This again draws attention to the tensions and contradictions of Leavitt's queer insights in this novel, and indeed to those conflicts of ideology in gay male writing that I have been exploring throughout this study. For without initiation into the language of the tribe the crane-child remains linguistically trapped, isolated within his own solipsistic worldview. Communication by means of a common language is necessary to break the isolation, but inevitably involves some loss of individuality. The central trope of the novel, then, insists that we are all unique, but that what we have in common, and can to some extent communicate, is just this sense of our personal uniqueness. It therefore tries to dissolve our sense of difference through concentration on our common experience of being and feeling different.

Cunningham's novel struggles with these same tensions and contradictions. On the one hand, its trio of protagonists, Bobby, Clare, and Jonathan, in their rejection of taboos and conventions, in their carnivalesque flouting of established social codes, in their refusal to label themselves sexually, personify a thoroughly postmodern outlook and indeed queer transgressiveness. In part, these characters adapt to, even feel at home in, the riot and disorder of contemporary New York, living together for several years "in a sixth-floor walk-up on East Third Street," which they have chosen for its cheapness and because it strikes them as "more interesting than the safer parts of town" (109). In flight from stifling provincialism and dysfunctional family life, they set about creating their own alternative social and familial arrangement. But the novel stresses that the particular characteristic that brings them together is their strong sense of individuality, their sense of being different and thus cut off from common experience. The main origin of Jonathan's sense of being different is of course his homosexuality; but like Philip in Leavitt's novel—and indeed, like Leavitt himself—he rejects the term "gay" as an all-embracing self-definition. He seems in fact reluctant, like them, to allow his sexual identity to subsume all his other identities.

What he and Bobby have in common is a sense of the perversity of their individual experience: a sense of that experience as lying outside the common currency of cultural and linguistic metanarratives, and as therefore condemned to—and only to be communicated through—silence. This feeling bonds them: they are at their closest after smoking a joint together, in the near-silent meditation and communion of a high. Behind their silence lies an inexpressible sense of loss. In Bobby's case, this stems from the death of his older brother Carlton in the traumatizing accident that leaves him marked and fixated for life: "But as long as she [Carlton's girlfriend] was in Cleveland, I could never look her straight in the face. I couldn't talk about the wounds she suffered. I can't even write her name" (37). In Jonathan's case, it results from the disintegration of his family that follows his mother's loss of her baby in childbirth, and the sense, in this painful aftermath, of his father's rejection: "Jesus Christ, Jonathan . . . What in the hell is the matter with you? *What?*" (19). For although in time his family returns to at least a semblance of normality, the novel suggests that it is this incident and the feeling that he is not the son his father would like him to be that leaves him with his permanent sense of outsidership: "He would ask me no more unanswerable questions, though his singular question would continue crackling in the back of my head like a faulty electrical connection" (19).

As I have indicated, however, these characters, like the novel they inhabit, are deeply conflicted. Alongside their strong sense of individuality and outsidership, there runs an equally strong need to belong: to embrace identity and become insiders. Hence their invention of "the Hendersons," the very ordinary, middle-American family they become when they go out together:

> We took to calling ourselves the Hendersons. I don't remember how it started—it was part of a line tossed out by Clare or Jonathan, and it stuck. The Hendersons were a family with modest expectations and simple tastes. They liked going to the movies or watching TV. They liked having a few beers in a cheap little bar. When we went out together, the three of us, we called it "a night with the Hendersons."

Clare came to be known as Mom, I was Junior, and Jonathan was Uncle Jonny. (155–56)

The Hendersons, then, are a private joke. But beneath the mocking playfulness there lurks a wistful longing. For the Hendersons suggest that Bobby, Clare, and Jonathan harbor aspirations to family status—indeed, that these three, in their guise of the Hendersons, constitute what traditionalists disparagingly describe as a "pretend family."

Moreover, there are other indications in the novel of the need in these characters to take on more conventional social and familial roles and identities. For instance, before Bobby joins them in New York, Clare and Jonathan live together for three years in a relationship very like husband and wife, the nature of which is immediately evident to Bobby, as his partly ironic use of the term *roommate* in his account of meeting Clare for the first time makes clear: "We walked through the big door and she called, 'Hello, dear.' Like a wife" (135). When Clare gets depressed (about her lack of identity, lack of achievement, lack of a conventional social role?) she and Jonathan even talk about having a baby together (111–12), although ultimately it is Bobby's arrival on the scene that provides her with the means of fulfilling her ambition "to do a better job with a child than my parents had done with me" (162). Furthermore, Jonathan's rejection of gay identity, his insistence that his relationship with Erich is merely a matter of sex, and his jealous sense of exclusion from the Henderson *ménage* as Clare and Bobby become bonded in parenthood, suggest that he and Clare are prey to similar anxieties: anxieties about the future (in which they claim not to believe); and anxieties born of a threatening AIDS-conscious world where people are again seeking old familiar structures, old securities:

> "Come on," I said. "Speak."
> He turned to face me. "The life I'd been preparing myself for has been called off," he said. "I thought I could stay unattached and love a lot of different people. You and Bobby included."
> "You can. You do."
> "I can't. It's a new age, everybody's getting married."
> "Not me, thank you," I said.
> "Yes you are. You're with Bobby now. I've got to find somebody of my own, and I don't feel like I have all the time in the world anymore. I mean, Clare, what if I'm sick?" (203)

Thus, in the way their concern with notions of home and family is undercut by an acute awareness of their individual differences, these characters experience and exemplify the conflicts inherent in the ideology they embody. Moreover, their attempt to create an alternative familial configuration is ultimately destined to fail, since their postmodern disavowal of identity and their focus on the perversity of individual experience can lead only to separatism, isolationism, and group disintegration. This process begins with Jonathan's long-term, if temporary, disappearance—an event triggered by his sense of a need "to find somebody of my own," and hence to buy into the security of a monogamous relationship and conventional pair bonding. Moreover, his sense of isolation, of being different, is increased through his awareness of AIDS and his own vulnerability. When Clare asserts that he is not sick, he replies: "You don't know that. We may not know for years" (203). Likewise, Clare's climactic elopement with baby Rebecca, which effects the final disintegration of the Hendersons, grows from a similar sense of separateness, isolation, and individual destiny. But in her case this feeling of difference is a matter of gender, for as "Mom" to the family, she feels that her role is largely functional: "Now I better understand why mothers appear so often in stories as saints or as monsters. We are not human in the ordinary sense, at least not when our children are small. We become monsters of care" (319–20). She thinks of herself as "Snow White living amongst the dwarfs," passing a life of domestic harmony but feeling otherwise unfulfilled; and she suspects that Jonathan and Bobby, loving each other more than they love her, are using her "without quite knowing it" (280). Furthermore, these suspicions are well founded, as some of Bobby's remarks make clear: "Jonathan and I are members of a team so old nobody else could join even if we wanted them to. We adore Clare but she's not quite on the team" (268).[7]

## END-OF-WORLD NOSTALGIA:
## POSTMODERN, POSTGAY TENSIONS

> Any new metanarratives that account for diversified subject position include gay and lesbian as two of many possibilities, as part of a variety that has become *status quo* even if nostalgia for the metanarratives of old continually tries to limit imagined gay/lesbian interference with familial order. (Roof 177–78)

Bobby, Clare, and Jonathan, then, not only personify a thoroughly postmodern outlook and queer transgressiveness, they also embody the inherent tensions and contradictions of their attitude and lifestyle. The relationship between the terms "queer" and "postmodern," as I note above, has been frequently remarked and discussed. Judith Roof, for instance, focusing in particular on the way these terms tend to overlap through an opening up of categories and dissolution of metanarratives, writes: "In the sense that queer tries to occupy an identifiably postmodern position in relation to modernist identity categories, queering might be seen as a postmodernist move" (180). But she goes on to examine one of queer's inherent contradictions: its tendency to become identified with the very categories it means to eschew. She points out that the term comes finally to stand for whatever is "not purely heterosexual or aligned with traditional gender categories" (180); and thus ultimately it comes to define itself in opposition to the larger metanarrative of reproduction and patriarchal family rather than create new metanarratives through absorption and transformation. The conflicting impulses that Bobby, Clare, and Jonathan experience—their attraction to, and flight from, the concept of "family"—originate from the contradiction Roof finds in queer generally: "Queer may well permit thinking beyond modernist categories, but because it is appended to those categories as their performative dislocation, it sometimes has a tendency to come full circle, not in enabling a wholesale rejection of sex/gender categories, but in finally enfranchising even heterosexuality as queer" (180).

In Cunningham's novel, this contradiction is dramatized in the portrayal of the central characters, and especially in their creation and adoption of the Hendersons and the role-play that accompanies it. For one strand of this role-play performs the same subversive function in respect of the traditional family structure as drag does in respect of traditional gender categories: that is, it satirizes, exposes, and rejects that structure through parody, stylization, and hyperbolic representation. Judith Butler has shown how drag, when impelled by a radical agenda, can reveal the constructedness of gender categories through parodic exaggeration of gender performativity, and her central claim that "there is no gender identity behind the expressions of gender; that identity is performatively constituted by the very 'expressions' that are said to be its results" (*Gender Trouble* 25) could be said to be the concept behind at least one aspect of the Henderson family role-play. Thus Bobby, Clare, and Jonathan, through their parodic invention, reveal (to themselves, at least) the hollowness behind the myths of middle-American family life: which is to say, the constructedness of the identities within the performance and expressions of that way of life. What their parody amounts to is a rejection of the essentialism that presupposes that a family has an essential constitution: a constitution, that is, formed from the essential identities of its members.

However, just as drag reveals the constructedness of identity and the possibility of self-invention—of our becoming the people we might wish to be—so the Henderson role-play reveals to Bobby, Clare, and Jonathan not only the constructedness of the family as a social unit but also the possibility of their self-invention as a family—the family that their identities traditionally disqualify them from becoming. Their parody, in other words, is rooted in nostalgic fondness: they are half in love with the thing they affect to find ridiculous. Indeed, their struggle to constitute themselves as a family, to build a home for themselves, suggests a striving for an ideal, for a way of life they feel they have lost or never quite achieved. Thus the main thrust of Bobby's motivation is his need to find a substitute for the home and family that suddenly and effectively came to an end on the day of his older brother's fatal accident. When Jonathan moves to New York, for instance, Bobby moves in with Alice and Ned, Jonathan's parents; and his fondness for Alice seems to stem from her role as a substitute for the mother who "died" on the same day as his brother. Likewise, Jonathan's sense of rejection in the aftermath of his mother's miscarriage (recall: "Jesus Christ, Jonathan . . . What in the hell is the matter with you? *What?*") results in a powerful need to replace the family that he feels have rejected him. Furthermore, when the substitute family seems also to have failed him, his sense of loss is revealed in his attempt to salvage something from the wreckage of the home he had known as a child—in his attempt, after the collapse of the family business and in the months of illness leading up to his father's death, to regain something of that former close bond with his father.

The tension produced by these conflicting impulses builds to a climax in Part 3 of the novel, and leads, as already intimated, through a gradual process of disintegration, to eventual breakdown. The tension is between, on the one hand, nostalgia for an irrecoverable past of secure sex/gender categories and familial roles and, on the other, a need to recognize a queer present, imagine a queer future, without such securities. Moreover, Jonathan's lover Erich, who becomes an object of care at the Woodstock home when he is dying of AIDS, comes eventually to symbolize one strand of this conflict, for in his dependency, he becomes a complement to little Rebecca—in effect, another child within the family, around whom familial bonding and role-play can develop. Hence, Clare's eventual perception is twofold. First, she sees that the gay male "family" of Jonathan, Erich, and Bobby (whose bisexuality and attraction to Erich is made clear in the text) is one that preserves the conventional sex/gender categories and therefore excludes her—or at least subordinates her to a functional female role. But second, with a kind of brutal clarity of vision, she sees that Erich, who is dying of AIDS, and Jonathan, who has probably been infected by the same virus, belong to the past: a past that, rooted in the sixties and symbolized by Woodstock, vanished with the coming of AIDS; and a past that, in any case, has failed to deliver on any of its promises. Her account of her last sight of Bobby and Jonathan, as she makes her secret elopement with Rebecca, makes this clear: "In their sunglasses and T-shirts and unruly hair they looked like they were standing on the brink of the old cycle: the 1960s about to explode around them, a long storm of love and rage and thwarted expectations" (327).

Not until the final pages of the novel, with the brief epiphany that Jonathan receives as he stands in the ice-cold lake with the dying Erich, do these tensions become, if only fleetingly, resolved. For what Jonathan experiences here, with the collapse of the metanarratives that have hitherto cramped and distorted his vision, is a moment of pure postmodernist liberation. With the knowledge that he might himself die soon from the very same virus that is even now carrying off the visibly ravaged Erich, what he grasps here, in a flash of relativist perception, is that truth, bounded by human limitation and confined to the isolated moment, is always contingent, partial, transient. In this moment of spiritual rebirth, he discards his sense of a unitary end of history and shakes free of the progressivist, positivist notions, the self-referential systems, by which he has evaluated his own life: "Something cracked. I had lived until then for the future, in a state of continuing expectation, and the process came suddenly to a stop while I stood nude with Erich and Bobby in a shallow platter of freezing water" (342). Indeed, his perception here could be seen as reflecting and encapsulating the postmodernist, and especially the Foucauldian, attack on concepts of absolute truth, objective knowledge, identity, and selfhood.

Thus the moment, as he experiences it here, is fundamentally antiessentialist in that it declares itself to be without essential quality, value, or meaning. It declares itself, in fact, to be simply itself. Just as history, in Foucault's account, must be conceived as an overlapping series of discontinuous fields, and discourse as "a series of discontinuous segments whose tactical function is neither uniform nor stable" (*History* 100), so this particular moment—and, by extension, his life and sense of selfhood—becomes for Jonathan an experience the quality, value, and meaning of which cannot be finally ascertained or fixed, and which therefore can only be experienced for itself alone:

> I was nothing so simple as happy. I was merely present, perhaps for the first time in my adult life. The moment was unextraordinary. But I had the moment, I had it completely. It inhabited me. I realized that if I died soon I would have known this, a connection with my life, its errors and cockeyed successes. The chance to be one of three naked men standing in a small body of clear water. I would not die unfulfilled because I'd been here, right here and nowhere else. (342–43)

So the moment does not presage the future or imply any comment on the past. It exists outside the constraints of modernist metanarrative, in what has been styled the "faultlines" of discourse and power (to recall my earlier discussion of Alan Sinfield's social constructionist theory). It could therefore be said to constitute one of those innumerable points of resistance to discursive practice that Foucault describes as being always present wherever power exists: a resistance "coextensive with [power] and absolutely its contemporary" ("Power and Sex" 122). Despite its tensions and contradictions, then, its oscillation between social-sexual identity and queer difference, its attraction to and flight from the concept of family, Cunningham's novel, like Leavitt's, seems to lay its ultimate stress on its confrontation with the perversity of individual experience and to come down finally, albeit with a kind of rueful honesty, on the side of the queer present.[8]

## KINDRED SPIRITS OF THE LIVING AND THE DEAD: THE GAY FAMILY

In *Cranes* and *Home*, Leavitt and Cunningham struggle with the problem that too much emphasis on the perversity of individual experience leaves the individual isolated. Philip and Jonathan, in their wish to celebrate their identities without having to move into a gulag, are divided characters, pulled in opposite directions. Their desire to assimilate, to find common ground, to be absorbed into the concept of family, exists alongside an acute awareness of difference, of sexuality as "an extremely individualistic business," of each gay man and lesbian being gay or lesbian "in his or her own way." Moreover, both novels end on an equivocal note, with no sense of permanent reconciliation between these conflicting impulses, and with both characters on the brink of new departure, new uncertainty. Philip's coming out, so far from effecting reconciliation, shatters his parents' lives and leads to disarray, a greater sundering, a wrecked marriage. Likewise, Jonathan's assumption of familial roles, his strong desire to be a father and husband, leads eventually to the breakup of his adopted family, to the collapse of the metanarratives that have hitherto sustained him, and to a sense of being isolated within his own consciousness: of being alone with his own incommunicable personal experience.

I want therefore to devote the rest of this chapter to an examination of Robert Ferro's novel *The Family of Max Desir,* a mixture of realism, romance, and fantasy in which the writer goes some way to resolving the conflict between gay life and heterosexual forms through a set of emphases very different from those of Leavitt and Cunningham. The clue to the novel is in its title, which alludes both to Max's biological family and to his other family: the gay family. Through this joint allusion the title itself suggests a coming together, a reconciliation of opposites. But a strong sense of group identity is in any case already implicit in the main social ambience of the novel, since Max's extended and close-knit family is Italian in origin, and the suggestion in Ferro's depiction of this milieu is that such a family, through the operation of a strong support system, is better able to absorb individual differences than one framed on the postwar, nuclear, Anglo-American model.

In this novel, Ferro, like Leavitt and Cunningham, is wrestling with the problem of whether gay life (representing "perverse" desire) and family life (representing the main unit of social identity) are essentially irreconcilable. I use the word *perverse* here in its Freudian sense: to mean, as in Christopher Lane's gloss on Freud's use of the word, that "sexuality is fundamentally at odds with social identity" (Lane 161).[9] But Ferro, as I intimate above, is ultimately more positive than Leavitt, Cunningham, or indeed Freud. The novel charts Max's struggle to integrate—to blend into a whole—the disparate elements in his life: his relationship to his family; his long-term romantic attachment to Nick; his need to celebrate his sexual identity, follow his "perverse" desire, and fulfill himself as an artist. These disparate elements are suggested by the varied strands of the narrative: the realism, romance, and fantasy. Ferro's achievement here is to weave these diverse parts into an almost seamless entity; and the degree of integration achieved in the novel thus comes to suggest the extent to which Max manages to bring together these diffuse constituents of his life.

Ferro's way of integrating these varied strands of his narrative is to lay stress not on difference but on similarity. He focuses on the oddness of the familiar, while emphasizing the familiarity of what seems odd. Thus, the account of Danilo's visit to the mausoleum to see the crypts of his mother and the daughter who died in infancy is as bizarre, as weirdly gothic in atmosphere, as the account of Lydia's rescue of Max and Nick from *La Stella Nera*. Likewise, the account of Marie's wake and funeral, in the attention it gives to the mysterious rites surrounding the burial of the dead, is fully as strange in its details as the account of Max's involvement in voodoo, or his final, imaginative self-transformation into a river god. At the same time, Ferro adopts a plain, direct, colloquial style throughout the novel, the effect of which is to domesticate, to make familiar, the strange and fantastic parts of his narrative.

He also makes evident his integrative tendency, his assimilative approach, through a deliberately drawn contrast: that is, by placing it purposely against a backdrop of *dis*integration. Thus he presents the Desir family as a dysfunctional, collapsing structure, to which he opposes the life-affirming potency of Max's slowly awakening sexuality and desire, which grow to full confidence in the course of the narrative. The novel opens, for instance, with a description of the motoring accident that effectively ends the life of Max's uncle Dan, who thereafter lies in a coma in the intensive care unit of a hospital. It then focuses for the remainder of its length on the lingering death from an inoperable brain tumor of Max's mother, Marie. These lines of narrative form the negative undertow of the novel: Dan's symbolic death and Marie's actual death embody Max's nihilism and despair, his sense of the futility of life.

Ferro draws together these opposed tendencies, and thus confirms the pull of his narrative, by showing the disintegration of the Desir family as in part due to the conflict engendered within it over Max's sexuality and his long-term relationship with Nick. The attitudes of Max's father, John, are the origin of this conflict. John's objection to Nick's name appearing on the embroidered family tree next to Max's—and especially to the embarrassment it causes him through its open display in the Desir summer cottage—creates a rift not only between Max and his father but also between Max and the rest of the family, who are inevitably caught up in the conflict. The novel thus makes a link between death and negative attitudes to sexuality, for the anguished passing of Marie, Dan's death-in-life, and John's stubborn refusal to accept Max and Nick as full members of the family are all presented as part of the same process of decay and fragmentation.

However, the novel resists its own movement toward disintegration in two ways: first, through its assimilationist approach to traditional, mainstream family life; and second, through its determination to identify with a wider network—the gay family. Thus, in the first instance, Ferro centers the action of his novel on Max and Nick's refusal either to keep their sexual identity secret from the family or to be marginalized by it. He focuses on their demand to be fully integrated into the family network and structure, symbolically represented in the novel by the embroidered family tree. Moreover, he lays stress on the theme and possibility of integration by underscoring the fundamentally romantic and monogamous nature of Max and Nick's relationship and its fifteen-year-long duration. Max and Nick's escape from *La Stella Negra* through the intervention of a powerful fairy godmother (Lydia) is a romantic episode that suggests, in its deliberate allusion to the love story of fictional romance, that their relationship is based on more than physical involvement—that it is, in fact, an affair of the heart.

This central strand of the novel, however, does not end with all tensions resolved. It seems to end, in fact, by acknowledging that gay life and traditional family life, though capable of a large measure of mutual understanding, are perhaps *not* fully reconcilable. For although John's attitude to Nick evolves in time from "coldly polite to cordial, and even to a level of respect" (94), he finds an unconditional acceptance of Max and Nick's relationship ultimately beyond him. But whereas Leavitt and Cunningham, reaching similar kinds of apparent impasse, leave their central characters isolated, cut off from others by the perversity of their individual experience, Ferro rescues Max by giving him, alongside a strong sense of family solidarity, an equally strong sense of having inherited, through his homosexuality, a different kind of ethnic identity. It is this aspect of the novel that lifts it out of its narrow, localized setting, transforming it from a grim, realistic account of a long, drawn-out, death-centered family feud into a confident vision of universal sexual and human liberation.

Max's split allegiances—to his biological family and to the gay family—are to some extent bridged by Nick. The Max–Nick relationship, combining both long-term romantic affection and sexual potency, allows Max to stay within the Desir family network—via the family tree, for example—while giving him the space, within the security of a singular attachment, to explore the wilder side of his nature and sexuality. This exploration begins with the scenes in the attic where Max and his school friend, Scott, have a series of wrestling matches that culminate in mutual masturbation—scenes that encapsulate the novel's positive charge, its exhilarated delight in the wild energy of mind and body: "Then making a quick turn of the hips, he released himself, and with a sound like a knock at the door, his semen hit the hollow attic wall" (47). The explosion of physical and mental energy released in these scenes creates waves that expand to the final pages of the novel.

Thus, during his stay in Florence, Max extends his sense of his sexual identity through contact with—and exploration of—the homosexual subculture of that city. This experience is presented as valuable in itself, as a kind of reaching out to the vast network of possible relations lying beyond the narrow confines of the singular romantic attachment. It is also presented as a process of education and self-discovery that is necessary for the achievement of satisfactory relations and self-fulfillment. In Florence,

Max feels, for instance, that he must start afresh, rid himself of the poisons that have hitherto clogged his life: "He had put himself in the wrong places, learned the wrong attitudes—about himself, so that he didn't know who he was; about his education, so that he hadn't learned anything; and about sex" (54). Hence, he opens himself to new experience by exploring the life of the streets; and his determination to compensate for the mistakes of the past pushes his thirst for self-knowledge to the limit. In his resolve to allow "nothing to hold him back," he becomes "atrociously unfaithful with strangers . . . quite the little whore" (57). However, this novel, unlike *Cranes* and *Home,* does not suggest that such experience is sterile or life denying.[10] On the contrary, it suggests quite the opposite: for Max's eager exploration of his sexuality is presented, here and throughout the novel, in life-affirming opposition to the decay, disintegration, and deathward pull of the Desir family narrative. Indeed, his fascination with, his absorption into, the gay family is shown as a clarifying, self-defining process from which he gains new life and strength: "The imposition of a secret, vast and unorthodox sex life upon an Edwardian schedule gave him a vivid sense of being, and an absorbed interest in the goings-on that he had never before known" (57).

This process of opening up to new experience extends much further, however. For if the novel suggests, as I indicate above, that Max's split allegiances can never be fully reconciled in the real world, it goes on to suggest that he can and does achieve integration through movement into another dimension. Thus, through the introduction of magical and supernatural elements, the novel achieves a spatial and temporal expansion that transcends the narrow, earthbound realism of its main narrative strand and gives it ultimately a visionary quality. Focusing on this aspect of the novel, David Bergman writes: "The gay family is not the biological family of the heterosexual novel. The gay family is made up of kindred spirits of the living and the dead, real and imaginary" (*Gaiety* 198).[11] Bergman's analysis of the novel goes on to suggest that, whereas the heterosexual man becomes naturally integrated into the community through the begetting of children, the homosexual man, lying outside the biological continuum, must seek integration through giving himself to the whole tribe, by making himself "an agent of a greater spiritual world, a vessel of the gods and the voices of destiny" (199).

The novel's blending of realism and the supernatural thus functions like the mixing of such radically different elements in magic-realist fiction generally: it breaks boundaries, transcends limitations, and gives access to remoter, and perhaps higher, areas of experience. The voice that Max hears while shaving one morning, for instance, which identifies itself as from Iala, the third orbiting planet of the Star Arcturus, has the effect of lifting us out of the fundamental drabness, the four-square solidity, of the novel's realistic mode. Indeed, since the voice reports that the Ialans observe our civilization with bemused detachment, rather as we watch TV, it has the effect of allowing us to glimpse Max's human predicament under the aspect of (something like) eternity. Likewise, Max's involvement with Clive, who propitiates his voodoo goddesses with "sweets, colored beads, liquor and money" (104) and who takes Max to see a Haitian woman who acts as a medium for a child named Gedde (178–79), interrupts the relentless march to oblivion that dominates and oppresses the realistic parts of the narrative. Gedde's message is uplifting, carrying Max beyond the narrowness of his earthbound perspective:

> Gedde is feeling sweet today. He likes you. He says *deux femmes,* two women protect you. He sees your spirit. You are a good spirit. Your luck is bad just now. You must take a good luck bath. You must think to yourself that things will get better. In the meantime, some delay. A woman in your family is going to have a baby. (179)

This visionary quality comes finally to dominate the novel: its closing pages are flooded with light. Here, Max finally manages to integrate the conflicting elements of his life and make himself whole through the exercise of his imaginative and visionary gifts: for by these means, quite simply, he turns himself into a god. This apotheosis is initially suggested by a story in the journal of John Braithewaite, who, as a young man, accompanied Darwin on the first voyage of the Beagle in 1831—a story that Max hears from his friend Arthur. This story is of a blond Englishman, who, as the first white man to enter the *Mato Grosso* region of the Amazon, is mistaken by the natives for a river god. *The Tribe,* the fiction that Max constructs from this story, is written, significantly, in the first person: for, as Ferro explains, "To Max the sensibility at the heart of the story is no less personal than a journal" (194). Moreover, as "a sexual deity," the Englishman travels "from tribe to tribe" (199) and is thus an integrating force: he has given himself over to the community as "a vessel of the gods."

But *The Tribe* is merely a stage in this process of Max's self-discovery: for in the final short section of the novel, which appears as a kind of postscript, Ferro dispenses with fiction as an intermediary device altogether. Here, Max does not imagine himself a god: he becomes one. Here, the first-person testimony is given even greater immediacy and intensity by its removal from the narrative framework that encloses his experiment in fiction. Max, the Englishman, and the river god fuse into a single being. The primitive, potentially destructive, Dionysian forces—sexual potency, creative energy—that have hitherto threatened to tear Max apart are here harnessed to the service of the community. Indeed, as an agent of the spiritual world and a guide to the deepest compulsions of life, he becomes central and essential to that community.

The close of the book strongly suggests that Ferro is using this deified image of himself as a powerful metaphor for his general conception of the position of the homosexual artist and writer in society—or, in other words, as a metaphor for what he sees as his own role in the community. Clearly, one way in which Ferro found fulfillment and achieved a level of integration and wholeness in his life was through writing. Thus the metaphor seems to work in this way: by reason of his skin coloring, blond hair, and blue eyes, the river god, like the homosexual artist, is different, set apart; and yet, by reason of his special gifts—his insight, intuition, communication with the spirit world—he is also central to the tribe and partakes of its joy and suffering. The river god, like the homosexual artist, is the vessel of all the gods—that is, a conduit for the whole panoply of human experience: "Depending on the moon, I am the flood, the harvest, the hunter's god—whichever is white in their imaginations" (217). Furthermore, as a sexual deity, his special gifts are linked to the power of creation and fertility. He is thus worshipped as one with access to the heart of all that is mysterious and taboo: "All that cannot be explained makes me holy—my arrival, my nature, my skin, my gold hair, my eyes, my placid acceptance of all attentions and offerings" (218).

*The Family of Max Desir,* then, like *Cranes* and *Home,* has strong assimilative tendencies. Unlike those novels, however, it manages ultimately to achieve a degree of integration—some reconciliation of its conflicting impulses—through the power of its final transcendent vision. It avoids, in David Bergman's words, "the received heterosexual conception of gay man's fate" by being directed "toward the visionary, the ancestral, the communal" (*Gaiety* 200). Whereas Leavitt and Cunningham leave their central characters isolated, neither fully integrated into the heterosexual family structure nor with any strong sense of gay identity, Ferro's vision of Max is that of "the gay man who has not rejected his family, but has transcended it by giving himself to the entire community, to the whole tribe" (199). In other words, it is the vision of a man who has assimilated to mainstream culture without surrendering his independent sexual and cultural identity.

## SUMMARY

The feature that binds the novels discussed in this chapter is their concern with gay men in relation to the wider social scene. Indeed, in *Cranes* and *Home,* this social inclusiveness blurs the precise focus of attention, making it difficult to say who the central protagonists are. Thus Leavitt is as much concerned with Rose as with Owen and Philip, while Cunningham gives roughly equal attention to Bobby, Jonathan, Alice, and Clare. The title of Ferro's novel is significant, too, since it suggests that Max is not the absolute center of Ferro's interest, nor even Max in the context of his family—but rather, precisely, *The Family of Max Desir.*

Yet concern with family and assimilation to social norms in these novels exists alongside a strong sense of difference. In *Cranes,* for instance, Philip struggles toward an independent identity against the backdrop of his parents' disintegrating marriage, while in *Home,* Bobby, Jonathan, and Clare, in flight from dysfunctional middle-American families, attempt an alternative social arrangement. Again, in *Max Desir,* the conflicting tendencies are revealed in two distinct strands of the novel: the realism of the family narrative and the fantasy of Max's "other" life. However, in this novel, Ferro achieves some degree of reconciliation between these warring impulses through the transcendent power of his final vision.

The assimilative impulse nonetheless predominates in the fiction that we have just explored, in spite of internal tensions. In another strain of fiction, however, the reverse is true; and this fiction is the subject of my next chapter.

# 5   The Gay Outlaw
## Sexual Radicalism and Transgression

My argument is that by not accepting and radically reworking the different identity of sameness—by rejecting the whole concept of identity—we risk participating in the homophobic project that wants to annihilate us. Only an emphasis on the specifics of sameness can help us avoid collaborating in the disciplinary tactics that would make us invisible. In other words, there *is* a "we." But in our anxiety to convince straight society that we are only some malevolent invention and that we can be, like you, good soldiers, good parents, and good citizens, we seem bent on suicide. By erasing our identity we do little more than reconfirm its inferior position within a homophobic system of differences.

—Leo Bersani, *Homos*

[T]he transgressive spiral tends to become simply cyclical and circular, going neither up nor down but simply biting your own tail, or to put it more elegantly, disappearing up your own orifice.

—Elizabeth Wilson, "Is Transgression Transgressive?"

The Queer movement has been, and continues to be, strenuously opposed. Its critics attack what they see as its assimilationist effects, its blurring of identity and image, and its consequent weakening, through dispersal, of homosexuality's potential to confront and disturb. They argue that queer's challenge to dominant ideology, through its denaturalization of heterosexuality and stress on the constructedness of all sexual categories, does little to undermine the power of that ideology—indeed, that such strategy demobilizes and weakens opposition to heterosexual hegemony by effectively erasing the subject or source of resistance. Moreover, they decry what they see as the ever-widening gulf between signifier and signified: Leo Bersani's claim, for instance, that "the epistemic and political regimes that have constructed us . . . don't need to be natural in order to rule; to demystify them doesn't render them inoperative" (*Homos* 4) seems to contain the suggestion that much of the talk that goes by the name of queer theory is mere sterile intellectual quibbling and academic pedantry.[1] It is thus a thought-provoking irony in the debate between supporters and detractors of the Queer movement that both sides accuse the other of blindly upholding and maintaining the dominant heterosexual order and system of oppression they wish to undermine.

The central paradox here is surely that a movement calling itself "queer" should be associated with assimilationist effects and a failure to confront and disturb. *Queer,* after all, is a word that still strikes terror in the hearts of many older gay men, for whom it retains a violently abusive power that puts it beyond reclamation. David Link, for instance, confesses: "I have wrestled with myself over whether, as a gay man, I am Queer. I have decided I am not. *Queer* is the word of the Other, of the Outsider." Similarly, Craig Johnston writes: "'Queer' is anti-homosexual. The 'queer' community does not exist. Queer is the enemy. When I hear 'Queer' I reach for the Kalashnikov" (quoted in Jagose 114–15). There is, of course, a generation-gap factor to take into account here: many young people today, it seems, are quite happy to call themselves queer, which suggests that the project to readopt and rehabilitate the term has been at least partially successful. But it seems likely that, for society at large, *queer,* as the word of "the Other, of the Outsider," is still resonant with a sense of fear and loathing, and retains much of its original force as a term of extreme abuse.

Whatever critics say about its effects, then, the Queer movement, I would argue, clearly intends to confront and disturb. Moreover, the feelings aroused by its name alone suggest that it has the potential to do so. However, one can see how that purpose and potential might be eroded, since the very act of attempting to reclaim the word *queer* tends, precisely through the process of re-evaluating and recentering, to reduce the word's oppositional force. Queerists counter this argument by claiming that the extent to which queer signifies "resistance to regimes of the normal" (Warner xxvi) guarantees it immunity to domestication. Eve Kosofsky Sedgwick, for instance, writes:

> The main reason why the self-application of "queer" by activists has proved so volatile is that there's no *way* that any affirmative reclamation is going to succeed in detaching the word from its associations with shame and with the terrifying powerlessness of gender-dissonant or otherwise stigmatized childhood. If queer is a politically potent term, which it is, that's because, far from being capable of being detached from the childhood source of shame, it cleaves to that scene as a near inexhaustible source of transformational energy. (Quoted in Jagose 105–06)

Here, Sedgwick puts her finger on what critics of the Queer movement see as its self-contradictory project: for if the word *queer* can never be detached from its shameful associations, in what sense can it be reclaimed? What Sedgwick seems to be suggesting is that the word can only be legitimated and affirmed within a marginalized group or subculture: in other words, among people who wish to be agents of transformation within a continuously evolving society and who thus choose to remain in permanent opposition to the standards of normativity demanded by its legitimate institutions of power. Implicit in her remarks is a critique of the lesbian and gay movement for its acquiescence within the larger system: for its attempt to seek legitimacy from within the wider culture.

In response to this, gayists, such as Leo Bersani, would no doubt observe that to readopt the word *queer* as a means of subverting the wider culture is a self-defeating strategy, since its effect is merely to reveal one's implication in, and subordination to, that culture. This brings us back to Foucault's so-called "theory of entrapment," which Raymond Williams, Alan Sinfield, and others explore in their writings and which I discuss in Chapter 1. The issue these theorists raise is this: how subversive is subversion? To overthrow the norms established by the dominant culture, they argue, is a very difficult undertaking, and any attempt to do so is bound to reveal the power of those norms. Hence, to call oneself "queer," Bersani implies, is merely to remind oneself of one's powerlessness and marginality: of one's dependence on terminology invented by others. "[R]esignification," he writes, "cannot destroy; it merely presents to the dominant culture spectacles of politically impotent disrespect" (*Homos* 51).

Bersani's central critique of the Queer movement recalls those remarks of Judith Roof, quoted in Chapter 2, about queer's tendency "to come full circle . . . in finally enfranchising even heterosexuality as queer." Lack of specificity, which those who align with queer see as its strength, is, for Bersani, precisely its weakness. In learning to deconstruct themselves—and queer is self-evidently a poststructuralist enterprise—gay men, in Bersani's view, have effectively erased themselves. Some readers might scoff at this, suggesting that a stroll down Old Compton Street on a warm June night would soon scotch any silly notions about "the new invisibility." But this would not be fair: Bersani's argument, after all, is about strategies for resistance. Becoming a gay consumer, his argument suggests, is not confrontational or ultimately liberating, since it keeps gay men politically quiescent through apparent absorption into the mainstream. It should be seen, rather, as part of the tendency to assimilationism that is the effect of the Queer movement, and hence to be resisted.

Queer's lack of specificity, Bersani implies, is grounded in a denial of sex. The writings of queer theoreticians, he observes, have a tendency to overlook what seems most obvious to a naive observer of the social scene: namely, that gay men like to have sex with other men. "You would never know," he writes, "from most of the works I discuss, that gay men, for all their diversity, share a strong sexual interest in other human beings anatomically identifiable as male" (*Homos* 5–6). In saying this he is not advocating a return to the kind of essentialist thinking that sees erotic preference as producing, or as being produced by, a certain characteriological type. On the contrary, as I indicate in Chapter 1, he welcomes the post-structuralist inquiry into "gay identity," and his summary of its critique of identity politics suggests that he fully recognizes the force of, and is generally persuaded by, the main lines of constructionist argument. Bersani's objection to queer is rather that its constituency is too broad and elusive to be politically effective. Furthermore, if queerness is characterized by a determined "resistance to regimes of the normal," to recall Michael Warner's phrase quoted above, rather than by a specific set of erotic tendencies (suggesting that "queer" should be taken as delineating a political rather than a sexual affiliation), then gay men disappear into what Steven Seidman calls a "millennial vision" of domination's demise ("Identity" 137). Bersani's understandable suspicion of this utopian lack of realism recalls Edmund White's insistence in his writings that it is their sexuality, and not their other affiliations, that drives gay men to political action, and that the already considerable achievements of the gay movement should not be dismissed in the current queer climate: "It is our sexuality that is contested, not the color of our hair. To build a political identity around this is therefore no mean feat" (quoted in Dellamora 113). Moreover, Bersani's fears about gay self-erasure and the de-sexualizing of politics sound like an echo of White's warnings, in "Esthetics and Loss," about AIDS, the new moralism, and the possible collapse of gay political organization and action for change: "[W]hen a society based on sex and expression is de-eroticised, its very reason for being can vanish" (*Burning Library* 214).

## SEXUAL ADVENTURISM

In the previous chapter I looked at the work of writers who, even when the subtexts of their writing suggest the opposite, seem impelled by the belief that gay life and family life are at least to some extent compatible. The writing I examine in this chapter, on the other hand, seems founded on the premise that gay men cannot avoid their outlaw status, are inevitably otherized by their sexuality, and should therefore embrace and celebrate their outlawry and otherness as positive identifications. But is it clear which of these two kinds of writing more closely reflects "queer" notions of sexuality? As we saw from the previous chapter, the central characters in *The Lost Language of Cranes* and *A Home at the End of the World* have no strong sense of "gay" as an ethnic identity, and the novels themselves seem to be informed by an antiessentialism that, like queer theory, lays stress not on identity but on difference: they recall Leavitt's remark that "each gay man and lesbian is gay or lesbian in his or her own way." These are novels, in other words, that Leo Bersani, to judge from his antiqueer polemicism, must deplore. Yet if these novels are "queer" in their rejection of essentialist notions, their suspicion of sexual categories, and their refusal to identify as "gay"—in short, in ways that Bersani sees as blurring the image of homosexuality and weakening its potential for disturbance—they go absolutely against the signification of "queer" as given above by Michael Warner, since they show a strong attraction to "regimes of the normal" and a tendency to focus not on the otherness, but on the very ordinariness of homosexuality. What this therefore seems to show is that "queer," as I indicate above, is an ambiguous, elusive, and paradoxical term that is open to a wide range of interpretation. It also lends support to Judith Roof's argument about queer's circularity.

The fiction I explore in this chapter, then, is "queer" in a sense of the word very different from its possible application to the fiction of Leavitt and Cunningham. Applied to the fiction discussed in this chapter, the use of the term suggests a deliberate exploitation of homosexuality's potential to confront and disturb. Moreover, the focus on sexual radicalism and transgression of this fiction links it to that current literary exploration of liminality, abjection, and otherness to be found at its most fiercely and dynamically perverse in the queer vampire fictions of contemporary Gothic. This link is well exemplified in the novel I want to discuss next: Alan Hollinghurst's *The Swimming-Pool Library*.

The long-established and widespread use of the vampire image as a metaphor for homosexuality has been explored by a number of writers.[2] Richard Dyer, for instance, notes that the "vampire returns again and again in popular gay writing" (47–48), and goes on to inquire into the reasons for this association, some of which, he suggests, are historically specific. Thus, since the early nineteenth century, the blood-sucking vampire has evoked a socially decadent aristocracy: "the weight of the past as it lays on the present" (54). This in turn suggests homosexuality since "much of the development of a public face for homosexuality and/or decadent sexuality was at the hands of aristocrats—de Sade, Byron—or writers posing as aristocrats—Lautréamont, Wilde" (53). Yet in the long term it is the wider metaphorical possibilities of the vampire, he argues, that best account for the strength of the association; and of these the most obvious is the sexual symbolism (54). The quintessential vampiric act—the bite on the neck—resembles a kiss. Moreover, it "takes place in private, at night, most archetypally in a bedroom" (55). But what make vampirism particularly amenable to homosexual interpretation, Dyer claims, are the additional characteristics of voyeurism and secrecy, the suspense in the vampire tale concerning the discovery of the vampire's secret nature being analogous to "the suspense of a life lived in the closet" (59). Drawing attention to the shared imagery of vampirism and homosexuality, he points out that the tell-tale signs of both—languor and paleness of complexion—derive from the idea of decadence, with its intimations of sickly bloodlessness and furtive nocturnality.

Mention of voyeurism brings us to a further link in this chain of associations. As Ken Gelder, Paulina Palmer, and others have noted, the queer vampire in contemporary Gothic fiction often bears a marked resemblance to the nineteenth-century figure of the flâneur as defined by Walter Benjamin in his famous study of Charles Baudelaire (1973). This is especially true of the vampires in the novels of Anne Rice. In Benjamin's account, the flâneur is a male individual "who strolls the streets contemplating the dream-like appearance of the urban spectacle" (Palmer 131); and this is very like Lestat de Lioncourt in Rice's *The Tale of the Body Thief* (1992), for instance, who has "a Parisian background . . . refined sensibilities . . . with leisure enough to watch the world go past and skill enough to read its various 'commonplace' signs" (Gelder 120). Like the flâneur, Lestat is a city stroller and performer: charming, cultivated, dandified, sexually voracious, and abnormally aware.

Moreover, these characteristics of the flâneurian vampire are exactly those of William Beckwith, the narrator-protagonist of Hollinghurst's novel. Beckwith is a young aristocrat who has no necessity to work for a living. Hence, like the vampire, he leads a loitering, leisure-class way of life that could be seen as parasitic. The very opening paragraph of the novel, for instance—which shows him journeying home on the last tube train of the night in the company of a couple of London Transport maintenance men—draws attention to his streetwise vigilance and lustfulness:

> The black was looking at his loosely cupped hands: he was very aloof, composed, with an air of massive, scarcely conscious competence—I felt more than respect, a kind of tenderness for him. I imagined his relief at getting home and taking his boots off and going to bed as the day brightened around the curtains and the noise of the streets built up outside. He turned his hands over and I saw the pale gold band of his wedding ring. (1)

Moreover, this attraction to black and working-class men suggests a further affinity with the vampire figure, one of whose most striking characteristics, after all, is an ability to break down barriers, cross boundaries, and disrupt notions of identity. Just as the vampire thrives on his gift for social adaptation and mobility, so Beckwith, in the passage quoted above, shows a desiring identification and imaginative empathy with the black transport worker, who, in different and more opportune circumstances, might have become his prey.

This passage also suggests a taste for the dark underside of life: for what is taboo, forbidden, and repressed. First, the fact that one of the men is black evokes all the Caucasian cultural connotations of blackness: evil, danger, crime, uncleanliness, and rampant sexuality. But second, there is the significance that both men work underground (on the London Underground) and at night. Indeed, as if alluding metaphorically to the relationship between the conscious and the unconscious mind, between what is openly acknowledged and what is repressed, the writing draws special attention to the way the work of these men functions as an invisible, if indispensable, counterpart to the visible, overground world of the London commuter: "I looked at them with a kind of swimming, drunken wonder, amazed at the thought of their inverted lives, of how their occupation depended on our travel, but could only be pursued, I saw it now, when we were not travelling" (1). This opening paragraph, then, announces what ultimately emerges as the central theme of the novel: namely, the continuity between, the closeness and interdependence of, the above-ground, daylit, metropolitan world of respectability and power and the dark, surreptitious, subterranean world of queer, vampiric, and parasitic outlawry.

Later episodes of the novel, however, suggest further parallels with the flâneurian vampire. For example, as Paulina Palmer points out, Benjamin's study of Baudelaire also establishes the relationship between the flâneur and the detective, a relationship elaborated by later writers.[3] The flâneur's streetwise watchfulness, Benjamin argues, makes him especially suited to the identification of criminals and the solving of crimes. Moreover, *The Swimming-Pool Library* is fundamentally a detective story, in which Will plays both sleuth and quarry. His investigation into the life of Lord Nantwich brings to light a self-incriminating family secret: namely, the unsettling discovery that Lord Nantwich was sentenced to a term of imprisonment for gross indecency as a result of the political ambition and homophobic malice of Will's own grandfather, who was the Director of Public Prosecutions at the time of the arrest. This finding himself implicated in the scandalous injustice of Nantwich's downfall, this revelation of his own culpability, understandably discomposes Will's confident sense of being in control. Commenting on the situation of the lesbian flâneur-sleuth in the contemporary lesbian Gothic thriller, Palmer remarks that, in appropriating "the male prerogative of the gaze . . . she simultaneously makes herself vulnerable to the gaze of others" (131). Will's situation is similarly double-edged, and the insecurity of his position is dramatically encapsulated in the episode of his encounter with the skinheads, an episode in which he finds himself suddenly "in danger of becoming an abject presence on the city streets, vulnerable to ridicule and assault" (131).

Clearly, then, there is a strong, if subtle and complex, link between this novel and those late nineteenth-century fictions of Stevenson, Wilde, and Stoker—*The Strange Case of Dr Jekyll and Mr Hyde* (1886), *The Picture of Dorian Gray* (1890), and *Dracula* (1897)—each of which has been examined separately in a contemporary critical study that highlights its homoerotic content.[4] In the light of this attention, these novels suggest a fictional group: a group characterized by the now much-elaborated concept of homosexual panic. "So-called 'homosexual panic,'" Eve Kosofsky Sedgwick writes, "is the most private, psychologized form in which many twentieth-century western men experience their vulnerability to the social pressure of homophobic blackmail" (*Between Men* 89); and partly as a result of the Foucauldian scholarship to which she has contributed, the late nineteenth-century focus on sexual taxonomy is now seen as the origin of a crisis in the male psyche, arising from a sense of beleaguered masculinity.[5] This focus, as we saw, resulted in the invention and initial use of the term "homosexuality" by the German-Hungarian social reformer Karl Maria Kertbeny in 1869, and led eventually to the ban on acts of "gross indecency" between men instituted by the Labouchère Amendment of 1885. Hence, in each of these novels, what is perceived as a threat—not only to masculinity but to the entire heteropatriarchal order—assumes a monstrous shape. I shall take up this theme again later, but to return to my current concern, what Hollinghurst's novel suggests (through a veiled allusion to these other novels within a panoramic survey of homosexual life in Britain since the 1880s) is that this perception of homosexuality has been consistently present throughout the past one hundred years and more of homosexual history, and is still with us.

The difference between *The Swimming-Pool Library* and these earlier fictions, however, is that in the latter, homosexuality, in whatever monstrous shape it appears, figures as the feared Other that must be exorcised. In Hollinghurst's novel, on the other hand, the relationship between homosexuality and heteropatriarchy is shown as much more complex: for here, the presentation of homosexuality as a submerged, otherized, and threatening presence within the established social order is mixed with a celebratory element. This is why the novel also relates to those contemporary Gothic novels that subvert the conventions of traditional horror fiction through a straightforward celebration of the monstrous and the abject. The celebratory element in *The Swimming-Pool Library*, however, is complicated and undercut by what, as I indicate above, is clearly its central focus: namely, homosexuality's complicity in—its collusion with—the heteropatriarchal system within which it figures as monstrous and abject. Indeed, with this complex allusiveness in mind, Joseph Bristow writes of the novel's "compelling ambivalence" (*Effeminate England* 178). The novel as a whole could therefore be seen as a dramatization of those conflicts of ideology, concerning notions of identity, difference, and strategies for resistance, outlined at the beginning of this chapter.

These tensions are signaled early in the text. Thus Will writes: "My life was in a strange way that summer, the last summer of its kind that was to be. I was riding high on sex and self-esteem—it was my time, my *belle époque*—but all the while with a faint flicker of calamity, like flames around a photograph, something seen out of the corner of the eye" (3). As most commentators find, the oblique reference to AIDS in this passage is impossible to miss. Indeed, Joseph Bristow sees the epidemic as the probable genesis of the novel, precisely because it is never explicitly named in the text. This absence, he argues, is testimony to the traumatic impact of AIDS and a reflection of the fact that the name of the epidemic is—for many gay men—literally unutterable. Thus Bristow sees the novel as "both a tribute to a distinguished tradition of homophile writing and a troubling work of mourning for a brief period of liberated sexual practices that—in the light of the epidemic—came to an end" (*Effeminate England* 172). From this point of view, the novel, although written from a quite different temporal perspective, displays the same tensions and forebodings as some gay male fiction of the 1970s, and recalls my discussion of *Dancer from the Dance* and *Faggots* in Chapter 3.

Ross Chambers, on the other hand, cautions against too narrow an interpretation of this passage. He feels that the reference to the "last summer of its kind" is quite appropriately read as an allusion to AIDS, but points out that the passage as a whole lays stress on continuity rather than rupture. In his view, the metaphor of the *belle époque* reinforces the link, constantly underlined throughout the novel, between contemporary and traditional patterns of gay men's lives, represented on the one hand by Will Beckwith and on the other by Lord Nantwich, whose biography Will has been requested to write and whose span of memory reaches back nostalgically to the 1880s. The "faint flicker of calamity," according to Chambers, does not refer simply to AIDS but has a wider suggestiveness that relates to the central theme of the novel. Rather, the flicker is in Will's conscience: the faint but ever-present realization, like "something seen out of the corner of the eye," of his own lack of heroism, of his failure to perform "the radical acts that would profoundly change the world" (208), of his "complicity with controlling power" (217).[6]

## HOMOSEXUALITY AND TREACHERY

Within this persuasive reading, the novel suggests, as I intimate above, an engagement with the issues both inherent in and surrounding the ideology and politics of transgression. This inevitably raises the specter of Jean Genet, the controversial figure at the center of these tensions, whose most powerful challenge to customary attitudes must surely be his professed admiration for treachery. In an attempt to grasp the nettle of Genet's trangressiveness, Leo Bersani asks us to consider the idea that Genet, in embracing betrayal as a moral achievement, uses the terms of the dominant culture "not to rework or subvert those terms, but to exploit their potential for erasing cultural relationality itself (that is, the very preconditions for subversive repositionings and defiant repetitions)" (*Homos* 153). In other words, Bersani is presenting Genet's celebration of betrayal as an attempt to escape the transgressive spiral to which Elizabeth Wilson alludes in the quotation at the head of this chapter. Hence, Alan Sinfield, in his own attempt to meet the challenge of Genet and in debate with Bersani, begins by acknowledging the problem: "It is a commonplace of post-structuralist criticism that transgression is always in danger of being limited by that which it transgresses" (*Gay and After* 141). But what, he wonders doubtfully—and clearly not relishing the idea—would lie beyond "cultural relationality"?

Bersani presents his argument about Genet in a discussion of the latter's *Funeral Rites*, which is set in Paris during the German Occupation and was inspired by the death of one of Genet's lovers, Jean Decarnin, a young communist resistance fighter who was shot in 1944, just before the Liberation of Paris, by the collaborationist militia. In this novel, Genet chooses to mourn Jean by showing desire, love, and admiration for the young collaborator he imagines to have been Jean's killer: in short, by embracing, in a Christ-like gesture, his worst enemy. He writes: "My hatred of the militiaman was so intense, so beautiful, that it was equivalent to the strongest love. No doubt it was he who had killed Jean. I desired him" (48). Is this betrayal, or, in Bersani's words, "an original act of mourning" (*Homos* 157)? For Bersani, however, the answer to this question is less interesting than the related idea, raised here and elsewhere in *Funeral Rites,* that "homosexuality is congenial to betrayal and, further, that betrayal gives homosexuality its moral value" (153).

Bersani argues that Genet's celebration of the alleged treachery inherent in homosexuality lifts him into an imaginary space beyond the transgressive spiral. Genet, he maintains, is not interested in resignifying the terms of the dominant culture, but in getting beyond the social and moral constraints of relationality altogether. But why does Genet allege that homosexuality and treachery are closely related? In answer to this, Bersani suggests that Genet's view of homosexual love lays stress on its sterility and on its "renunciation of intimacy" (170); and he pursues his argument with reference to passages in *Funeral Rites* that describe certain sexual practices particularly associated with gay men: namely, rimming and *coitus a tergo,* or fucking from behind. While admitting that these are also heterosexual practices, Bersani claims that Genet presents them not only as *essentially* homosexual but also as acts of betrayal, and in this way underlines his view of the link between homosexuality and treachery. In *Funeral Games,* Bersani argues, rimming is presented as an act of betrayal through its alleged reduction of the lover to waste matter. Similarly, *coitus a tergo* figures as betrayal through its alleged denial of intimacy: its antirelational turning away, in lovemaking, from the eyes of the other.

But an even more puzzling and disturbing question is why Genet sees these alleged acts of betrayal as cause for celebration. Bersani's explanation is that, when Genet embraces what he calls "evil," he is not using the term as commonly understood, that is, as distinct from "the good." Rather, he is using the term to signify a solitary self-sufficiency beyond conventional social categories: to express what he sees as the value of emptiness and solitude. From Genet's use of the term "evil," Bersani suggests, a new possibility emerges: "evil . . . not as a crime against socially defined good, but as a turning away from the entire theatre of the good, that is, a kind of meta-transgressive *dépassement* of the field of transgressive possibility itself" (163). This suggests a celebration of "evil" based on the notion that loyalty to the self comes before loyalty to the tribe. However, Bersani credits Genet with more than a simple desire to bypass the social. Genet destroys, he suggests, in order to reconstruct. In other words, Genet collapses social difference in order to imagine a reconstituted sociality—although, as Bersani admits, it is not entirely clear what form this reconstituted sociality would take: "Erik and Riton are positioned for a reinventing of the social without any indication about how such a reinvention might proceed historically or what face it might have" (171).

Sinfield, in a generously skeptical examination of Bersani's argument, takes issue with many of these claims, although he is mainly concerned to resist Bersani's idea that *Funeral Rites* uncovers some essentially treacherous property of homosexuality. Sinfield sees Genet's fascination with treachery as the inevitable outcome of his experiences in the reformatory at Mettray and in prison, where male–male relations were characterized by hatred, self-hatred, and a brutal denial of queerness. He argues, moreover, that this impression of human relations as inherently treacherous must have been confirmed and indeed strengthened by Genet's experience of Nazi-occupied France. "For in this context," he asks, reminding us that *Funeral Rites* is set against this background, "who were the traitors?" (*Gay and After* 136). As he points out, day-to-day survival in France at this time often depended on some form of collaboration with the occupying forces, while many of those fighting in the Resistance were communists, and therefore viewed as "destructive of established social relations" (136). In this context, Sinfield argues, Genet, an already branded thief and homosexual outlaw, was given ample opportunity to develop his "defiant attitude to France and conventional morality" (136).

But in a further development of his argument, Sinfield denies that Genet's general stance in this novel *is* antirelational. On the contrary, the center of the novel is Genet's love for Jean, he argues, while the other relationships in the novel are deflections from that love. Moreover, he sees Genet's attempt to remain "outside a social and moral world" by choosing to be "a traitor, thief, looter, informer, hater, destroyer, despiser, coward" (*Funeral Rights* 157) as deluded, since all of the chosen identities on that list *in themselves* imply a social and moral involvement. For Sinfield, "there is no human life beyond the social" (141) and thus no escape from social and moral involvement, not even for those who, like Genet, live within a criminal subculture. The problems of social engagement, Sinfield insists, must be confronted from within the social. Genet's alternative—solitary, transcendent self-sufficiency—is, he implies, mere romantic gesture.

The Bersani–Sinfield debate is fascinating, but what interests me here is how Genet's transgressive ideas, and the controversy surrounding them, are fictionalized and re-examined in *The Swimming-Pool Library*. In the first place, as the Ross Chambers reading emphasizes, betrayal is clearly the central theme of Hollinghurst's novel. Like *Funeral Rites*, it evokes a world of social and moral confusion: a world where ruling elite and criminal underworld are so entwined that the distinction between them is blurred. In this context, then—as in that of *Funeral Rites*—to whom is loyalty due? Or, as Sinfield might put it, who are the traitors? Will and Lord Nantwich, though born into the ruling class, are also, on account of their sexuality, members of a criminalized subculture. Are these two worlds reconcilable? Can one fight injustice from a position of privilege and power? Or, to put it yet another way, in Bersani's words: "Should a homosexual be a good citizen?" (*Homos* 113). This is the issue these characters face, and the dilemma Hollinghurst explores in his novel.

*The Swimming-Pool Library* thus addresses the same questions as those raised in the controversy surrounding Genet. Its central concern, after all, is Will's discovery that he is not free of social and moral responsibility, as he has supposed, but deeply implicated in gay history. Will, the novel implies, is not only sexually promiscuous but a man who pursues casual sex as a way of life—a way of life invoked in the scenes depicted on the frieze adorning the remains of the Roman bath in Lord Nantwich's cellar. These scenes are a reminder not only of the long history of homosexuality but of the link between the Roman world and the contemporary gay scene. Our attention is drawn to the continuity between the idealized, male-centered, pagan way of life shown in these scenes (a way of life soon to be displaced by a family-focused Christian ideal) and the ambience Will encounters daily at the Corinthian Club swimming baths. As Nantwich himself remarks: "This little bit of the baths is all that's left to show how all those lusty young Romans went leaping about. Imagine all those naked legionaries in here . . ." (80; ellipsis in original).

But there the analogy must stop. The Roman baths, after all, were part of "the pagan accommodation between sex-for-pleasure and sex-for-reproduction" (Sinfield, *Gay and After* 1). Will's pursuit of casual sex, on the other hand, is presented in the novel as resistance to full human involvement. His attraction to working-class and black youths, for instance, is shown as bound up with class-conscious and racist attitudes: attitudes that present a barrier to full human contact, since they maintain a power structure within a relationship that casts the other as outsider. Will's taboo breaking is thus fueled by an attitude to sexual partners that is socially regressive, and indeed imperialist. This is made clear at several points in the novel. In the opening chapter, for instance, Will comes home, after an evening spent in the company of his friend James, to find his current lover, a black youth called Arthur, slumped on the ground outside the door of his apartment. Arthur has been badly injured in a knife fight with his brother. Will tends him and bathes him, but seems less interested in his plight than in taking sexual advantage of the situation: "There was something repulsive and careless about him . . . But at the same time he was utterly defenceless: everything about him spoke of need" (21–22). Arthur's vulnerability, signaled here by the blood seeping from his wound into the bath water, is, the episode suggests, sexually arousing for Will, who also notices that Arthur has an erection, possibly because Will's hand is already on his cock. Will then wanks Arthur slowly, "the ripples slapping rhythmically against the side of the tub" (23). The elements of this scene—Will's predatory interest, the mixing of blood and semen—thus bring to mind my earlier comments about the suggestions of vampirism in the novel.

Will's imperialist and exploitative attitudes, however, are even more graphically exposed in later episodes of the novel. When, for example, after a period of separation, he catches up with Arthur again at a disco club, he pushes him roughly into a toilet cubicle and, without conversational preliminaries of any kind, uses him sexually in a manner close to rape: "I prised open the top stud of his trousers . . . yanked down the zip, pulled them round his knees" (203). Likewise, his relationship with Phil, the young working-class barman from the Queensberry Hotel, is based on the assumption that an object of desire exists to service sexual requirements. He therefore takes the dominant role in all their relations with the primary purpose of satisfying his own needs: "Nothing was going to get done unless I took command . . . I gripped his jaw, turned his head towards me and kissed him" (105). Indeed, at a later stage in this relationship, the younger man is treated as a sexual plaything. This occurs in Will's apartment, where, after a pint at the Volunteer, Phil is "busting for a piss." Holding on to him, Will removes Phil's shirt, slips his hands between his legs and, squeezing his balls, whispers to him "to let it go." The climax of this episode not only draws attention to Phil's passivity and submission but seems to resonate beyond the immediate event to the wider social scene and power structure within which Will operates: "An abundant, infantile puddle spread on the lino, and when he had finished I went behind him, pulled down his trousers, pushed him to the floor and fucked him in it like a madman" (163).

How closely, then, does Will's transgression resemble that of the characters in *Funeral Rites*? Given, for example, that betrayal is clearly the central theme of Hollinghurst's novel, is it significant that the incidents of near-rape described in the previous paragraph involve the very sexual practices—rimming and *coitus a tergo*—that Genet associates with the treachery allegedly inherent in homosexuality? Actually, alongside such resemblances, there are equally clear differences. Certainly Will shows no social or moral responsibility toward those with whom he is sexually involved. But unlike Genet's various personae he is not an intellectual, nor does he attempt to explain his behavior in rational terms, as if it stemmed from a conscious ideology. If Genet's political radicalism, as Bersani claims, "is congruent with a proclaimed indifference to human life as well as a willingness to betray every tie and every trust between human beings" (*Homos* 172), Will's treatment of his sexual partners, in contrast, is the result not of proclaimed indifference, but of simple carelessness. Indeed, his transgression is not political at all; it is merely expedient and opportunist.

There is thus an essential difference, in respect of transgressiveness, between Genet's attitude of conscious commitment and Will's ambivalence. Where Genet transgresses out of conviction, Will does so by instinct and with a faintly troubled conscience. *The Swimming-Pool Library*, as I have already suggested, is in part a celebration of Will's way of life and in part a critique of it. Ross Chambers calls it "a novel of compromise" (208).[7] Indeed, it could be said to reflect, in its equivocation, both sides of the Bersani–Sinfield debate. On the one hand, Will, like Genet, is drawn to a life of amoral, transcendent self-sufficiency, beyond the social as it has been understood. He aspires (at an intuitive level, rather than with Genet's rationale) to "replace the rich discursiveness of good-and-evil with what might be called the empty value of solitude" (Bersani, *Homos* 168). His instincts, in short, are antirelational. In the course of the novel, however, he learns that the life of absolute freedom that he aspires to is an illusion. Relationality, he discovers, is part of the human condition and therefore inescapable. If the Nazism of *Funeral Rites,* as Bersani claims, "is the apocalyptic appearance in history of an impulse to erase history" (169), what Will finds, as he explores the Nantwich diaries in response to the request to "write about me" (81), is that this impulse is mistaken, since history cannot be erased.

*The Swimming-Pool Library,* then, presents the main patterns of gay men's lives in the twentieth century through a complex and subtle blend of celebration and critique that avoids crude didacticism. Thus, on the one hand, in its celebratory mode, it relishes the transgressive pleasures of gay eroticism, and therefore, in this aspect at least, reflects Bersani's antiassimilationist stance. Yet, on the other, as we have seen, it suggests a critique of the social—or more accurately, asocial—relations and power positions implicit in that eroticism; and here it reflects the Sinfield side of the debate. For instance, as the title of the novel intimates, the pattern of Will's relations is established at Winchester College, the all-male institution in which he is raised, and in this respect he resembles Genet, who, as Sinfield stresses, was formatively influenced by the kind of male–male relations he saw at Mettray and in prison. At Mettray, as we know from Genet's writings, sexual relations between boys were coercive and followed a pattern in which, to use Sinfield's phrase, "big boys had little boys" (*Gay and After* 139). It is this pattern of relations, *The Swimming-Pool Library* implies, that is the basis of Will's experience at Winchester and the background to his attitude, character, and behavior.

There is consequently a link between Hollinghurst's presentation of Will's power-inflected relations and Sinfield's account of Genet's attraction to fascist hoodlums. For the defining moment of *The Swimming-Pool Library,* it could be argued, is that previously mentioned episode in which Will is beaten up by a gang of skinheads at whom he has been gazing with lust and admiration: "Cretinously simplified to booted feet, bum and bullet head, they had some, if not all, of the things one was looking for" (172). Indeed, this episode brings to mind my earlier discussion of what Bersani calls "Genet's original and disturbing notion that homosexuality is congenial to betrayal" (*Homos* 153): for Will's betrayal here, it could be said, is a constituent part of his sexuality in that he is attracted to those forms of masculinity that would like to annihilate him. His homosexuality is therefore an inherent form of self-treachery in that it is bound up indissolubly not only with the betrayal of friends and lovers but of a way of life and a cause. This betrayal is precisely caught in the episode's culminating image, which pictures a boot slamming down on "my beautiful new copy of *The Flower Beneath the Foot*" and "grinding the pages into the warm-smelling spilt rubbish" (174). Here, homophobic violence meets and destroys its polar opposite; and the conjunction suggests that Will is driven by a self-destructive impulse that is integral to his desire. Hence, in his antirelationality, Will reminds us of Genet, whose desire for Riton in *Funeral Rites* is, as we saw, also a form of self-betrayal.

Again, just as Sinfield takes Genet and Bersani to task for their tendency to turn moral failings into virtues, so Hollinghurst passes implicit critical judgment on Will for his failure to recognize that we cannot escape social involvement: that to be fully human we must engage with others and with history. Thus, Genet's fascination with Nazism, Bersani maintains, has nothing to do with "territorial politics" or "any specific genocidal ideology"; it is rather that Genet sees in Nazism a transcendental myth: "a myth of absolute betrayal—the betrayal of all human ties, the attempted murder of humanity itself" (*Homos* 167). But, argues Sinfield, the ideology of Nazism cannot be dissociated from the atrocities it legitimized. What Genet admires in Nazism, he claims, is not its mythic potential but its essence. In his view, the "myth of absolute betrayal," which Bersani sees as the source of Genet's fascination with Nazism, is "not something other than fascism, but an evocative summary of it . . . [not] something for which fascism might be a metaphor, but a distillation of fascism" (*Gay and After* 141). And all this finds an echo in *The Swimming Pool Library*, which is concerned to expose a similar self-deception in Will's thinking and attitude to life: a similar belief in freedom from responsibility, from moral and social involvement, and indeed from "all human ties."

In his provocative essay "Is the Rectum a Grave?" Bersani defends gay male promiscuity precisely on the grounds that it rejects the heterosexual model of sexual relations and thus "[resists] being drawn into mimicking the unrelenting warfare between men and women" (218). Bersani's argument here is centered on the notion that sexual relations cannot be dissociated from power relations. Thus he writes: "Human bodies are constructed in such a way that it is, or at least has been, almost impossible not to associate mastery and subordination with the experience of our most intense pleasures" (216). The thrill of gay male sex, he argues, is grounded in the sense it gives of violated male power; and he sees this sense as likewise the source of homophobia. "*To be penetrated,*" he writes, "*is to abdicate power*" (212). But this abdication of power, together with the shattering of selfhood that results from it, is, in his view, a salutary pleasure that should be valued. Sinfield's argument suggests, however, that the power relations inherent in sexual relations sometimes lead, as in the case of Genet, to an unsalutary worship of power that is treacherous, antisocial, and to be resisted.

In its ambivalence, *The Swimming-Pool Library* mediates between these viewpoints. Will's sexual adventurism, after all, does lead, via numerous revelatory self-shatterings, to greater self-knowledge. Moments of insight are gained when he is forced to recognize that his own male power—the homosocial power with which he has been complicit and that he has taken for granted—can be violated. Thus his sexually charged encounter with the skinheads, in the episode discussed above, suggests, in reflection of the way he himself experiences it, an act of rape. Abdication of power occurs, too, in his lustful submission to Abdul, the handsome head waiter of Wick's, a man he regards as his social and racial inferior: "I waited greedily, and yelped as his hand came down . . . tenderising my ass with wild, hard slaps" (262). Again, there is a similar moment of realization when he discovers that Colin, a policeman he greatly desires and knows to be "as queer as—whatever is very, very queer: me, you" (222), has entrapped and arrested his friend James for soliciting in a public toilet. But the culminating revelation, of course, is the discovery that his own grandfather, Lord Beckwith, was responsible, as Director of Public Prosecutions, for Lord Nantwich's imprisonment for the same offense. At these critical moments he is forced to recognize not only the homosexuality inherent in homosocial power but also his own impulse to self-violation.

But what the novel makes clear in its final illumination is that the homosocial power from which both Will and Lord Nantwich derive their wealth and privilege is something that neither man is willing to relinquish. Nantwich, rather than buck the system, devotedly serves the state all his life; and although Will, a younger man with a more modern outlook, has twinges of conscience and sporadic attacks of moral indignation, his allegiance to the homosocial network that allows him his comfortable way of life is never put seriously to the test. Thus the transgression explored in the novel is sexual, not social. This is underlined in the final pages, where Will's feeble attempt to expose Colin's hypocrisy and treachery fizzles out in its encounter with the noncooperation, inscrutability, and "diplomatic ignorance" of Nantwich, Staines, and circle (288). The novel leaves us, then, with a sense of changelessness and circularity. In the final paragraph, his moment of conscience having passed, Will drifts back to the Corry, where life, the writing insists, is going on just as before: "And going into the showers I saw a suntanned lad in pale blue trunks that I rather liked the look of" (288).

## THE RETURN OF THE MONSTROUS

> Well, all right then—if I can't fit, I'll be an ozone boy, more rarefied, more peculiar. I'll breathe the atmosphere of my own elevation; I will be doggedly devoted to my own peculiarity. I'll show you how to be alone!
>
> —Mark Doty, *Firefly*

As I have said, a central feature of the writing I have chosen to examine in this chapter is its deliberate exploitation of homosexuality's potential to confront and disturb. In my view, the most disturbingly confrontational of contemporary gay writers is Dennis Cooper. However, I want to approach his novel *Frisk* by way of a related form: namely, the kind of contemporary Gothic fiction I alluded to earlier in my discussion of *The Swimming-Pool Library*.

The defining mark of Gothic writing, it could be argued, is its rejection of classic realism: its attempt to get beyond classic realist conventions and limitations. These conventions and limitations have been critically examined by Roland Barthes, for whom the classic realist text is essentially an expression of bourgeois values and ideology. Barthes, in distinguishing between readerly and writerly texts, draws attention to way the authorial voice tends to dominate in classic realist narrative, thus discouraging a plural reading.[8] This authoritarianism, he suggests, also blocks oppositional thinking by blurring the distinction between signifier and signified. Language therefore becomes not a medium of discourse, but the means whereby the reader confronts "truth" and "reality." In this way, classic realism blocks out those aspects of human experience that do not accord with its worldview. Or, to use the psychoanalytic term—since what it blocks out usually emanates from the unconscious—it "represses" them.

Gothic writing, on the other hand, is characterized by a refusal to repress. In its determination to risk new areas of experience, to explore the dark and buried regions of human nature, and to push to the far reaches of the mind, it crosses imaginative, discursive, and moral boundaries. But its fascination with the bizarre, the macabre, and the horrific, and its focus on other and aberrant states of being, comes in two modes. The distinction between these modes is made clear in the following passage by Clive Barker, a best-selling gay author of mainstream popular fiction, whose novel *Cabal* I now want to discuss:

> My books are completely opposed to those of James Herbert and Stephen King. Their books are death-driven, mine are life-driven. I write about the strangeness you see from the corner of your eye—actual adventures waiting to happen. James Herbert and Stephen King want your blood. Their books have a bourgeois mentality manifested by the view that if it's strange, *shoot it*. They're terrified of diversity and think that if it's different, it belongs on the dark side; if anything's different, it's after them. Their books are all about reinforcing the status quo. Deeply conservative. (Quoted in Woods, *History of Gay Literature* 245 emphasis in original)

The proposition here is that one mode of Gothic writing (Barker's own) is radically challenging and transgressive, while another (that of James Herbert and Stephen King) is more closely related to the repressive authoritarianism Barthes finds in classic realism—and indeed, perhaps the reverse side of it. Barker's reference to "a bourgeois mentality," for instance, suggests that this latter mode of Gothic derives not from sympathetic interest but from a sense of horrified fascination, and is concerned not to extend its vision but to shore up its defenses.[9] Paulina Palmer also draws attention to this polarity: with regard to the way the contradiction is reflected in contemporary lesbian fiction, she writes that some Gothic narratives "challenge realist perspectives" while others "reproduce the values of the dominant culture" (3).

This distinction seems to me a valid one, and not just for contemporary Gothic writing but for Gothic writing in general. However, I want to add that the death-driven and life-driven modes are often to be found within the same work, thus producing an internal tension that suggests a split in the writer's psyche. This is perhaps most evident in Stevenson's *The Strange Case of Dr Jekyll and Mr Hyde,* where the thrilling, lustful energy that drives the narrative eventually gives way to the writer's death-driven need to kill his sexual and creative impulses. At least, this is what is suggested in Christopher Craft's remarks on the novel, which point up the tension in it between decorum and desire. Craft sees the text as motivated by a "fundamental ambivalence," in which "a pleasurable . . . thrilling anxiety" finally gives way to a "requirement that the monster be repudiated and the world of normal relations restored" (216–17). William Veeder, on the other hand, taking a psychoanalytic approach, reads the story as an indictment of Scottish patriarchy, rooted in Stevenson's own oedipal conflicts. For Veeder, the central tension of the text is not the struggle between decorum and desire, but rather the hidden warfare between professional men, beneath whose civilized veneer rages "the regressive emotions of oedipal sons and sibling rivals" (109).

Despite this difference in emphasis, however, both Craft and Veeder locate an anxiety in the text around repressed sexual desire—desire that, as Veeder convincingly argues, is predominantly homoerotic. Why, Veeder asks, are there are so few women in the story? And why are the central characters all professional men as well as celibates? These questions are clearly related, and Veeder's reply to them suggests a link between the misogyny in the tale and the submerged homoerotics of the male relations. "Men antagonistic to women are attracted to men," he writes (143), thus making it clear that he is referring to the specific homoeroticism of patriarchal male bonding, for which he finds ample evidence in the text. Hyde, for instance, is called Jekyll's "favourite" (Stevenson 27). Is this why his being Jekyll's beneficiary looks to Utterson like the result of a particularly coercive form of blackmail? And what is the relationship between Utterson and Jekyll? Does Utterson's obsession with Hyde's power, together with his proprietorial interest in Jekyll's will, spring from feelings of jealousy?

But the way that Veeder's essay relates to the distinction identified above (between conservative–radical, or death-driven–life-driven, forms of Gothic writing) emerges in his consideration of the reasons for the misogynistic, patriarchal celibacy at the center of the story. The patriarchs fear mature relationships "with peer-aged women," he argues, because such relationships betoken parenthood—"patrilineal succession"—which in time leads to "a handing on of [their] status to a younger successor and a going on to death" (147–48). Thus, what Hyde and his transgressive energies finally represent, Veeder suggests, is defiance of human limitation and escape from mortality. In this respect he resembles the mythic figure of the vampire, a figure that (like the queer desire with which it is associated) strikes at the very core of heterosexist society, and in Sue-Ellen Case's words, "punctures the life/death and generative/destructive bipolarities that enclose the heterosexist notion of being" (4).

As Veeder's study demonstrates, the patriarchs' sense of violent recoil from Hyde exists alongside a feeling of kinship with him. Thus, shortly after witnessing the incident in which "the man trampled calmly over the child's body and left her screaming on the ground," they take breakfast with him (Stevenson 9, 11). In Jekyll's case, this feeling of kinship—which figures in the text as a father–son relationship: "Jekyll had more than a father's interest; Hyde more than a son's indifference" (68)—proves fatally unnerving, for the knowledge that Hyde is part of himself becomes finally insupportable and leads to self-murder. Ultimately, he, like the text, can only "contain" the knowledge by obliterating it. As David Punter writes: "There is an underlying pessimism in the book which results from Stevenson's difficulty in seeing any alternative structure for the psyche: once the beast is loose, it can resolve itself only in death" (*Literature of Terror* 5). Here, then, is a psychic drama of internal conflict in which a need to set demons free is at war with a need to annihilate them, a conflict mythically embodied elsewhere in literature and folklore—in Mary Shelley's *Frankenstein,* for instance, and in the tale of the sorcerer's apprentice. Moreover, a similar tension can be felt in Wilde's *The Picture of Dorian Gray* and in Bram Stoker's *Dracula,* where the figure of the vampire, Gina Wisker writes, "embodies the feared Other which, in the narrative trajectory of horror, must be exorcised" ("Queer Vampires" 77). In all these narratives, as in those of James Herbert and Stephen King, transgressive energy is finally defeated—and expelled or destroyed—in its war with conventional order.

But this distinction between radical and conservative modes of Gothic writing is also valid, it seems, when we come to consider the relationship of Gothic writing in general to the Bakhtinian concept of carnivalization. All Gothic writing, it could be argued, is imbued with the spirit of carnival, at least to the extent that it imagines a world in which conventional order is radically discomposed or even threatened with destruction. This accounts for the centrality of the vampire figure to this tradition of writing, for, as many writers have remarked, the vampire, in the Gothic imagination, is the creature most powerfully equipped with transgressive potential. Infinitely mobile and able to shape-shift, transmogrify, and dematerialize, it can cross all boundaries, defy all human limitations, and break all physical as well as moral laws. It is also, in common with many writers, a lover of freedom and pleasure rather than of authority and decorum, which perhaps explains its appeal to disaffected and rebellious youth, and especially to the so-called blank generation of young people for whom certain writers in the Gothic mold—Poppy Z. Brite, for instance—have become spokespersons.

The conservative mode of Gothic writing, however, unlike its radical counterpart, views the spirit of carnival as an indulgence, a passing phase, an interruption to normal life. Its movement is always toward a restoration of conventional order. It flirts with carnival, enjoys the titillation of subversive ways of thought, but from within the security of established authority. It is never tempted to cross the line, but simply watches voyeuristically from the other side. In this way it contrasts with writing like Clive Barker's, to which the spirit of carnival is central. This latter mode of writing is written from within the carnival, not from without; and from this vantage point it is the bourgeois mentality of conventional order that looks strange. Moreover, this opposition runs historically through all carnivalized literature, as a tension both between writers and within them. This is why critics differ as to whether the emphasis in Shakespearean forms of the carnivalesque— *Twelfth Night,* for instance—is on subversion or its containment.

In Barker's novel *Cabal,* the drama of these conflicting viewpoints is projected through the fantasy of the narrative. The story, as Barker readily acknowledges, is a gay allegory. The monstrous inhabitants of Midian embody not only "the strangeness you see from the corner of your eye," but also the strangeness, the feared Other, we glimpse in ourselves. In this novel, the distinction between the familiar and the strange, the normal and the monstrous, constantly collapses, as the horror of Midian that grips the representatives of law and order is revealed as their recoil from self-recognition. Decker's greatest fear is that the mask he hides behind, not only to deceive others but to conceal himself from himself, will be torn away. This happens figuratively when Boone, exploiting Decker's vulnerability, exposes the man beneath "the Mask" by addressing him directly, using his real name: "'You're a dead man, Decker!' the monster cried" (119). Decker's response to this is indicative of that psychic split, that divided and warring self, we have noted in Gothic writing generally: "'I'm not Decker,' the Mask replied, and fired again" (120). Thus, in his wider meaning, Decker is representative of the main focus of Barker's critique in this novel: namely, the psychic disorder that lies behind our general social and cultural malaise.

Psychic health in this novel can be achieved only by those who recognize that civilization is itself a mask. These, as Boone perceives, are the wholesome people of Midian, who accept and flaunt, rather than curb, their primal energy and elemental being: "It was only the monster, the child of Midian, who actually altered its flesh to parade its true self" (58). Lori has similar moments of insight: "But yesterday she'd thought beasts were beasts" (111). This is the driving theme of the novel. Thus for Boone, the magnetic attraction of Midian, we infer, stems from his need to be psychically healed: "Boone the man and Boone the monster could not be divided" (42). For Lori, too, Midian holds the key to spiritual survival and wholeness:

> And matching dust against flies, she knew which she favoured; knew ... that if Midian died ... then *she,* dust herself one day, and touched by Midian's condition—would have nowhere to be carried, and would belong, body and soul, to the flies. (178 emphasis in original)

Indeed, the novel's constant refrain is that respectability, with its semblance of orderliness, pursuit of "normality," is but skin-deep, paper-thin, a matter of appearances only. Decker, for instance, even as he confesses to serial murder, "[looks] sane, in his well cut suit" (57) and Lori wonders how her testimony will stand up against his. *He,* after all, is "the one with ... the doctorate and the friends in high places"; and furthermore, "the *man,* the voice of reason and analysis" (157 emphasis in original).

*Cabal* could be seen as a fictional dramatization of contemporary theorizing around the related concepts of marginality, abjection, and othering. Diana Fuss, for example, writes: "The philosophical opposition between 'heterosexual' and 'homosexual' ... has always been constructed on the foundations of another related opposition: the couple 'inside' and 'outside'" (*Inside/Out* 1). If the outside has usually been associated with absence or lack, she points out, more recent work on sexual subjectivity has begun to view this association as the consequence of a recognition of lack on the inside. To avoid such recognition, the theory goes, the self, in a defensive move, ascribes its internal lack to the Other, which it invests with a negative image and around which it erects well-patrolled borders. The process is therefore deflective, the Other being made to embody the lack that the self descries within. This would explain not just the closeness of homosexuality and heterosexuality but also the sense both have of being too close for comfort. As a result of this mutual interdependence, Fuss suggests, these oppositions haunt each other, which is why many contemporary theorists are fascinated with "the specter of abjection" and preoccupied with the figure of the homosexual "as specter and phantom, as spirit and revenant, as abject and undead" (3).[10]

Abjection, as Julia Kristeva defines it in *Powers of Horror,* is that which "disturbs identity, system, order," that which does not "respect borders, positions, rules" (4). And although the abject, in her account, can be experienced in various ways, it is most often associated with bodily waste, decay, sickness, and death. So the corpse, "seen without God," is "the most sickening of wastes," the "utmost of abjection" (3–4). It is the body without a soul and therefore devoid of meaning. Existing outside the spiritual orbit that the self inhabits, it represents the thing that "I" am not; and since it "draws me toward the place where meaning collapses," it must be driven away or destroyed (2). Moreover, it is this drawing toward that constitutes its greatest threat, she implies, for the seductive power of nihilism and its attendant "evil" (to recall Genet's use of the term) can destroy our belief in morality and spiritual values. Thus the corpse is "death infecting life"; we would reject it but cannot, since it haunts us until our defences wither away. Indeed, it "beckons to us and ends up engulfing us" (4).

In *Cabal*, the undead of Midian disturb "identity, system, order" through their refusal to be categorized, their denial of the life–death divide. Midian itself is a ghost town, an enormous cemetery that both repels and attracts, and to which the living are spiritually drawn despite their fears. Those who enter Midian approach it in a spirit of openness and adventure (Boone, Lori) or of terror and hostility (Decker, Eigerman). It is, as its name suggests, a place of mediation between one state of being and another: a place where corporeal distinctions evaporate and moral certainties dissolve. In Midian, all values are put to the test and even the meaning of abjection is probed. For, in this context, who *are* the abject? Midian's undead are at least undeceived about themselves and prepared to challenge the narrowness of petty bourgeois mentality. "He who denies morality," writes Kristeva, "is not abject; there can be grandeur in amorality and even in crime that flaunts its disrespect for the law—rebellious, liberating, and suicidal crime" (4). It is Decker, on the other hand, who is the "in-between, the ambiguous, the composite"; who is "sinister, scheming, and shady"; who is "the criminal with good conscience . . . the killer who claims he is a saviour . . . the friend who stabs you" (4).

Indeed, in this novel, it is those on the inside who evince a sense of absence or lack, which they deflect into fear and loathing of those on the outside. Thus Decker's "treatment" of Boone is his way of externalizing his own killer instinct, while Eigerman's manic and brutal pursuit of law and order is his self-justifying mission, his mechanism for hiding from himself his own destructive urges and will to power. Likewise, Ashbery's adoption of a priestly role is a form of self-defense, his mode of cleansing himself of what he perceives as his sexual failings. For all of these three, the outside, the despised Other, is the means to self-esteem and self-definition. The undead of Midian, on the other hand (or the Breed, as they are known), have, in their self-acceptance, no need for such insider–outsider opposition. Hence Boone, in his ruminations, can find no way to describe them, for they exist outside the either/or of conventional discourse: "They didn't belong to Hell; nor yet to Heaven. They were what the species he'd once belonged to could not bear to be. The *un*-people; the *anti*-tribe; humanity's sack unpicked and sewn together again with the moon inside" (230).

*Cabal* is a celebration of Otherness. It exudes the spirit of carnival and crackles with subversive energy. It ends, however, on a muted note, for the revolutionary potential of the Breed is dispersed and consequently weakened in the diaspora that follows the destruction of Midian. And yet, even here, the spirit of carnival is not finally crushed. Diminished but not defeated, they retain a latent hope of resurgent powers. With patience, they *will* come through—or so they believe: "Their liberator would come eventually, if they could only survive the wait" (253). Meanwhile, in the austere words of the novel's final sentence, "It was a life" (253). But the accent here is on constraint rather than containment: on carnival suspended rather than authority restored. Thus radicalism, not conservatism, remains the driving force of the novel.

These themes are explored elsewhere in contemporary Gothic writing, although sometimes with different emphases. Poppy Z Brite's *Lost Souls*, for instance, also celebrates Otherness. Unlike *Cabal*, however, its final muted note is not temporary: for here, as the title implies, the spirit of carnival is, paradoxically, inherently sad, its savage subversion mere futile and consolatory rebellion against a world without meaning. In this novel, where the carnival parades and dances on a bedrock of nihilism, celebration is founded on despair. Indeed, blankness is registered in the very name of the novel's central character: Nothing. Moreover, Brite's protagonists, plagued by existential angst, are rebels without a cause. Their vampiric energy, though in part an assault on stifling social conformity, is chiefly directed at a perceived emptiness at the center of life, a void in the cosmos that their share of first-world plenitude tends to accentuate rather than disguise. Thus Nothing's agony arises from the inevitable tensions of existence: for, in that his needs demand that he must devour even his friends and lovers, he is daily confronted with the quandary that survival depends on betrayal—a predicament that again brings Genet to mind.

Indeed Nothing, in his confrontation with those aspects of experience that the "bourgeois" mind chooses to repress, embodies the youthful disillusion, disaffection, and tortured struggle of our contemporary Western world. His abandonment on the doorstep of a dull, if loving, couple in Maryland and his subsequent flight from the nightmare of suburban America metaphorically encapsulates our human experience of alienation: "*I've got to get out of this place,* he thought just before dawn, and the ghosts of all the decades of middle-class American children afraid of complacency and stagnation and comfortable death drifted before his face, whispering their agreement" (29). This alienation is signaled in the books he reads, for he is drawn to writing that penetrates the guise of the civilized world: "Plath . . . Bradbury . . . William Burroughs" (29). Hence, he alone of his classmates has access to the "primal magic" of Golding's *Lord of the Flies*, which moves and haunts him with its picture of "wild salty-skinned little boys . . . so young, grown old so fast" (30). In this way the novel affiliates with a whole generation of alienated young people and indicts mainstream America for its hollow pursuit of happiness, its attempt to expunge the tragic dimension of life.

However, Nothing's distress in Maryland is also partly attributable to his sense of being alienated from his own body. Like *Cabal*, *Lost Souls* engages with the notion that the body is the site of conflict between our pre-oedipal relationship to our mother's body, which will not deny "its debt to nature," and the prohibition placed on this relationship by the law of the father, which strives to cast out "the impure, the non-separate, the non-symbolic, the non-holy" (Kristeva 102). In Kristeva's account, it is the paternal (or phallogocentric) symbolic order, with its commitment to the binary opposition of man/woman, that abjects the female body and splits the human psyche. So, for Nothing, as perhaps for alienated youth in general, the appeal of the vampire way of life is its surrender to the pre-oedipal symbolic flux in defiance of this prohibition. Hence he gladly attaches himself to the androgynous Zillah, Molochai, and Twig, with their blatant disregard for distinctions of gender and sexuality, and readily acknowledges them as family, even though association with them exposes him to great emotional and spiritual anguish.

In *Lost Souls,* as in *Cabal,* the vampiric undead are abject because, like the ancient and symbolic mother figure, they maintain a close, accepting, and undifferentiating relationship with the body.[11] Thus, in violation of the paternal order that seeks to protect the holiness of the body from what it sees as polluting waste—in particular, blood secreted from the body, for this has broken its boundaries and is therefore impure—they feast on such "waste" as the wellspring of life. In her discussion of the long-standing injunction against such impurity, Kristeva (102–03) cites chapter and verse from the Bible:

> For it is the life of all flesh; the blood of it is for the life thereof: therefore I said unto the children of Israel, Ye shall eat the blood of no manner of flesh: for the life of all flesh is the blood thereof: whoever eateth it shall be cut off. (Leviticus 17:14)

But any exchange of body fluids, of course, is also sexually charged, and hence the drawing of lines and boundaries here is also related to sexual taboo. The feasting of vampires in *Lost Souls* is loaded with a sense of comprehensive sexual lawbreaking. Moreover, the relationship between food and sex is made quite explicit in the episode of Nothing's first kill, for his victim on this occasion turns out to be his first love, Laine, who has come from Maryland in search of him. Pleasure therefore becomes indistinguishable from pain, as the novel's carnival mode once again collides with its nihilistic undercurrents: "But Laine should have learned by now that when you have too much faith in something, it is bound to hurt you. Too much faith in anything will suck you dry. In this way, all the world is a vampire" (161).

## DESCENT INTO NIGHTMARE: DENNIS COOPER'S *FRISK*

> Literature is not innocent. It is guilty and should admit itself so.
>
> —Georges Bataille, Preface to *Literature and Evil*

These provocative words of Bataille raise huge philosophical questions concerning the nature and function of literature. In challenging Sartre's notion of literature as the instrument of engaged moral action, Bataille's book suggests that it is only through a knowledge of evil that literature can confront the totality of human experience; and moreover, that such knowledge, like the Fall, is inevitably guilty because it entails a loss of innocence. But if Bataille's use here of the terms *innocent* and *guilty* suggests a moral outlook based on binary opposition, his book as a whole explores the possibility of getting beyond such constricted thinking. Like Genet, Bataille challenges orthodoxy by laying stress on the value of "evil" as a liberating and creative force. But, again like Genet, the meaning he ascribes to the term calls for a reinvention if it.

A key to Bataille's ideas about evil, sexual passion, and the release of repressed desire is his essay on the Marquis de Sade (*Literature and Evil* 103–29). Bataille, in common with other French commentators, sees Sade as a tortured genius, who seeks, through the strange interrelatedness of his life and writing, to divine and lay bare the enigma, the last and darkest secrets, of the human heart. He draws attention to Sade's ever-shifting apprehension of the impenetrable mysteries of life and to the way his vision, like Genet's, transcends the arbitrariness of established moral codes. Thus he quotes from a letter of Sade's—a letter that is signed with the pseudonym "Des Aulnets" and (though the recipient is not given) was probably addressed to Mlle Rousset, a woman with whom Sade was briefly in love: "O man! Is it for you to say what is good and evil? . . . You want to analyse the laws of nature and your heart . . . your heart whereon they are engraved, is itself an enigma which you cannot solve" (110). This dissolution of the barrier between good and evil, Bataille suggests, is related to the conciliation Sade effects between life and death, passion and annihilation, desire and nothingness. In his will, as Bataille reminds us, Sade left instructions that he should be buried in a corner of his land and the surrounding soil sown with acorns, so that in time all "traces of the tomb will disappear from the surface of the earth as I hope my memory will vanish from the memory of men" (109).

As Bataille stresses, the central feature of Sade's *Les Cent Vingt Journées de Sodome* is its fascination with pain, suffering, and extinction. This book, in which the objects of desire "are invariably propelled towards torture and death" (116), is, Bataille maintains, the first "to express the true fury which man holds within him and which he has to control and conceal" (108). In this respect, it clearly relates to those forms of contemporary Gothic we have just been examining, for these, as we have seen, are also centrally concerned with our control and concealment of the elemental and irrational drives within us. But Sade's disturbing exploration of the relationship between torture, death, and sexual arousal goes much further than that of *Cabal* or *Lost Souls*. Indeed, his terrifying mockery, shocking defilement, and frenzied destruction of all civilized values goes, to use Bataille's words, "as far as imagination allows" (121); and this is all the more disturbing, Bataille argues, in view of the conscious control he brings to bear on the venting of what is apparently beyond controlled utterance. "In the solitude of his prison," he writes, "Sade was the first man to give a rational expression to those uncontrollable desires, on the negation of which consciousness has based the social structure and the very image of man" (120).

Bataille presents Sade's writing as a form of religious quest, a contemplation of the soul that is monklike in its concentration; and this relates to his suggestion that Sade cannot bring his desires and passions to full consciousness because they are ultimately unknowable. "One must read [his books] as they were written," he writes, "with the intention of fathoming a mystery which is no less profound, nor perhaps less 'divine,' than that of theology" (116). Moreover, he suggests that what Sade finds, at the end of his search for the ground of our erotic instinct, is death. Death liberates us from desires that cannot be satisfied and from the subordination of our finite being to the infinity that surrounds it. In short, it enables us to escape our human limitations and "returns [us] to immensity" (122). Hence, the full release of our passion leads us inexorably to the destruction of the object of our desire. The implication in Bataille's essay, then, is that Sade's obsession is related to the concept of Liebestod, or love-death.

This concept, as Kevin Kopelson has shown, is one that has strong associations with homoerotic writing, a conjunction he ascribes in part to "a curious late-nineteenth-century conflation of sadism and homosexuality" (30). At the center of this conflation, Kopelson maintains, is the figure of Gilles de Rais, the fifteenth-century marshal of France "executed for kidnapping, sodomizing, and murdering untold numbers of children" (31). Kopelson's examination focuses on the way that homoerotic writing of the fin-de-siècle employed the trope of Liebestod both as reverse discourse (by which it attempted to counter homophobic perceptions of homosexuality with idealized depictions of gay love) and as a means of articulating for gay readers "the otherwise inarticulable phenomenon of homosexual orgasm" (23). In this use of the trope, he suggests, the lovers figure as either victims or victimizers, according to viewpoint, for their forbidden love pushes them toward a self-immolation that re-enacts the power relations that oppress them. The murder-suicide of sadomasochistic relations, in other words, is embedded in its very concept. Moreover, this association of homosexuality with victimisation and death, Kopelson argues, has continued into our own time and is still with us. "[The] conflation and connection," he suggests, "may even inflect the sado-masochistic self-identifications of contemporary gays and lesbians who have never heard of Rais" (33).

Dennis Cooper's *Frisk* is a visceral ravaging of these ideas. In this novel, a young man, Dennis, is shown a series of fake snuff photographs by Pete, the owner of a pornographic bookshop with whom he has become friendly, and is disturbed to find himself sexually excited by them, especially since they awaken in him latent sadistic and murderous cravings that become obsessive and return to haunt him. Indeed, in time, he finds himself utterly possessed and driven to madness by them, as he testifies when he writes of "those images that went on to completely direct or destroy my life in a way" (30). Like Sade, Dennis achieves control, release, and exorcism of these passions through writing, and this begins with letters to friends, because, as he puts it, "I couldn't see how it [such writing] could ever fit into something as legitimate as a novel or whatever" (123).

At least this is what appears to happen in *Frisk*, for Cooper's metalinguistic blurring of the distinction between reality and fantasy leaves the reader in some doubt. Thus, in the letter that brings the novel to its gruesomely sensational climax, Dennis, writing to his friend Julian from his isolated windmill home in Amsterdam, describes how, with the help of two psychopathic German thugs, he casually picked up, tortured, and murdered a series of cutely vulnerable young men who took his fancy. Yet later, when Julian questions the truth of his story and urges him to come clean, he claims that these events are imaginary. His letters to friends, he submits, are not accounts of actual happenings but rather Sadean confessions of profoundly impure thoughts, written in the hope that the recipients will "either write back and give me some sort of objective analysis, or else relate to the fantasy, come here, and give me the courage or amorality or whatever to actually kill somebody in league with them" (123).

There is, then, an ambiguity at the heart of the novel, which is part of its deliberate attempt to unsettle and implicate the reader, for Dennis's account of his crimes is so disturbingly "real" that any doubt about their actuality seems academic and beside the point. Moreover, this dissolving of the barrier between repressed and fulfilled desire implies a parallel collapsing of moral distinctions, and thus brings to mind Bataille's transcendental use of the terms *innocent* and *guilty,* together with his challenging ideas about the liberating energies of evil. In *Frisk* (as in *Wuthering Heights,* to which Bataille devotes the opening chapter of his *Literature and Evil*) conventional moral concerns are swept up and annihilated in the whirlwind of the novel's fury and passion. For in the artfulness of its suspenseful plot, which leaves the enigma of Dennis's guilt or innocence unresolved, the novel accuses the squeamish reader of both complicity in Dennis's "crimes" (through disappointment at the possibility that they are mere fantasy) and of bourgeois pusillanimity and feebleness (or failure of moral imagination). Its accusation is thus an echo of Baudelaire's preface to *Fleurs du Mal:* "Hypocrite lecteur, -mon semblable, -mon frère."[12]

With all this in mind, it comes as no surprise to learn that Cooper's interest in the dark side of human sexuality began at an early age, nor that the writings of Sade, Baudelaire, and Rimbaud have helped to develop his taste for extremes of aesthetic expression.[13] At sixteen, it seems, he wrote a prose work in imitation of *Les Cent Vingt Journées de Sodome,* which he destroyed lest his mother should find it. In this regard, one aspect of *Frisk* that suggests indebtedness to Sade is the iron control of the writing. Like

Sade's work, this novel subjects its violence and hysteria to quiet, dryly rational expression, and hence its emotional content can be glimpsed only through the faultlines of its text, as the narrative voice here struggles to retain a sense of selfhood from within the prevailing ethos of reductive nihilism. Stranded between first-person and third-person modes of expression, between restricted viewpoint and omniscience, between presence and absence, corporeality and the void, it grapples with the liberal humanist concept of "the person," and its provenance, the divine mystery of "the soul," as if grievously reluctant to abandon them.

Indeed *Frisk* could be seen, as Bataille sees Sade's writing, as a form of religious quest, since Dennis's morbid fascination with pain, death, and material existence arises, according to his own account, from a kind of anguished and fevered metaphysical inquiry.[14] Thus, in conversation with Pierre Buisson, the porn video star and male escort he seeks out in New York—perhaps as a way of avoiding "the mess of real relationships" but more probably in response to "an urge that I don't understand" (44)—he says:

> I mean, I know there's no God. People are only their bodies, and sex is the only intimacy, etc., but it's not enough. Like you. I find what I know about you amazing, so amazing I can't get beyond my awe. So part of me wants to dismantle that awe or whatever, and see how you work. . . . I think of it [this feeling] as religious. Like insane people say they've seen God. I saw God in those pictures [the fake snuff photographs], and when I imagine dissecting you, say, I begin to feel that way again. It's physical, mental, emotional. (69–70)

Indeed, these speculations suggest that Dennis should be seen as a brooding Hamlet figure, suspended, in his contemplation of the human condition, between amazement and boredom, admiration and disgust, exaltation and despair. Cooper, as Edmund White writes, has "a terrifying gift for finding a death's head under every pretty face" (*Burning Library* 282). If Pierre, with his flawless good looks, represents for Dennis the quintessence of manhood, he is at the same time, although from a different angle, "this quintessence of dust." His beauty, like Ophelia's, is but skin-deep.

Moreover, Dennis's alternation between his conviction that "people are only their bodies" and his feeling that they are also possessed of something godlike suggests that he is also the site of a Kristevan struggle between nature and symbol, abjection and destiny, pre-oedipal flux and paternal law. This is reinforced by his attempt to explain, in high-flown symbolic terms, his fascination with Pierre's waste matter and bodily functions: "So could you use the toilet and not flush it? And piss into one of those glasses? . . . I'm not being abject . . . It's, like I said, information . . . It's really hard to articulate this . . . it's gotten so complex and clouded with daydreams, theories . . ." (69). By "information," he means factual imagery on which to construct his fantasies of dissection and murder—or so his words imply: "Uh, create a mental world . . . a situation where I could kill you and understand . . ." (69). This information builds ultimately into the "daydreams," indistinguishable from nightmare, described in his letter to Julian. Here, his rage to tear the entrails from his victims again points to internal conflict, suggesting on the one hand a desire to re-enter the pre-oedipal, presymbolic relationship to the (maternal) body, and on the other to abject undifferentiated materiality, cast out "the impure . . . the non-holy," and even destroy the site, or corpse, where meaning collapses.

The taboo breaking of *Frisk*, like that of *Cabal* and *Lost Souls*, is a push to the very limits of experience, the borderlines of possibility, in a search for some bedrock reality. It is also an attempt to lay bare the stultifying hollowness beneath the smug morality of mainstream contemporary Western, and specifically North American, culture: for Dennis, Cooper's alter ego, is a Californian and, like the protagonists of Poppy Brite's novel, part of an alienated generation of young people in violent recoil from the cultural logic of late capitalism. Thus, sitting with Julian in his parents' library, he registers his disgust at the prevailing ideology of his environment: "The shelves were crammed with Reader's Digest Condensed shit" (15). Moreover, his actions here suggest a bored effort to wrest meaning from the fragile instability and strewn detritus of the fragmented postmodern world: "I turned the dial of a clock radio, making rock opera from severed parts of announcements and ads and hit songs" (15). Like Hamlet, then, he is eventually provoked by his enervation and moral disgust into destructive behavior: into rending the veil of the sterile promontory he inhabits and letting loose its foul and pestilent vapors.

A large part of *Frisk*'s power to confront and disturb, however, derives from its anxious involvement with, and playful deployment of, the poststructuralist concept of the sign: for ambiguity, centered on the question of Dennis's guilt and the actuality of his crimes, is, as we have seen, at the heart of the novel. The only indication of his guilt, after all, is a series of signifiers, or meaningful marks on a page: namely, his letter to Julian. In their search for further evidence of the signified, Kevin and Julian find nothing substantial: there is no "teenage-sized skeleton" (122) in the bell-shaped room at the top of the windmill, although, teasingly, on another level, "[parts] of the floorboards were stained with a black substance, shimmery as a dance floor, presumably dehydrated blood" (112). The question of Dennis's guilt, therefore, becomes a matter of interpretation and reception. Indeed, the novel's self-inquiry and hounding of the reader here suggests a poststructuralist interrogation of moral precepts based on Saussurean semiotics. Thus it asks, what *is* the relationship between Dennis's letter and the crimes described in it? Or, to put it another way, how arbitrary, in this case, *is* the connection between signifier and signified?

These questions lead eventually to the novel's fundamental anxiety, which revolves around the concept of subjectivity and the philosophical implications of the signifier "I": a concern signaled, as I intimate above, in the novel's movement between third- and first-person narrative viewpoints. The unobtrusive entry of the signifier "I" at a midway point in the first chapter suggests a tentative, metalinguistic awareness of its precariousness and lack of fixity. Indeed, the narrative's self-conscious adoption of a new subject position here is like the trying on of a disguise. Behind this insecurity we glimpse the concept of language as social process that underpins Kristeva's study of abjection, for the arrival in this text of the signifier "I" seems to mimic the human subject's movement out of an infantile stage of development (or the pre-oedipal flux) and into a social role (or the phallogocentric symbolic order). Moreover, it could be argued that *Frisk*'s preoccupation with sexual torture and murder is, at root, a tormented wrestling with the relation between the signifier "I" and its signified: the mark on the page and the whole complex of biological and psychic processes that make up the human subject.

This brings us back to the notion of a religious quest. For if the signifier "I" makes possible the concept of the unified self within the flux of material existence, the development of poststructuralist ways of thinking in our time means, to quote Earl Jackson Jr., that the concept "lingers in an environment hostile to it" (79). Jackson suggests that Cooper's "I" is "arguably one of the most poignant and plaintive voices in contemporary literature" (79), and *Frisk*'s real or imagined acts of mutilation and murder become, within his reading, a frenzied, anguished search for the essential self. By way of illustration, he refers to the scene in the penultimate chapter where Kevin (a tenderly evoked younger self?) imagines the windmill to be haunted and attempts to conjure up the ghost of one of Dennis's victims—a scene made all the more affecting by his failure, for the ghost remains frustratingly elusive and the murdered boy simply will not materialize. According to this reading, Dennis's obsessions stem from a conviction that the objects of his desire are not coterminous with their physical makeup, and hence the novel's exploration of the wildest reaches of sexual passion "traverses (and blurs the boundaries between) religion and crime, worship and sacrifice" (81). However, to this I would add that, within its postmodern context and poststructuralist ways of thought, the novel also suggests an act of resistance to the Derridean assault on the notion of a final signified: to the deconstructive movement's stress on the endless deferment of meaning. It seems, in fact, to raise a visceral howl of protest against our contemporary preference for absence over presence: our eagerness to replace substance with the "hole" of nonbeing.

## SUMMARY

This chapter presents a strong contrast to the last, for the writers of the novels discussed here, in place of concern with family and social norms, are clearly drawn to homosexuality as a potentially dangerous and disruptive force. The danger remains potential, however, because the stress in each of these novels is on containment. Indeed each creates a sense of circularity: of the narrative building to a critical moment at which radical change, a breaking free of the circle, might occur, but then going into retreat and coming back to the point at which it began. In *The Swimming-Pool Library*, for instance, Will's near-acquisition of a social conscience, produced by the shock of reading Nantwich's papers and the news of Charles's arrest, is easily defeated in the final pages, his temporary oppositional stance feebly collapsing back into compliance with the status quo. Moreover, *Cabal* and *Lost Souls* end on a similar note of failure and inertia, with a return to the restricting patterns of life-as-before. In *Frisk* too, circularity and containment are suggested both in the novel's ending (the repeat of the "snuff" movie screenplay with which it began) and in the teasing ambiguity of the text as a whole: the blurring of the distinction between fantasy and reality, whereby the "danger" of homosexuality becomes no more than artful literariness, playful fictionality.

This stress on containment again points to internal conflict. Of course the subtext of the fiction examined here and in Chapter 4 is AIDS, and one obvious way in which the former differs from the latter is in sexual frankness. Thus the unbridled sex scenes of the novels by Hollinghurst and Cooper stand in sharp contrast to the erotic conservatism of those by Leavitt and Cunningham. The tendencies and internal conflicts of both strains of fiction, however, derive from their relationship to the new puritanism of the AIDS era. *The Swimming-Pool Library* and *Frisk*, for instance, are ambivalent, their defiant transgression in uneasy relationship with conventional moral stricture: for just as Hollinghurst's novel negotiates between conflicting impulses through the figure of Will Beckwith, so *Frisk*, through the figure of "Dennis," struggles to normalize the madness of its erotic compulsions. Moreover, the novels examined in Chapter 4, as we saw, are similarly conflicted, and hence the ambivalence revealed in the fiction examined in both of these chapters highlights the intensification of the conflict between assimilationism and radicalism that AIDS has produced.

But if the fiction we have looked at so far registers AIDS as subtext, there is another kind of fiction that looks directly at AIDS; and this is the focus of my next and final chapter.

# 6   The AIDS Epidemic
## Victory to a Virus?

In a very real sense, all writing today is AIDS writing in that it must consciously choose how to respond to the epidemic, whether by direct involvement or evasion.

—Suzanne Poirier, "On Writing AIDS"

Surely the truly responsible thing to do now would be to write sexy nostalgic fiction set in the period before the epidemic, safeguarding if only in fantasy the endangered gains of gay liberation?

Well, no. Even when I thought that the problems of writing about Aids satisfactorily were insurmountable, for me at any rate, I still felt that it would be a good thing, even politically, if the trick could be managed. Fiction might create a psychological space in which the epidemic could be contemplated, with detachment rather than denial or apocalyptic fear.

—Adam Mars-Jones, *Monopolies of Loss*

AIDS is now an unavoidable part of the gay male writer's mental landscape and the world he knows. Unavoidable because any attempt he may make to avoid it draws attention to his need to do so, and hence to the enduring stubborn fact of its existence. In short, AIDS in contemporary gay male writing becomes conspicuous by its absence. But if the early years of the epidemic were dominated by the fearful, paranoid, apocalyptic response to the crisis, the longevity of the disease and the advances in medical understanding and treatment of it have permitted a more measured approach. The problem here, though, is that this approach may lead in turn to a view of AIDS at an opposite extreme from paranoia, a view that could be termed "denial." According to this view, which places the epidemic within a long historical perspective, AIDS is an "irrelevance," to quote Adam Mars-Jones—an irrelevance (and the tone here makes its own deft point) "even to those whose lives it threatens" (*Monopolies* 2). In Mars-Jones's judgement, these extreme positions distort our view of AIDS, since "[the] present reality of the epidemic must lie somewhere in the middle," and thus what is needed to find a "truer picture" is writing that addresses the subject without recourse to either (1). In other words, if I interpret him correctly, we need writing that is both sufficiently involved to be able to bear witness to the impact of AIDS on the lives of individuals, and yet sufficiently removed to be able to view the epidemic with some degree of contemplative detachment.

In respect of AIDS, Mars-Jones and Edmund White, to go by their remarks and writings on the subject, have much in common. This is perhaps to be expected of two writers whose collaboration on a book of short stories—*The Darker Proof* (1987)—produced some of the earliest fiction about AIDS.[1] In "Esthetics and Loss," the essay he wrote while working on these stories, White proposes "tact" (*Burning Library* 216) as the first requirement of any artistic response to AIDS; and this suggests a standing back in order to obtain the necessary distance, breadth of outlook, depth of insight. Our response to AIDS in general, he implies, should mirror our response to AIDS in the lives of individuals: just as "we must not reduce individuals to their deaths . . . How someone dies says nothing about how he lived" (216), so we should not allow a health crisis and its surrounding moral panic to erase a culture and a history. Speaking of Larry Kramer, who once berated White for "wasting" seven years on a biography of Jean Genet, when AIDS, in Kramer's view, was the only possible subject for a writer in the current crisis, White remarks:

> I appreciate what he is saying, but it's the reduction of the whole of gay culture to a single issue, a medical emergency. And it's terrible to think that homosexuality was only de-medicalised for a brief period, about 20 years. What I wanted to do was remind people how much more there is to gay culture than disease. (Jenkins 32)

This stance certainly does not imply a lack of involvement, however, an avoidance of the gravity, terror, and "unspeakable scandal" of AIDS (*Burning Library* 216): White was diagnosed HIV positive in 1985 and most of the men who made up his world in New York in the seventies are now dead. His decision to collaborate with Mars-Jones was prompted by the belief that, as an insider with firsthand experience of the crisis, he had something valuable to contribute to a discourse that was losing sight of the fact that "actual human beings were suffering, watching their lives crumble, and having to confront very deep fears" (quoted in Dellamora 99). Like Mars-Jones, White favors an approach to AIDS that resists paranoia and apocalyptic brooding, while remaining sensitive to the change, personal suffering, and loss the epidemic has brought.

Hence, in his nonfiction writing, White explicitly opposes the new moralism of the AIDS era, a stance that is also reflected in his AIDS fiction. In "Esthetics and Loss," for instance, he mourns the fact that the confidence of the gay movement—the "brassy hedonism of a few years back"—has given way to a new "protective gay invisibility" (*Burning Library* 213). In the new moral climate, he argues, AIDS threatens not just the lives of individuals but the very existence of the gay movement itself, which against extraordinary odds has managed to build a political identity around sexuality: "[W]hen a society based on sex and expression is de-eroticized, its very reason for being can vanish" (214). Moreover, in the afterword to the 1986 reprint of *States of Desire* he argues that the new moralism, by ignoring the sexual needs of gay men and the *real* health dangers presented by the existence of the virus, can itself be seen as life-threatening (342).

Kramer was perhaps the leading AIDS activist and writer on AIDS in the early years of the epidemic, and his moral rhetoric has been carefully and dispassionately analyzed by David Bergman (*Gaiety* 122–38). Bergman, while recognizing the compassion and energy of Kramer's crusade, finds evidence in his writing of internalized homophobia and antieroticism. Indeed, his analysis of a passage from *Faggots* finds that it comes "perilously close to saying 'the wages of gay sin are death'" (126). Furthermore, Bergman finds an internal contradiction in Kramer's attitude to gay marriage and the family, since Kramer's recommendation of gay marriage ("Had we been allowed to marry, we would never have felt the obligation to be promiscuous" [*Reports* 178–79]) is clearly at odds with his perception of the state's manipulative use of the concepts of "family" and "family values," both as an excuse for remaining silent about AIDS and for the further stigmatizing of homosexuality.[2]

Kramer thus represents one extreme position, his approach to the epidemic being apocalyptic in tone, as indicated by the very title of the book in which he chronicles his experience as an AIDS activist in the early years of the epidemic: *Notes from the Holocaust*. Denial, on the other hand, is a less easily identified response, reticence being more ambiguous than outspokenness. Are silence and indirection necessarily evasive? Gregory Woods thinks not. He finds the stark choice presented by Suzanne Poirier (in the citation at the head of this chapter) too hard, narrow, and restrictive: "Surely there must be some alternative, or alternatives plural, to these two possible extremes" (*History of Gay Literature* 368). This is clearly related to Edmund White's warning about the reductive tendency of an exclusive focus on AIDS ("How someone dies says nothing about how he lived"), as well as to Mars-Jones's uneasiness about the power of the AIDS narrative, in fiction about the epidemic, to subsume all other narratives: "Aids doesn't deserve to be promoted up into the body of the book. It's only a bug, after all. Why flatter it?" (*Monopolies* 2). For these writers, then, the challenge of writing about AIDS is twofold. On the one hand the problem is artistic: how to transcend the stupefying predictability of the AIDS narrative. "They all died," writes White in *The Farewell Symphony* (471), as if bluntly demonstrating the difficulty. But on the other it is political: how to be true to the experience of the disease without giving added weight to the "homosexuality = AIDS = death" metaphoric equation.

For Joseph Cady, however, the measured, spare, tactful approach of White and Mars-Jones "runs the risk of ultimately collaborating with the larger cultural denial of the disease" (261). Cady favors direct involvement, or what he calls "immersive" writing: that is, writing in which "the reader is thrust into a direct imaginative confrontation with the special horrors of AIDS" (244). AIDS writing that takes an indirect approach to its subject he calls "counterimmersive," and suggests that such writing "typically focuses on characters or speakers who are in various degrees of denial about AIDS themselves" (244). Cady concedes that counterimmersiveness, through the tactfulness of its address, has the merit of not harrowing the denying reader into further denial, and he also recognizes that immersiveness, through the rawness of its account, may drive the denying reader away. But he gives his final endorsement to this latter kind of writing on two counts: for its "willingness to defy the dominant culture directly and fully," and for "its faithfulness to the emotional and social anguish of people affected by AIDS" (261).

Cady's essay is peculiarly pertinent to my own line of argument in this study in the way it links these two distinct strains of writing about AIDS to the wider ideological tensions of gay culture and politics, and hence to what I have been calling the central conflict of gay male writing since Stonewall. Thus Cady sees the prevalence of counterimmersiveness in AIDS literature by gay men as "rooted in a lingering depression about homosexuality and in stereotyped understandings of it" (258). In support of his argument Cady instances the case of Andrew Holleran, whose short story "Friends at Evening," chosen as a representative example of counterimmersive AIDS writing, he has already discussed earlier in the essay. On the evidence of this story and the novels *Dancer from the Dance* and *Nights in Aruba*, Cady contends that Holleran's work falls chiefly into what he calls "the concessive and ironic modes of gay male literature" (259), and he goes on to argue, I think rightly, that both of these modes involve a degree of complicity with the dominant culture. This is in general accord with my own view of Holleran's work, as my examination of *Dancer* and *Nights* in Chapter 1 shows. Indeed it would be difficult to argue differently, since Holleran makes his concessiveness and irony abundantly clear.

But while I go along with some of the lines of Cady's argument, I find others—and especially his final endorsement—more problematic. After all, in respect of AIDS writing, the issue that clearly engages White and Mars-Jones is whether a "willingness to defy the dominant culture directly and fully" through immersiveness is itself a form of complicity. Thus Mars-Jones writes: "At a time when media coverage tends to push the issues of Aids and homosexuality closer and closer together, as if epidemic and orientation were synonymous, how can you justify writing fiction that brings this spurious couple together all over again?" (*Monopolies* 2). Likewise,

White comments: "we must not fall into the trap of replacing the afterlife with the moment of dying. . . . we must not let the disease stand for other things" (*Burning Library* 216). For these writers, immersive AIDS writing, being directly confrontational, oppositional, and reactive, is too exclusively concerned with the denials of the dominant culture and hence too deeply implicated in its general response to the epidemic.

In my view Cady himself highlights the problem of immersiveness in offering Paul Monette's *Love Alone: Eighteen Elegies for Rog* (1988) as a classic example of it. In this set of poems about the illness and death of Roger Horwitz, his lover of twelve years, Monette appears to defy the dominant culture directly and fully by mounting an aggressively blunt and harrowing assault on its denial of AIDS. Yet it could equally be argued that, paradoxically, he defers to that culture in allowing *its* response to the epidemic to dictate and narrow his content. Indeed, these poems exhibit a tendency that Edmund White finds in Monette's work as a whole. White comments:

> I've sometimes felt that Paul Monette, encouraged by Larry Kramer, had a sort of trumped-up politicised anger, which is no doubt very therapeutic in the sense that it's better to be angry than to be depressed. But the truth is that there aren't many people to be angry at right now. The main thing to be angry at is a virus. So I think that Paul Monette's writing is what's called author-manipulated. In other words, you feel that the action is constantly being wrenched out of shape in order to express a politicised anger and to point up themes of oppression and so on in a kind of textbook way. It feels, in fact, very programmatic. (Brookes 39)

These remarks bring us back to Gregory Woods, for behind them, surely, is the suggestion that indirection is not necessarily evasion: that, on the contrary, it may be a way of establishing a culturally independent viewpoint.[3]

## CONFIRMING THE MODEL OF THE SELF-DESTRUCTIVE PERVERT?

I want to turn now to Oscar Moore's disturbingly frank and hugely controversial novel *A Matter of Life and Sex* (1992), which, in respect of homosexuality and AIDS, is undeniably writing of direct involvement, as its title indicates. Indeed, in the Joseph Cady sense, this writing is immersive, in that "the reader is thrust into a direct imaginative confrontation with the special horrors of AIDS and is required to deal with them with no relief provided by the writer" (Cady 244). It is also notable for its willingness, in Cady's words, "to defy the dominant culture directly and fully" (261) through its refusal to keep silent on a subject that a majority of people would prefer not to think about. But, as we have seen and as Cady concedes, writing of this kind has its risks as well as its merits. In any case, as I hope to show, the immersiveness of Moore's novel is quite different, in both expression and effect, from that of Monette's writing.

Structurally, *A Matter of Life and Sex* is a classic case of what Gregory Woods calls "before-and-after fiction." This is fiction in which the central character is first shown growing up, coming out, and enjoying "the sexual carnival of gay liberation in the 1970s" (*History of Gay Literature* 368). Then, at about the midway point of the novel, the AIDS epidemic arrives in the form of a distant rumor, but is soon experienced more palpably—a development that begins with the loss of friends and lovers, and ends perhaps with the death of the central character himself. This kind of fiction, then, follows what is, as Mars-Jones points out, the remorseless logic of the long AIDS narrative, which is constrained to allow a biographical and historical footnote (as the epidemic might be called, taking a long-distance view) to engulf whatever else is of interest in the story. However, *A Matter of Life and Sex* partly escapes this structural fix through its avoidance of strict chronology. Thus the novel opens with the letter from "Oscar Moore" (the novel's implied author and narrator) to Hugo's mother. From this the reader immediately learns the end of the story—Hugo's death from AIDS—and with this move the narrative is released at a stroke from its seemingly preordained shape, becoming free to place a different set of emphases on a story that is conventionally seen as laid down by fate. Moreover, this playing with chronology is maintained throughout the novel, the narrative skipping back and forth, from scenes at Hugo's final sickbed to critical episodes in his life. However, the freedom achieved in this way is only partial, of course, since the essential ground-plan of the long AIDS narrative, although rearranged, remains substantially in place.

Hence, as with AIDS writing in general, the central question that arises in respect of this novel is whether its effect—whatever its purpose—is to challenge or underwrite the dominant culture's view of the epidemic. Thus the form and tone of the novel suggest, at first glance, a cautionary tale or rake's progress, together with the conventional moral judgments that accompany such storytelling. But on closer inspection, what kind of caution is being given here, and to whom is it addressed? After all, from the opening words of the novel Hugo's lying and sex-obsession are shown as the inevitable outcome of his conventional suburban upbringing, as the natural, humanly sympathetic reaction to its dullness, repression, and hypocrisy: "Hugo was a liar. Of course, he lied to escape punishment and ended up being punished for lying, but he was also a fantasist whose lies invented a world where everything was extraordinary" (5). In other words, he lies not only because the culture he inhabits requires him to do so, but also because he needs to feed his naturally voracious and exuberant imagination.

Moreover, the tendency of this novel as a whole is to show that, given his character and sexuality, rebellion against the social and sexual codes of the dominant culture is the only course open to Hugo. He thus becomes habituated to sex in public toilets because this is the one form of sexual outlet available to him. His fumbling attempts to forge other forms of relationship meet only with rejection and betrayal. Sam, his best friend at school, breaks off their friendship as soon as he becomes aware of its basis in sexual attraction—attraction that the subtext of the letter he later sends to Hugo suggests might be mutual. Sam's admission, for instance, that he has spoken of the relationship "only in moods of spite which I deeply regret now" (79) hints at an internal insecurity, a fear of taint by association. But whether mutual or not, what the episode shows is that Hugo's finer feelings, his first adult intimations of erotic tenderness toward another human being, are crushed by this culturally induced homophobic reaction. Indeed, as the writing makes plain, the wounding he receives here is a permanent one: "He never stepped so far out of his shell for anybody again as he did for Sam. . . . Hugo from that time changed from the liar to the secret" (76).

This exposé of the psychological damage that a homophobic culture wreaks on a young, impressionable gay man is further developed in the episode of Hugo's relationship with Charlie. This episode reinforces what Hugo has already learned from his involvement with Sam: namely, the dangers of self-revelation and the need to keep his desires shrouded in secrecy and lies. In his relationship with Charlie, he opens up, drops his alias (David) in favor of his real name, and shows a natural impulse towards a better, purer, more trusting and generous way of life: "[Now David] was gone, Hugo felt relieved . . . He had taken one step towards the truth. . . . He had just cut his way through part of the mesh" (122). But Charlie is a man Hugo has met in a public toilet: in other words, a man whose life and relationships, like Hugo's, are shaped and stunted by the oppressions of a homophobic culture. For in such a milieu gay men learn to define themselves as they are defined in the culture generally—that is, by their sexual needs only. And even these needs, since they are not publicly recognized, must be satisfied furtively. Thus, what the whole episode poignantly dramatizes is the raw pain of looking for love in a world of undercover casual sex and transient relations.

But the novel also challenges the dominant culture in its critical presentation of Hugo's home environment and upbringing. Indeed, Hugo's self-destructive perversity (to describe his behavior from the viewpoint of the dominant culture) is shown as, in large part, the outcome of his parents' failure: failure to offer him understanding and support; failure to love one another; failure to function as rounded, compassionate human beings. Thus the moral bullying of Mrs Harvey, which bears down on all the family and receives no correction from her kindly but weak-willed husband, is revealed as the offspring of a bad conscience. Her inquisitorial prying, her insistence that her children tell her the truth about everything, stems, the novel suggests, from a hypocritical need to cover her own tracks; and this dishonesty is fully exposed when Hugo, not long before his death, accidentally finds out that she has had a secret lover.

Moreover, her moral outrage on reading the "secret" contents of her son's diary—in which he recounts his sexual adventures, describing his partners "by their bellies and chests and hair and how hot the sex was" (98)—points to a fundamental dishonesty in this mother–son relationship, and indeed in the family relations as a whole. First, Mrs Harvey lies about her discoveries. She does not admit that she has read Hugo's diary. She claims to have learned about his behavior by report: "You were seen on several occasions. Coming and going. It's a disgrace. You're nothing more than a filthy prostitute" (108). But, more important, there is her failure to confront squarely the issue of her son's sexuality, for her line of attack, here and elsewhere, suggests that the main bone of contention between herself and Hugo is the matter of his deception. In fact, neither she nor her husband is able to face up to the main point of their concern: namely, that their son enjoys having sex with men. Instead they allude to it indirectly, through a process of displacement. Indeed the whole family is afflicted by an inability to discuss sex and sexuality openly and honestly; and in this way it resembles the homophobic culture to which it belongs: a culture that is (I am arguing here) a central focus of the novel's critique.

What drives this novel, then, is anger and indignation at hypocrisy and repressive British attitudes. This is particularly clear from the letters that appear between its chapters, with their dry, satirical exposure of the dominant culture's slant on homosexuality and AIDS. Indeed the novel at times resembles Forster's *Maurice* in its bite and mordancy. The letter from Doctor Wilkinson to Hugo's mother, for instance, brings to mind—and may be an allusion to—the episode in Chapter 31 of Forster's novel where Maurice attempts to gain some understanding of his homosexuality by requesting a private consultation with Doctor Barry. For, as the letter reveals, Doctor Wilkinson's attitude to homosexuality, even if coped in more "enlightened" medical terminology, is based, like Doctor Barry's, on ignorance and prejudice. Behind his careful circumlocutions, after all, is an unspoken assumption that homosexuality is a lure that should be resisted. His belief that Hugo's lack of interest in heterosexual relations is "down to basic shyness," his admission that he still cherishes "hopes that Hugo will find himself a girlfriend" (157), and the implied doubt in his letter about whether or not Hugo's attraction to men is the result of an "incurable" defect of character (158), suggest a viewpoint not very far removed from the one that informs Doctor Barry's advice on hearing of Maurice's homosexual inclinations: "Now listen to me, Maurice, never let that evil hallucination, that temptation from the devil, occur to you again" (Forster 139).

Yet the novel also exemplifies the risks that Cady, White, and Mars-Jones identify as attaching to immersive AIDS writing generally: the risks of reinforcing the link between homosexuality and AIDS, of underwriting the dominant culture's view of the disease and, in short, of suggesting in subtext that "the wages of gay sin are death." Moreover, in *A Matter of Life and Sex* the problem is particularly acute since the novel's oppositional stance is counteracted by its fatalism. For instance, in the letter to Hugo's mother that opens the novel, "Oscar Moore" (the implied author of the "manuscript" that follows, and hence of the novel as a whole) writes, in a clear reference to AIDS: "All along he [Hugo] knew the sweets behind the glass were poisoned, but he enjoyed them too much to put them down" (2). Now, the question that immediately arises here is whether "Oscar Moore" is to be taken as a reliable witness and narrator. In other words, how close is his viewpoint to that of the novel's real author? Actually, there *are* suggestions in the writing that his letter and manuscript should be read with a degree of skepticism. First, if we are to believe the "Oscar Moore" whose signature appears at the end of this opening letter, Hugo was addicted to sex in public toilets long before there was any knowledge of AIDS. But, more tellingly, there is the admission in the opening paragraph of the manuscript that Hugo was a "liar" and a "fantasist" (5), for this immediately casts doubt on the accuracy and truth of what follows, much of which is presumably based on evidence provided by Hugo himself.

Nevertheless, "Oscar Moore" and Oscar Moore have the same name, a correspondence that implies an affinity of outlook. Moreover, in "PWA" (Person With AIDS), a regular column he wrote for the *Guardian* between 1994 and 1996, Moore refers to his novel as "an autobiography thinly disguised as a novel" (xxxii). Hugo, in other words, is Moore's alter ego, and "Oscar Moore" is simply a different projection of himself. This kinship makes it difficult to dissociate the fatalism of the novel from the viewpoint of its real author. For while there may be a degree of ironic detachment in Moore's view of himself, it is surely unlikely that he would tell his own harrowing and deeply felt story in such a way as entirely to disguise his true feelings about it. The novel suggests, rather, that Moore is using his framing devices not to distance himself from his life but to see it more fully: not to disguise his true feelings but to project them with more honesty and clarity.

I therefore take the remark about the poisoned sweets behind the glass to be an expression of Moore's own fatalism. Hugo, after all, is Moore's protagonist and second self; and we are told quite explicitly that "Hugo was a fatalist" (145). This fatalism pervades the whole novel. Hugo's reflections on his life and character, though punctuated with brief moments of excitement and celebration, are almost all gloomy, guilt-laden, and negative. Why, he wonders at one point, would anyone suppose him to have chosen his sexuality: "Who would have chosen this? All the hiding, all the covert watching, all the childlessness, all the expensive presents bought for other people's children" (144). Moreover, these thoughts culminate in a clinching statement of belief that reinforces the link between homosexuality and AIDS and coincides absolutely with the way both are seen from the viewpoint of the dominant culture: "It was a future with loneliness sewn into the seam and death woven into the fabric; unseen until too late, a single sinister thread" (144).

This fatalism counteracts the novel's oppositional force by turning the energies of the writing away from the oppressions of the dominant culture and into a sense of tragic destiny. Furthermore, within the fatalism, there is also, as I intimate above, an element of self-accusation, even though Hugo denies any sense of guilt, preferring to see his sex addiction as the responsibility of his libido: "He knew where the blame lay. It lay between his legs" (144). Thus the novel comes close at times to resembling the plain cautionary tale it appears to be at first sight: the simple, moralistic message that certain critics accuse it of being.[4] The effect of Hugo's guilt displacement, however, is to turn the story at other times into a doom-laden scenario in which morality, as in the novels of Thomas Hardy, is beside the point. For, in his self-examination, Hugo sees himself as a man trapped between a rock and a hard place. To enjoy sex, he concludes, is to take poison; yet to resist it is to deny the life instinct:

> Sex had been his making and his undoing. He had drunk too long, too far, too fast from the fountain and caught the germ that hid within the pipe. But he would have died of thirst had he not drunk. Sex was instilled in his blood like an addiction and it led him down the path to rack and ruin, laughing and gurgling all the way . . . (145; ellipsis in original)

But whether the tendency of the writing at these points is to self-accusation or to a sense of tragic destiny the effect is the same: namely, to underwrite the viewpoint of the dominant culture on homosexuality and AIDS.

In his challenging essay "Is the Rectum a Grave?" Leo Bersani gives further support to the thesis, already convincingly expounded by Simon Watney, that the AIDS epidemic, as well as being a medical emergency, "involves a crisis of representation" (*Policing Desire* 9). Thus he examines, with reference to what he sees as society's general aversion to sex, some of the ramifications of Watney's argument that the AIDS epidemic "is effectively being used as a pretext throughout the West to 'justify' calls for increasing legislation and regulation of those considered to be socially unacceptable" (*Policing Desire* 3)—a category that comprises not only male homosexuals, but also IV drug users, many of whom, as he points out, are already socially disadvantaged, being poor blacks and Hispanics. For Bersani, AIDS has literalized the link, as commonly perceived, between homosexuality and death, a link that derives from a notion of male homosexuality as involving the loss of the sense of male selfhood, of "the masculine ideal . . . of proud subjectivity" ("Rectum" 222). "Passive" anal sex in male–male relations, he argues, is imbued with a psychic, social, and political significance that relates to the abdication of male power. Moreover, just as venereal disease in the nineteenth century gave rise to "a fantasy of female sexuality as intrinsically diseased" (211), so AIDS in our time feeds a fantasy of gay men as self-destructive killers. Hence, to summarize in Bersani's own words, AIDS reinforces "the heterosexual association of anal sex with a self-annihilation originally and primarily identified with the fantasmatic mystery of an insatiable, unstoppable female sexuality"(222).

If the fatalism of *A Matter of Life and Sex,* as I have been arguing, undermines its oppositional stance, the ideas discussed in Bersani's essay suggest some other ways in which Moore's novel might be seen as adding to Watney's crisis of representation. Thus, in the first place, it could be said that the novel bolsters the widespread belief that homosexuality, HIV infection, and sexual promiscuity are inextricably, even causally, linked. Hugo's insistence that sex has been his "undoing," that it runs in his blood "like an addiction," brings to mind Bersani's discussion of nineteenth-century male fears and fantasies about female sexual insatiability, and therefore suggests that gay men are the source of HIV infection, rather than just one of the principal groups of carriers and victims of it. For just as the spread of syphilis in the nineteenth century, as Bersani points out, fostered a view of female sexuality as intrinsically diseased, so the current epidemic promotes a spectacle of homosexuality as intrinsically HIV infected. Hence, in these fantasies, promiscuity, as Bersani writes, "far from merely increasing the risk of infection, is the *sign of infection.* Women and gay men spread their legs with an unquenchable appetite for destruction" ("Rectum" 211).

But it could also be said that the novel contributes to damaging misrepresentations of the disease in the way it seems to set out, with willful perversity, to create a comprehensive stereotype of a "socially unacceptable" person with AIDS. Thus, in the reckless life he leads before the sickness begins to show itself, Hugo progresses from pornographic model to male hooker, associated roles that relate him to that nineteenth-century representation of prostitutes "as contaminated vessels, conveyancing 'female' venereal diseases to 'innocent' men" (Watney, *Policing Desire* 33–34). Moreover, the novel's slide into lurid darkness after the death of Chas underscores Hugo's role as self-destructive killer, for, as an IV drug user, shooting up and sharing his needles with Larry, he becomes another kind of "contaminated vessel." However, the homophobic fantasy of AIDS, as Bersani delineates it above, is given maximum reinforcement, in the climactic chapter of the novel, where, in the darkroom of a nightclub in New York, Hugo participates in the kind of "self-destructive" orgy of anonymous sex that figures in those paranoid responses to AIDS collected in Watney's *Policing Desire.* Bersani cites one such response from Richard Wallach of the New York State Supreme Court in Manhattan, who, in issuing the temporary restraining order that closed the New St. Marks Baths, remarked: "What a bathhouse like this sets up is the orgiastic behavior of multiple partners, one after the other, where in five minutes you can have five contacts" ("Rectum" 199).

*A Matter of Life and Sex,* then, is an odd mixture of attitudes, for its biting social critique, its defiant radical edge, and its black humor are undercut by its sense of tragic destiny. Like Monette's *Love Alone,* it surrenders itself, through immersiveness, to the immediacy of its anger and pain, confronting the world's denial with terrifying honesty, yet in the very intensity of that confrontation it necessarily sacrifices historical perspective and detachment. As we have seen, Joseph Cady defends immersive AIDS writing both for "its willingness to defy the dominant culture directly and fully" and for "its faithfulness to the emotional and social anguish of people affected by AIDS" (261). However, there is good reason to feel that the immersiveness of Moore's novel does not so much defy the dominant culture as confirm its worst prejudices; and moreover that its faithfulness to the emotional and social anguish of people affected by AIDS (unlike that of Monette's *Love Alone*, for instance) gives precious little hope and support to those people as readers.

## FINDING A TRUER PICTURE

> I struggled to turn Aids into a countersubject, to give it an appropriate status, neither ignored nor holding centre stage. That seemed the best way of rendering HIV its due, no less and no more.
>
> —Adam Mars-Jones, *Monopolies of Loss*

Is the suppression of the word *AIDS*, in fiction about the epidemic, evidence of collaboration with the larger cultural denial of the disease or a defensible strategy for divesting the subject of damaging cultural connotations? Joseph Cady takes the former view, while Adam Mars-Jones, explaining the absence of the word in his own AIDS fiction, appears to take the latter. Thus Cady, using this fiction to substantiate his own argument, writes: "The narrator of Mars-Jones's 'Slim,' for instance, announces at the start that 'I don't use that word. I've heard it enough. So I've taken it out of circulation, just here, just at home'; instead he substitutes the title word, the colloquial African term for AIDS whose implication of mere dieting blurs the ruinous realities of the disease" (261). Mars-Jones, on the other hand, admits that it was at his suggestion that the word *AIDS* did not appear in *The Darker Proof* (the collection of short stories by himself and Edmund White) and defends the decision as a necessary disempowering device. He also reports that the move was successful, since after the publication of the book he found that he could use the word "without a qualm" (*Monopolies* 4).

The Darker Proof reflects the belief of its authors that immersive writing encourages paranoia and a sense of hopeless defeat through an exclusive focus on AIDS that concentrates on immediacy and misses the wider view. In the Preface to *Love Alone*, for instance, Paul Monette writes that he wants his poems "to allow no escape, like a hospital room, or indeed a mortal illness" (xii); and Joseph Cady, while allowing for the attendant risks, approves this tactic as a way of unsettling the complacent reader. Part of the problem with this argument, however, is that the reader of AIDS literature is unlikely to be complacent, as Cady himself acknowledges in a parenthetic qualifier. A much stronger objection, however, is that this same reader understandably and legitimately *needs* some means of escape—escape, that is, in the form of support, encouragement, affirmation. Furthermore, this is a need that Monette, as if to thwart his own purpose, recognizes and attempts to meet. Thus, in *Love Alone*, his emphasis on the devastation brought by the disease is offset by an attempt to give sustenance to those stranded in the wreckage, and especially to his community of fellow gay men. In these poems the general sense of havoc is interspersed with passages that show a defiant attitude to the forces of gay oppression, and also with moments intended to fortify the spirit of people affected by AIDS by alleviating their feelings of isolation. In the final poem of the sequence, "Brother of the Mount of Olives," for instance, Monette, reconstructing an episode from his life with Rog, tells of their visit to a Benedictine monastery while on holiday in Italy, where they have an almost mystical experience of belonging to a worldwide and long-established community of gay men; and this epiphany, this recovered moment of shared happiness, is offered as a "historical, public and private [occasion] to take heart" (Cady 252).

Thus Monette's inclination "to allow no escape" is contradicted by his effort to offer the reader these moments of consolation and encouragement. Cady again recognizes the problem, however, and seeks to resolve it within the terms of his general argument. He admits that this heartening episode is "framed by representations of loss and discord in the poem as a whole," and that Monette "sustains *Love Alone*'s overall note of wreckage even in the book's most 'solidifying' poem" (252). This is because Monette sees his foremost duty, he suggests, as that of "relentlessly immersing [his denying readership] in the disease's devastation" (253), and hence support, encouragement, and affirmation must in the end give way to the more pressing need to document the havoc of AIDS. This sense of priority wins Cady's approval for the reasons given above: that is, for "its willingness to defy the dominant culture directly and fully and its faithfulness to the emotional and social anguish of people affected by AIDS." Yet his warning about the risk of immersive writing—that "its raw embodiment of the wreckage of AIDS could defeat its chief purpose" (261)—is in this case a telling one, for the contradictoriness of Monette's approach is self-canceling: its "blunt harrowings and wrenchings" (261) may, by the end of the sequence, have driven the denying reader away, leaving Monette's community of fellow gay men and others affected by AIDS still mired in confusion and chaos.

In Mars-Jones's fiction, on the other hand, the approach to AIDS is indirect and counterimmersive, and thus diametrically opposed to that of *Love Alone*. So are his stories in *The Darker Proof*—to judge according to the harsh alternatives of Suzanne Poirier—evasive? Moreover, are they, as Cady's account of counterimmersive writing suggests, "rooted in a lingering depression about homosexuality and in stereotyped understandings of it" (258)? I want to argue here that they are neither—indeed, that they manage, through the very indirection of which they stand accused, to counter both denial and a sense of apocalyptic doom. For the primary focus of these stories is not disease but people; not death from AIDS but ways of living with it and perhaps through it; not cultural annihilation but cultural survival. In short, theirs is an alternative approach to the epidemic, neither evasive (like Holleran's) nor fatalistic (like Moore's) nor yet divided and self-defeating (like Monette's).

With reference to his general strategy in *The Darker Proof*, Mars-Jones writes: "The programme of my four stories was, first, to look directly at Aids—with 'Slim'—and then to edge it into the background. I wanted to crown HIV with attention and then work to dethrone it" (*Monopolies* 4). This edging into the background, then, is progressive, for with each story in the sequence the reference to AIDS becomes more oblique. Thus, after the comparative directness of "Slim," "An Executor" is concerned less with Charles's death from AIDS than with the difficulty of carrying out his instructions as to the disposal of his property. But AIDS is edged even further into the background in "A Small Spade," the story that follows, for here the center of attention is a gay weekend in Brighton, a generally enjoyable break for Bernard and Neil, interrupted on occasion by poignant reminders of Neil's antibody status. In "The Brake," however, the status of AIDS is reduced to an absolute minimum, for here we catch just a glimpse of it toward the end of the story, where it hovers in the wings, a mere (if ominous and disturbing) rumor from America that is never allowed star billing.

Yet this treatment of AIDS is not evasive. On the contrary, it replaces negativity and reaction with a positive, proactive approach, for it purposely sets out to give AIDS an "appropriate status." Cady contends that counter-immersive AIDS writing "typically focuses on characters or speakers who are in various degrees of denial about AIDS themselves" (244), although his main complaint is that such writing "does not press its audience to experience the subject in any way that significantly differs from its characters' stance" (257). But except in "The Brake," where the stance of the central character is in any case countered by the narrator's point of view, the characters in these stories of Mars-Jones are not in denial about AIDS. To be sure, they confront the extremity of their situation, like the stories themselves, with a very English kind of restraint; but this, as I hope to show, is not necessarily a denying response.

Gareth, the central character in "An Executor," for instance, is certainly not in denial, and a large part of the story is concerned with his need to confront the denial of others. This becomes especially evident in the episode at Charles's funeral service where Charles's brother, on behalf of the family, requests him not to mention the cause of death—a request that carries with it the suggestion that Gareth, for the sake of the family, should also keep silent about the nature of his relationship with Charles. Gareth confronts this denial first by turning down the invitation to the funeral itself and then by talking loudly about Charles with Amanda, a nondenying guest at the postfuneral buffet lunch. Amanda is an actress "with a mane of hair and huge hoop earrings" (49), who, in daring to appear at the event in the very boots she has worn on a sponsored walk to assist research into AIDS, boldly confronts the denial of the other guests and flamboyantly defies "the taboo laid on Gareth" by Charles's brother and family (50). Gareth is drawn to her, if somewhat nervously, for this very reason: he finds her company supportive and her rebelliousness exhilarating precisely because there is "a sort of satisfaction to be had . . . in defying human pressure, after months spent railing against nature's strong extinguishing push" (50).

Nor is there any sense of denial in Bernard and Neil, the central characters of "A Small Spade." Indeed, so far from being evasive, this pair is shown as managing the fact of Neil's HIV status with level-headed realism and quiet responsibility. Thus their nonfatalistic approach to the disease is indicated in the opening page of the story by the circumstances of their meeting: "The place was a pub in Nine Elms which hosted an evening, every two weeks, for people who had been exposed to a virus" (67). For their attendance at a support group meeting of this sort suggests an attitude to the disease that neither discounts the risks nor exaggerates them, that neither wallows in nostalgic illusion nor in a sense of romantic doom. It implies a view of the epidemic that recognizes that no way of life is risk-free; that not all sexual activity, whatever the dangers of the virus, is life-threatening; that, in short, allows for the eroticization of safer sex. "[Those] evenings," Bernard muses, "were for anyone who put a high priority on healthy sexual living" (67–68).

Moreover, "A Small Spade" refuses to collude with the denying reader in other ways, since Bernard and Neil, like Gareth in "An Executor," are also shown as having a need to confront ignorance and denial wherever they find it. In the restaurant where they have dinner, for instance, both men are moved to anger by a group of fellow diners whose uninformed ideas about the disease they overhear. But Bernard decides not to challenge them, sensing that they would simply resent any violation of their right to bigotry, and that the action would prove counterproductive. In the hospital, however, he does confront the doctor who is preparing to remove the splinter from Neil's finger, since her remarks suggest to him that she is reluctant to treat someone who is antibody-positive; and although the story suggests that he has misunderstood her and is therefore tilting at windmills, his confrontational approach to what he perceives as her lack of professionalism makes it clear that he and Neil, so far from being in denial, are constantly engaged in a quiet kind of AIDS activism: "I think anybody who doesn't work with people who are antibody-positive should be sacked on the spot, not because they're prejudiced but because they must be incompetent to be taking any risks" (115).

In contrast, the story called "The Brake" focuses on Gregory, who by implication *is* in denial about AIDS. But what matters here, surely, is the narrative standpoint, for in this story Gregory and the culture of denial he inhabits are viewed with an ironic eye and critical detachment. Thus the story dryly comments on the way that Gregory's friends defend themselves and excuse their risk taking with absurd self-justifications: "I could live like a saint and still be run over by a bus" (158). In similar scathing fashion, it shows how AIDS, in the relatively early days of the disease, was seen in Britain as a specifically American problem. Thus Gregory witnesses an incident in a bar off Oxford Street where a handsome young American is given the cold shoulder because his loudly advertised Americanness casts him in the role of alien invader. Although Gregory himself condemns this irrational behavior, the denial of the friend to whom he relates the incident is witheringly exposed: "He [the friend] spoke as if the virus—it had to be a virus, didn't it? Didn't everything point to that?—would be refused a visa by the authorities when it applied for one, and that would be that" (158).[5]

Moreover, there is nothing in these stories to suggest that they are "rooted in a lingering depression about homosexuality and in stereotyped understandings of it," to recall Cady's critical analysis of counterimmersive writing. On the contrary, stress is laid on the affirmative, assertive, defiant qualities of the characters and their relationships. In "An Executor," for instance, Gareth opposes a suppressed desire he detects in Charles "to backslide into reconciliation with his family": Charles's family are Catholic, and Gareth is only too aware that, in such circumstances and with the knowledge that one has a fatal illness, a need to be closer to family brings with it a growing temptation "to relapse into absolution" (32). Indeed, this tension is the central conflict of the story, for against the sense of closure and betrayal that Charles's late decision to be received back into the Catholic Church brings with it, Gareth struggles to celebrate the alternative meaning of his friend's life, to keep alive and set free what family and Catholicism seek to obliterate. This is the significance of his solution to the problem of how to dispose of Charles's "kinky relics" (23), dramatized in the final pages of the story. For here his generous impulse in allowing Andrew Gould, a man he detests, to lay claim to some items of leather gear (souvenirs of former motorcycling days that would offend Charles's mother if discovered in the flat) stems from a realization that any attempt on his part to impose meaning on his friend's life would be to collude with the powers that wish to obliterate that life. He sees, in fact, that any attempt "to stamp the gesture with his meaning, and no other, was more in the nature of a murder than a resurrection" (63).

Nor is there anything depressing or stereotyped about the tenderly evoked love relationship of Neil and Bernard in "A Small Spade." The story ends on a note of sudden poignancy, but this derives not from the attitudes of the characters nor from the nature of their relationship but from the distress and potential heartbreak of the illness that threatens them: "A tiled corridor filled with doctors and nurses opened off every room he would ever share with Neil" (118). What characterizes this relationship is the sense of protective, near-parental concern the two show for each other. In bed, for instance, after their nightclub visit, Bernard asks "Neil . . . have you had a piss since we got back?" in the manner of a father checking his child's daily program; and when Bernard cries out in his sleep, Neil puts his arm around him and murmurs "I'm here" (102–03). Indeed, these two characters are markedly independent and self-possessed in their attitudes, for they do not concede to the dominant culture by conforming to stereotype, nor do they react to it through the inversions and ironies of "camp." They are thus reflections of the author's own explicit viewpoint, for Mars-Jones writes that he hopes his stories "are free of fatalism even when they refer to fate, that they belong, rather to a tradition of Stoicism" (*Monopolies* 6). This hope is certainly realized in "A Small Spade," where Neil and Bernard keep their feelings under strict control, even at times of acute anxiety. In this story, feeling is intimated rather than stated, and often not in what the characters themselves say or do but in the interventions of the narrator: "It was as if he had been pierced in a tender place which he had thought adequately defended, by a second splinter, not visible" (119).

"The Brake," however, again provides a different and more oblique angle of vision in that it centers on a character who is not directly affected by AIDS and who in some respects *is* representative of the general cultural denial of the disease. Yet there is no suggestion in this story of complicity with this denial, nor indeed, where homosexuality and AIDS are concerned, with the dominant culture generally. This is not just a matter of narrative standpoint, for the story's independent stance is also finally embodied in this central character, Greg, whose own independence of mind is quickly established in the opening pages. On his first visit to a gay bar, for instance, Greg stands very still and keeps his eyes "fixed firmly on his beer glass," and even on later visits, he is "full of suspicion" and unwilling to give his real name (127). Moreover, the small provincial circle of gay men to whom he is introduced are puzzled by him because he has "none of the pliability of personality they [value] in someone of his age" (130).

In London, he eschews fashion, invents a number of schemes to tackle his sexual dysfunction, and pursues architecture as a means of making a living rather than a career, since his eccentricity, nonconformity, and reluctance to be "tied down" tempt him "to remain uncommitted for ever" (143). Meanwhile, he ignores his doctor's advice about burning the candle at both ends and the need to put a brake on his way of life: "You can have a good time with your . . . cock . . . or you can eat too much, drink too much, smoke a lot, take drugs. But you can't do both" (139). Then, toward the end of the story, he is shaken out of his complacency when he experiences a mild heart attack. He thus moves from a position of denial to one of greater awareness and more realistic responsibility. This movement parallels the way gay men have experienced and responded to AIDS in general, but in particular it mirrors the experience and response of gay men in Britain. So although "The Brake" is not directly concerned with AIDS, it is informed by the epidemic, to which it alludes metaphorically. The essential point, however, is that Greg, as the embodiment of the story's stance on AIDS, emerges as a strong, likeable individualist, who is in no way reliant on the dominant culture. As an independent character, capable of development, he learns from his experience and eventually overcomes his denying impulse.

The indirection of these stories, then—to summarize my argument here—is not evasive, nor does their counterimmersiveness collude with the wider cultural denial of AIDS. Rather, they quite deliberately take an oblique approach to their subject in order to see it within a broader context and to find "a truer picture." Here, AIDS is not viewed as an inextricable part of homosexuality, and hence as further confirmation of a fatal flaw in the physical makeup of gay men. Nor is it seen as an irrelevance, for the writing does not shirk its responsibility to show the sense of change and loss that has resulted from the epidemic. So, although individuals are lost to AIDS in these stories, the underlying emphasis here is on cultural survival, and on a final redemptive vision that rescues and reaffirms "the endangered gains of gay liberation."

## BEARING WITNESS TO THE CULTURAL MOMENT

> Should I record my fears obliquely or directly, or should I defy them? Is it more heroic to drop whatever I was doing and look disease in the eye or should I continue going in the same direction as before, though with a new consecration? Is it a hateful concession to the disease even to acknowledge its existence? Should I pretend Olympian indifference to it? Or should I admit to myself, "Look, kid, you're scared shitless and that's your material"?
>
> —Edmund White, "Esthetics and Loss"

I return at the end of this study to the writer with whom I began. In respect of my central inquiry this is appropriate, for the stories by Edmund White in *The Darker Proof* are a further wrestling with the conflict explored in *Forgetting Elena*. White's first novel, as we saw, immediately engages with the central theme of gay male fiction since Stonewall: the conflict between gay sensibility and gay politics; between the impulse to assimilate to the dominant culture and the need to celebrate an independent identity. In White's stories about the AIDS crisis, this conflict is still the central focus of the writing, although the novel and the stories reflect different stages in the writer's engagement with it. Thus *Elena* ends with an act of betrayal, and the protagonist's discovery that he is the prince of the island community depicted in the novel ("a closed society that has allowed the cult of beauty to replace genuine moral concerns") is a dramatization of White's own internal conflict, split allegiance, and sense of guilt. Here, surrender to the island's aesthetic code is presented as a process whereby hard political and moral decisions are resolved in favor of personal gratification and convenient self-interest. In the short stories, on the other hand, the conflict is resolved differently, for here there is no surrender to the dominant culture and gay identity is reasserted in a context in which AIDS itself figures as an oracular utterance offering possibilities of renewal to gay men through new modes of intimacy and sociality.

The three stories by White that appeared together for the first time in the second edition of *The Darker Proof* (1988)—"An Oracle," "Palace Days," and "Running on Empty"—reflect gay life in the mid-eighties (or at least a segment of it, since the central characters here are mostly affluent American WASPs) and are overshadowed by the presence of AIDS.[6] But in accordance with White's belief that there is more to gay culture than disease, they address the crisis sometimes directly and sometimes obliquely; and their common theme is survival. The characters in these stories, like the culture they inhabit, are positioned, in Richard Dellamora's words, "between one existence and another yet to be envisaged," a crisis deepened by the fact that the onset of AIDS in 1981 marked a break with a way of life that, although a fairly recent formation, had quickly established itself and "come to be taken for granted as normal" (Dellamora 98–99).[7]

But this new existence, although "yet to be envisaged," is clearly not a return to a way of life based on heterosexual patterns of living. Indeed, the uneasy relations with home and family that the characters in these stories experience (even when mixed with feelings of regret, resentment, exclusion, and loss) are founded on a perception of the impossibility of return, and hence on an attitude of realistic and deliberate rejection. In White's stories illness and bereavement become the agents of a learning process that reveals the narrowness and inadequacy of the traditional concepts of home and family, and the life-diminishing effect of a lifestyle based on such concepts. At the same time, intimacy between men is valued as an extension of friendship, a means of forging a new kind of homosociality. However unpromising, even bleak, the contexts in which they appear, White's characters, through the very extremity of their situation, are forced to question and extend the meaning of their lives, to find home and family elsewhere. Returning to what, as we have seen, is a central theme in gay male writing since Stonewall, these stories present a challenge to that cozy view of traditional domesticity and sentimental attachment to heterosexist values that underpins Holleran's fiction.

Thus, in "Running on Empty," Luke's need in his illness to re-establish links with his family is accompanied by an acute fear of losing his independence from it, of "becoming critically ill here in Texas" (308). From the opening pages Paris takes on symbolic significance as Luke's spiritual home and the center of his independent, freewheeling lifestyle. In this opening scene Paris is instantly embodied in the healthy, good-looking, youthful Sylvain, whom Luke meets, along with Sister Julia, on his flight to New York. But the story moves from the civilized tolerance of this opening scene, in which the three interlocutors openly discuss and enjoy their differences, to an ambience in which differences—between Baptist and Catholic, gay and straight, the sick and the healthy—are dogmatically asserted, perceived as a threat, and viewed in accordance with strict moral judgments. Hence, holding on to Paris and the ideal it represents is Luke's means of protecting himself from the life-denying spirit of Texas, from the meanness, malice, and *Schadenfreude* of his family. Moreover he remains loyal to this ideal and is sustained by it even when, in the final pages, it has shrunk, poignantly, to a patch of damp soil, a brown stain in the dust.

In Texas the sympathy between Luke and his Baptist missionary cousin Beth is not quite strong enough to surmount the cultural differences between them. Her restraint and tact cannot quite disguise her moral disapproval: "She loved family, and he was family, even if he was a sinner lost—damned, for he'd told her ten years ago about his vice" (295). But damaging though this difference is, what finally drives a wedge between them is Luke's illness, which puts his side of the argument in their moral debate, his choice of lifestyle, at a disadvantage, since it allows Beth to imagine he is having "to pay for his follies with his life" (307). Beth is ultimately incapable of the kind of tact that White identifies in his essay "Esthetics and Loss": the kind of tact that does not "let the disease stand for other things"; that recognizes that "how someone dies says nothing about how he lived"; that does not read "illness as metaphor" (216).

However, though Luke weeps bitter tears of humiliation that a virus has been permitted to win an argument, ultimately the story vindicates his stance in not conceding this victory. In his nocturnal jog Luke relieves his anger and frustration through a reassertion of his identity and independence, and his review of his life becomes a self-validating exercise in which he refuses to deny his sexuality or lifestyle. His search for the spot where "the redhead had pissed a brown circle" and his touching the dirt to his lips in an attempt "to recuperate his past if not his health" is a small act of private courage and defiance that gives him a new burst of energy. Moreover his reflections on human relations are a stoical defense of that shared social and sexual intimacy that he has sought with working men all his life—on building sites, in gyms, bars, and bowling alleys: "the impermanence of sexual possession was a better school than most for the way life would flow through your hands" (309).[8]

Some of White's remarks in an interview with myself shed light on this story and on the other stories in this collection:

> I think that there have been two great strains in gay politics since Stonewall. One is assimilationism, which is the David Leavitt brand—and you see a lot of it now in the work of these new gay conservatives, like Andrew Sullivan and Bruce Bawer. Their effort is to say: "Well, really we should disband. There's no longer any reason for gays to be a political entity, or even a cultural entity. We should just meld back into the crowd. We have achieved what we want, which is to be accepted, and now we should become ordinary bourgeois householders

like everybody else, with our adopted children and our Volkswagen or
whatever" . . . At the other extreme is someone like Martin Duberman,
who feels that gays have a special mission and can teach heterosexual
society something, that they're on the cutting edge of psycho-sexual
and cultural exploration, that there are new forms of association, new
forms of love or freedom from possessiveness and jealousy unique to
gay society. (Brookes 37–38)

If, as we saw, the assimilationist strain in Leavitt's fiction is a more complex matter than these remarks allow, it is true that he examines the lives
of his characters broadly from within the framework of traditional family
and literary values. White's fiction, on the other hand, representing the
opposing strain, lays stress on the distinctiveness, otherness, uniqueness of
gay experience. In this respect, and particularly in their celebration of gay
eroticism and homosociality, his stories have an affinity with the poetry
of Thom Gunn. In his collection *The Passages of Joy* (1982), for instance,
Gunn is often trying to capture the special quality of gay life—the distinctive atmosphere of a gay bar, the unique aura of gay desire—and in the final
section of *The Man with Night Sweats* (1992), the poems, like White's stories in *The Darker Proof* and the later collection *Skinned Alive,* are elegies
for friends that concentrate on the particular quality of gay friendship.

In White's stories, then, the search for new forms of association in the
era of AIDS must not be abandoned. Indeed, as the crisis deepens, this
search becomes all the more necessary, urgent and inevitable. Thus Mark
in "Palace Days," like Luke in "Running on Empty," is forced to review
and change his life, to seek new ways of relating, ways of surviving. Survival is conceivable only within the context in which he finds himself; there
can be no return to home and family. Like Luke, he has a dread of losing
his independence; he would rather "kill himself beside the Ganges" than
"end up back home in Charlottesville. . . . to be pitied by his father's Baptist kin" (228). "Home," for him and Ned, is essentially that New York gay
male culture of the seventies that finds its symbolic expression, the story
suggests, in the Robbins–Balanchine ballets presented at the New York
State Theater: ballets "in the elaborate *enchainements*" of which "we, yes,
*we* Americans saw . . . a radiant vision of society" (234). When this home
is threatened they seek it elsewhere, although in their AIDS-haunted world
"home" is becoming an increasingly elusive idea, a dwindling concept. He
and Ned move to Paris because "they hoped the party would go on in
Europe as it had before in the States" (203); and the word *party* here points
to that attitude of privileged self-indulgence, typical of a certain class of
American gay male in the previous decade, that White castigates in *States
of Desire* and elsewhere as a betrayal of Stonewall and liberationist ideals.
It suggests, too, that White's treatment of the AIDS crisis in these stories
is in part an engagement with the Forsterian concept of the undeveloped
heart—a consideration I return to below.

The symbolic significance of Paris in this story—unlike in "Running on Empty"—is ambiguous. For at the heart of its civilized tolerance there is a cold indifference; its charm is seductive, but not spiritually nourishing. It seems to stand for that idea of "Europe" that exists only in the American imagination: that venerating view of an older civilization that in White's novel *Caracole* expands into a nightmare of corruption and intrigue. Symbolically it is opposed to the radiant vision of society embodied in the Robbins–Balanchine ballets. This vision represents the hope and promise of the New World, the American dream of progress and enlightenment, supremely embodied in Stravinsky's *Apollo*, which by extension includes the hope and promise of the gay movement. The significance of these ballets is underlined by *Violin Concerto*, the other work that Mark and Ned see at the Paris opera house, the last movement of which "was clearly both Stravinsky's and Balanchine's homage to the square dance" (234). Together with Robbins's *Dances at a Gathering*, they evoke for Mark that American ideal of community life—that dream of a society with a just and fair democracy, an unsophisticated "goodness"—that stands in contrast to Parisian disillusion and world-weariness. As he watches them and the bored Parisian response, Mark is reminded not only of the home he has lost but of the vanished ideals of the gay movement, betrayed and abandoned in the panic and aftermath of the AIDS crisis: "Mark wept at this old mirror, leprous with flaking silver, that was being held up to reflect the straight young features of Balanchine's art" (234).

"It has been suggested," writes Soshana Felman, "that testimony is the literary—or discursive—mode par excellence of our times" (Felman and Laub 5). As with the other traumas of the twentieth century, there has been at the heart of the AIDS epidemic a "crisis of truth," which, "larger, more profound [and] less definable" than that which obtains in a legal context, has brought testimony "to the fore in contemporary cultural narrative" (6). Post-AIDS gay fiction has been faced with an enormous responsibility, so great and many have been the needs it has been required to meet. "Written by anguished writers for readers in disarray" (to recall White's words) it can be compared only to other extreme categories of writing: "Holocaust literature, exiles' literature, convicts' literature—these are the only possible parallels that spring to mind" (*Burning Library* 283). To be sure, Felman's discussion of Camus's *The Plague*, which alludes to the Holocaust and to "a radical human condition of exposure and vulnerability" (5), does not refer directly to AIDS. Nevertheless, it suggests, by extension, that Camus's metaphorical use of disease could be read as a pre-echo of "gay plague." It also suggests that post-AIDS gay literature has been in the position of Camus's physician-narrator, Dr. Bernard Rieux, who decides that it is "up to him to speak for all . . . [to] bear witness in favor of those plague-stricken people; so that some memorial of the injustice done them might endure" (quoted in Felman and Laub 4).

In "An Oracle," White, like Camus in *The Plague,* tries to comprehend the historical dimension of his testimony. "An Oracle" is the story of Ray, who accepts the offer of a holiday in Crete in an attempt to reorient himself after the death from AIDS of his long-term partner, George. Here, the setting puts contemporary trauma into historical perspective, for in Crete it is not only Ray's sexuality that is reinterpreted within a Greek context—a context that comprises "a number of different social formations . . . urban and rural modern Greek, Homeric, classical Athenian, Minoan, Dorian, and Hellenistic" (Dellamora 103)—but also his personal crisis and state of mourning. Ray experiences this crisis in terms of a loss of self ("'You must look out for yourself,' George had always said. But what self?" [243]); and this loss of identity following the death of George reflects the way gay identity, in a time of gay plague, is under great pressure. Indeed, Ray's crisis is that of the gay movement generally. Of course the stigma of AIDS, which has driven gay men to question "whether they want to go on defining themselves at all by their sexuality" ("Esthetics and Loss" 214), has been the main cause of this pressure. But there has been an additional factor, for the epidemic, as I have stressed throughout this study, has been accompanied by developments in poststructuralist ways of thinking that have been as threatening to the notion of gay identity as the epidemic itself. Thus, though notions of unitary identity have been necessary in post-Stonewall gay politics for the creation of a movement, one project of deconstructive theory is to show that an apparently integral entity such as "the self" is marked by internal contradictions.

In approaching this story and the crisis it represents, Richard Dellamora makes use of Foucault's *History of Sexuality* and Derrida's essay "Of An Apocalyptic Tone Recently Adopted in Philosophy." In particular, he focuses on Derrida's suggestion that the attack on the notion of unitary identity that characterizes one aspect of the deconstructive project requires supplement by a second or affirmative phase "that enables the subject in distress to begin to make the gains that are possible only when one begins to differ from one's customary sense of self" (Dellamora 100). For Derrida, such disruption of self-identity is an oracle, and occurs when "the tone of another . . . [comes] at no matter what moment to interrupt a familiar tonality" (quoted in Dellamora 100). In refusing to specify who "another" might be, however, Derrida leaves unspoken the relevance of affirmative deconstruction to particular groups. Hence the principal thrust of White's story, Dellamora suggests, is to make this relevance clear: "By siting the possibility of oracular utterance within the history of gay existence at a moment that is fraught with suffering, confusion, and anxiety, White supplements Derrida's reflections with others that open upon the possibilities of personal and social renewal" (101).

As White outlines it, Ray's career runs parallel to and is hence representative of recent American gay history, both before and after Stonewall. Thus his "marriage" to George is presented as a betrayal of the ideals he had once held as a gay activist in the early seventies, since it is semicloseted and partly based, despite his "ideological horror" (249) of such an arrangement, on the role-playing heterosexual model. Moreover he is denied the possibility of fully mourning George's loss, since his current mode of gay existence is not one within which George's death from AIDS can be fully acknowledged. He cannot speak of it to his boss, Helen, for instance. His story is therefore a dramatization of the distress felt by the gay movement from the dual onslaught of the AIDS crisis and the Foucauldian critique of gay identity. However it also echoes Derrida in pointing up the need for the deconstructive project to be followed by a supplementary phase of affirmation; and, again like Derrida, it asserts the gains that can result from an oracular disruption of self-identity.

One way in which Ray's customary sense of self becomes disrupted is through his reading of Loring M. Danforth's book *The Death Rituals of Rural Greece,* and in particular the account in that book of a Greek mother's loss of her daughter. Though Ray draws inappropriate analogies between this woman's experience and his own, it does prompt him to reflect on his responsibility, and that of other gay men, to women who mourn. Moreover, it affords him an insight into the situation of women generally, and particularly of women who mourn women, whose position *does* partly resemble his own, in that their loss, lacking recognized forms of expression, forces them to invent ways of showing the meaning of their relationship to the person who has died. It is a necessary insight and one that opens up the possibility of personal and social renewal in Ray, whose "marriage" to George has blunted his sensitivity to others and seduced him into a privileged male lifestyle of culture and affluence. Though Betty is Ray's "best friend" (239), for instance, his inability to communicate his feelings to her suggests that the self-identity he has acquired within the Ray–George partnership has become a block on his personal and social development. Indeed his relations with Betty intimate an anxiety about gender inversion indicated elsewhere in the story: being too close to her might seem to confirm his role as George's "doll" (250), a perceived identity that manages to offend both his political conscience—his rejection of role-playing—and his "'phallocratic' hang-up" (246)—his need to be socially and sexually on top.

In this story White implicitly questions the post-Stonewall concept of gay identity by exposing the narrowness of its focus. Thus the narrative continually undermines Ray's self-understanding by laying stress on difference: on different constructions of sexuality, different male–male traditions and sexual practices across time and space. In his involvement with Marco, Ray finds himself at a point where these differences converge, since there are implications within the relationship of many different patterns of male intimacy. However, the possibilities for growth suggested by this convergence are initially blocked for Ray, since the cash nexus of his relationship with Marco repeats the pattern of his earlier life with George.

"Look out for yourself," the refrain that returns throughout the story with ever-changing meaning, is, as delivered by George on its first appearance, an injunction to get a good job, to provide for oneself materially. This meaning of the refrain and its corrupting influence on Ray is further underlined in the passage that satirically reveals the source of the couple's material prosperity. George, for instance, specializes in expensive face-lifts for "one major corporation after another" (240), while Ray has accepted a job found for him by George. This is a "gig" in public relations for Amalgamated Anodynes, a dubious corporation that has "a lousy record with women and minorities" and that had once "produced a fabric for children's wear that had turned out to be flammable" (244). In short, their employment reflects their complicity in "a late capitalist 'we' contoured along lines of race, gender, nationality, and class" (Dellamora 104).

Ray's sense that this visit to Crete will help him "escape, start something new or transpose his old boyhood goals and values into a new key, the Dorian mode, say"—indeed, that everything in Crete is conspiring to "re-orient him, repatriate him" (280)—is evidence of his awareness that his life has taken a wrong turning. Yet as an effect of his cultural conditioning, he fails to recognize differences and nurtures a fantasy of establishing a relationship with Marco based on the pattern (and specifically on a reverse or mirror image) of his "marriage" to George. However, a means of escape is at least suggested by his encounter with Homer: for Homer, as the name indicates, is the character in the story who best understands and respects these differences. Thus, in his platonic friendship with this sixty-year old Classics professor, Ray is made aware of his insularity and alerted to the possibilities of cross-cultural fertilization. The gulf that separates Ray from Marco and from male–male traditions in modern Greece is illuminated, Dellamora suggests, by Foucault's account in *The Use of Pleasure* (Volume 2 of *The History of Sexuality*) of the patterns of sexual relations in ancient Greece, where the classic model of pederastic love is shown to be an essentially ethical tradition: a tradition in which "the uses of the pleasures" are codified so as to produce an individual who is "an ethical subject of sexual conduct" (32). As Dellamora points out, although Foucault does not offer this tradition as an alternative to contemporary modes of gay existence, he does suggest that the problem the Greeks had with the relations between ethics and aesthetics (that is, between moral considerations and the pleasure principle) demands attention and promises to be of some use in current gay self-reflection:

> Recent liberation movements suffer from the fact that they cannot find any principle on which to base the elaboration of a new ethics. They need an ethics, but they cannot find any other ethics than an ethics founded on so-called scientific knowledge of what the self is, what desire is, what the unconscious is, and so on. I am struck by this similarity of problems. ("On the Genealogy of Ethics" 343)

In Foucault's account, the classic model of pederastic love is based on respect for "the virility of the adolescent" and for "his future status as a free man" (*Use of Pleasure* 252). In becoming master of his pleasure, the adult male has to allow for "the other's freedom . . . in the true love that one bears for him" (252). Furthermore, the model excludes the exchange of money (217–19). In contrast to this, the concept of love that allows Ray to imagine, despite years of consciousness raising, that he can "have" Marco in a possessive love relationship derives from the condescending asymmetries of his earlier relationship with George, who "saw [Ray] obviously as a sort of superior home entertainment centre" (248). It also derives, as the final paragraph makes clear, from the clichés of pop song. Moreover, the cash nexus of the Ray–Marco relationship, as in the earlier case, is vitiating; and this point is driven home in the final pages where the gold necklace that Ray chooses for Marco as the gift to accompany his letter is characterized, in an echo of Ray's colonizing attitude, as "the sort of sleazy bauble all the kids here were wearing" (281).

Marco's refusal of the gift shatters the fantasy Ray has been nurturing. Indeed, his response to Ray's letter, in words that call up the ghost of George, has the force of oracular utterance. This is because "the tone of another" (Marco? George from beyond the grave?), interrupting "a familiar tonality," has effected a Derridean disruption of self-identity. Here, the refrain "You must look out for yourself" acquires a quite different meaning. In this context, it suggests "a number of traditions of desire between men in Greece," of which the most important is "the ethical model described by Foucault, in which what mattered was 'the use of pleasure' in 'the care of the self'" (Dellamora 114). Marco also uses the word *love*. But this again requires translation. In this context, "I know you love me" suggests that Marco fully understands Ray's concept of love, the kind of domestic arrangement he has in mind, and that such love—particularly in Xania, which is both "no good" for Ray and "too small" to accommodate such an arrangement—is doomed to claustrophobic failure (282). Consequently his follow-up—"And I love you"—suggests a future in which each, in order to come of age and acquire a fresh sense of self-identity, must "look out for [him]self."

Thus, in this final encounter with Marco, Ray, in a confusion of "grief and joy," at once buries the recent past, completes his act of mourning for George, and looks forward to an uncertain future with a renewed sense of challenge and hope (282). Through the medium of an oracle he has gained sudden insight into the life of another, insight that promises to repatriate him to the idealism of his youth. The story ends, however, with no clear indication as to the route his repatriation will take. White hints that renewal may come through writing (279), a route taken by White himself and by other gay men affected by AIDS. White's identification with Ray in this regard is suggested in the text, since the "story about Marco" (279) that Ray begins is effectively the one that White tells.[9] Julia Blazdell's study of the role of writing in the current HIV/AIDS crisis, *AIDS and the Borders of Postmodernity* (1994), sheds light on this aspect of the story through an examination of writing by Derek Jarman, David Wojnarovich, and others as examples of textual resistance and forms of AIDS activism. On the other hand, "Watermarked," one of White's later stories, suggests possibilities of renewal through caring for PWAs and active participation in other organized responses to AIDS.

The suggestion in "An Oracle," however, is that White's principal stress here, as in his other short stories, is on renewal through an affirmation of gay identity: an identity that is radical, revolutionary, and antiassimilationist, since founded, as White has frequently asserted, on sexual desire. This affirmation, White insists, is particularly necessary in the context of AIDS. Indeed, in his short stories, AIDS itself figures as an agent of change and renewal, and therefore as reason in itself to celebrate intimacy between men. More exactly, it figures as the unfamiliar "tone of another," which in Derrida's account disrupts one's customary sense of self. This disruption, taken in conjunction with the deconstructive project of self-interrogation generally, forces gay men to acknowledge their differences and redefine themselves. In short, in these stories White is interested in exploring the possibility that the AIDS crisis might establish closer and better relations between gay men from those that existed before the epidemic—a possibility that brings to mind some words of Jeffrey Weeks, quoted by White in his afterword to the 1986 reissue of *States of Desire:* "It would be a nice irony of history if a moral panic directed largely at homosexuals were to end up strengthening the ties of solidarity of the gay community" (*Sexuality and Its Discontents* 53).

## SUMMARY

AIDS, I have argued throughout this study, has caused the long-standing antagonism between assimilationism and radicalism within gay culture and politics to become yet more conflicted. This hardening of the divide is suggested in the stark alternatives of "direct involvement or evasion" set out by Suzanne Poirier in the quotation at the head of this chapter, a suggestion reinforced by Joseph Cady's clear-cut distinction between immersive and counterimmersive AIDS writing in his contribution to the same volume of essays. Like Gregory Woods, I find these alternatives too harsh. I am much more persuaded by the balanced view of the issues surrounding the writing of AIDS given by Adam Mars-Jones in his introduction to *Monopolies of Loss.* His account here of how *The Darker Proof* came to be written suggests a broad convergence of viewpoint between himself and Edmund White, a viewpoint aptly summed up in the remark about the need to give AIDS "an appropriate status, neither ignored, nor holding centre stage" (4).

The radically transgressive impulse that I have been exploring in this study is vividly exemplified in *A Matter of Life and Sex*. But this angry, confrontational novel also demonstrates the risks of immersive AIDS fiction: for in its determination "to defy the dominant culture directly and fully" it becomes all too implicated in the dominant, reinforcing media coverage by bringing that "spurious couple [epidemic and orientation] together all over again" (Mars-Jones, *Monopolies* 2) and hence reconfirming the latter's inferior position "within a homophobic system of differences" (Bersani, *Homos* 42). Moore's novel—raw, honest, deeply felt—is undoubtedly faithful to the experience of many people affected by AIDS, but its fatalism is not the whole picture. For a more balanced view we need the stories in *The Darker Proof,* which manage to be faithful to the experience of AIDS while avoiding fatalism.

# Coda
## Pressures of the New Millennium

This chapter is offered as a tailpiece rather than a conclusion. "Conclusion," after all, is a problematic word: it suggests closure, when what most investigations uncover is lack of closure. So in the case of my own research, there is no sense of a tidy ending. But this is to be expected and welcomed: it accords with our contemporary notion of sexuality as a fluid, challenging, and troublesome force, and confirms the study of same-sex desire, whether in literary or other disciplines, as a place of ongoing, indeed permanent, contestation and disruption. The inconclusiveness here is at least twofold. First, the findings themselves open up into new lines of inquiry, suggesting, indeed offering, points to be questioned, gaps to be filled, boundaries to be crossed. But second, the conflict that is the focus of this study—and the fundamental antagonism, as I see it, in the history of homosexuality—is a continuing, ever-present, fruitfully productive tension. Indeed, the dispute today is as keen as ever: it is, after all, closely bound up with the question of gay identity, which in recent times (following the ravages of the AIDS epidemic and the demolition work of queer and deconstructive discourses) has been under enormous pressure to change.

I began this research with quite simply a strong interest in gay male fiction of the post-Stonewall period. This is fiction that in its reflection of different aspects of my own experience has influenced me formatively. So how, I initially asked myself, is this literature different from its parent literature? How, in other words, does it reflect the new gay culture, politics, and consciousness of the post-Stonewall era? Here, what inspired me, in addition to the strong personal element, was the idea of writing that rejected guilt, secrecy, and torment in favor of a liberationist outlook. It was, after all, the fiction of Isherwood and Baldwin—with its pioneering, pre-Stonewall expression of such an outlook—that had first fired my imagination. Hence, my initial questions were an attempt to test Richard Hall's claim that, since 1945, gay writing had evolved from "a literature of guilt and apology to one of political defiance and celebration of sexual difference" (1).

The clearest way in which post-Stonewall gay fiction reflects the changed consciousness of the new era to which it belongs (to respond directly to this initial line of questioning) is in its depiction of a much brighter, stronger, and more self-confident subculture. The gay characters here, in general, move in a more upbeat, cohesive, and supportive milieu. They are social as well as private beings. In this, they contrast sharply with their counterparts in earlier fiction: Jim, in *The City and the Pillar*, for instance, who drifts, alienated and self-contained, from one anonymous gay scene to another, making only fragile connections and sustained, in the absence of any sustaining reality, only by fantasy; and even George, the hero of *A Single Man*, who—significantly as the protagonist of a proto-liberationist novel—survives his long-term partner only to enter a lonely afterlife (and the "single" of the title is indicative here) *with no gay friends*. In short, the heroes of post-Stonewall gay fiction are in general more at ease, both with themselves and socially, than their predecessors.

Moreover, this social ease often extends into the wider social scene beyond the subculture. To recall a remark from my introduction, the first entreaty of gay liberation was to come out, a process often described as one of gradual expansion: one first comes out to oneself, then to others like oneself, then to the whole world. These, then, were the stages by which the movement grew, and the development of gay fiction in the post-Stonewall period reflects this process. Thus the key gay novels of the 1970s are nearly all inward-looking self-diagnoses, exclusively concerned with the new gay subculture. An exception is Armistead Maupin's *Tales of the City* (1978), a novel that deserves more attention here than space allows. In this series of interlinked tales about a group of eccentrics living together in a bizarre family configuration, the gay subculture and the wider culture interact, a cross-fertilization perhaps partly explained by the West Coast origin and setting of the novel, San Francisco being the center of so much countercultural activity in the 1960s. Whatever the explanation, Maupin's novel, although often dismissed as entertainment rather than serious fiction, anticipates the future development of gay writing. This development is shown in the work of the Violet Quill, that self-named group of writers (there were seven in all, including White, Holleran, and Ferro) who, in the 1980s, came together occasionally to read to each other from work in progress. These writers began to produce fiction in which gay characters are shown in the round: as members of families, as friends and lovers, as part of a mise-en-scène extending well beyond the ghetto. Thus, in White's *A Boy's Own Story*, Holleran's *Nights in Aruba*, and Ferro's *The Family of Max Desir*, gay fiction itself comes out, driven by an impulse toward openness. Indeed, like the act of coming out, this fiction suggests an attempt to heal the divided self: to reconcile inner and outer experiences, and bring together segregated worlds.

My initial inquiries, however, soon moved on. After all, gay fiction since Stonewall reflects not only the changed consciousness of the new era to which it belongs, but also its conflicts. In other words, as well as marking a break with the past, it also shows continuity with it. I remarked right at the beginning of this study that my prevailing impression, on first encountering the gay subculture in the 1970s, was of a community riven by conflict; and indeed the history of homosexuality since Stonewall, as even the most cursory glance shows, has been one of rapid change, constant turbulence, and sense of crisis. Of course, the AIDS epidemic, as the central event of the period, has played a key role in this development. Nevertheless, as this study shows, the 1970s were not years of uninterrupted celebration. In this decade, the new movement was already being confronted by the challenge of difference, a challenge that was essentially a questioning of the cultural and political meanings of "gay" as a self-created identity. These tensions—the inherent and surrounding tensions of the new gay identity—are embodied in the gay male fiction of this decade. Thus, in *Forgetting Elena,* the Fire Island scene, figuratively envisaged as a community of aesthetes, is critiqued as a narrow and exclusive society of enforced regulation: as a self-defined and self-serving world, hostile to all kinds of otherness. Moreover, a similar critique, as we saw, drives both *Dancer from the Dance* and *Faggots.* In the former, this is implicit in Holleran's reworking of Fitzgerald's *The Great Gatsby,* as well as the letters that frame the central narrative. In the latter, it is blatant in the bludgeoning satire.

If these novels embody the tensions of the decade as an inner conflict, however (for in each there is a mixture of fascination and censure; in each the Fire Island scene both attracts and appals) gay fiction since Stonewall, taken as a whole, articulates the same tensions as an external conflict—or, in other words, in the opposition of two quite different strains of fiction. To be sure, both of these strains struggle with internal tensions too. In general, however, they show a strong inclination toward one side or other of the long-standing ideological divide between assimilationism and radicalism. Thus *The Lost Language of Cranes, A Home at the End of the World,* and *The Family of Max Desir* (Chapter 4) suggest a strong impulse toward the creation of an integrating myth, by means of which a reimagined and self-defined homosexuality can be drawn back into the general framework of heterosexual norms. This is in marked contrast to *The Swimming-Pool Library, Cabal, Dead Souls,* and especially *Frisk* (Chapter 5), which suggest an absolutely contrary motivation: an urge, that is, to reject heterosexual norms and explore the otherness of queer experience as the dangerous cutting edge of psychosexual adventure. In this way, these opposed strains of fiction in post-Stonewall writing show their lineage: on the one hand, the line of fiction represented (in Chapter 2) by Forster, Vidal, and Isherwood, in which there is a general attempt to make homosexuality fit into categories validated by heterosexuality, as against, on the other, the line represented by Wilde, Genet, and Burroughs, in which there is a violent, exultant overturning of such categories.

The AIDS epidemic has intensified this conflict—indeed pushed it to a point of crisis—and since 1981 all gay fiction has been written in its shadow. Moreover, the tensions of at least two novels of the 1970s—*Dancer from the Dance* and *Faggots*—seem partly grounded in a premonition of its outbreak. Hence, in gay fiction of the past three decades, AIDS has been strictly speaking unavoidable. In fact, its deafening presence is perhaps most keenly felt in those novels—*The Swimming-Pool Library,* for instance—where it is never actually named. If writers have responded in various ways, some have addressed the subject more or less directly; and here the tensions of post-Stonewall gay culture and politics are reflected again in two opposed strains of AIDS fiction (Chapter 6). Thus, in *A Matter of Life and Sex,* AIDS figures as the fate that Hugo, the rebel-hero of the novel, dangerously invites and finally embraces in a lone gesture of ultimate defiance. This is in marked contrast to the treatment of AIDS in *The Darker Proof,* for in these short stories White and Mars-Jones reject romantic fatalism in favor of balance, objectivity, and sober reflection.

One important conclusion that clearly emerges from this study is that the conflict embodied in these opposed strains of gay fiction is closely bound up with the issue of the function of literature, of what literature is for. As the novels examined here show, the assimilative impulse in gay fiction leans in the direction of morality, reason, humanity, and positive social values. It is part of the process by which homosexuality begins, in those now familiar words of Foucault, "to speak in its own behalf, to demand that its legitimacy or 'naturality' be acknowledged, often in the same vocabulary, using the same categories by which it was medically disqualified" (*History* 101). But, as this study also shows, gay fiction, like literature in general, often has no such function. Indeed, more often than not, it is a medium of dangerous knowledge, opposed to humane values and driven by the intractable forces of fantasy and desire. For Bruce Bawer, "the Gay Novel at its best addresses a high moral question: how does one live honorably as a homosexual in a world that considers homosexuality itself dishonorable?" (198). This defence of gay fiction accords with that widely held view of art that sees it as the most exalted expression of civilized life. Others, however, would dismiss this view as a domestication that robs art of its power to challenge and disturb: the very quality that makes art valuable in the first place.

This conclusion about the conflict in gay writing being grounded in a disagreement about the function of literature emerges particularly strongly in the case of fiction about AIDS, as the sharpening of tension in the era of the epidemic might lead us to expect. In the face of such devastation, how should writers respond? The general view would seem to be that the sheer horror of the disease, and the enormity of public reaction to it, calls for some kind of special literary response: response, that is, that ignores, or goes beyond, what might be considered the usual function of literature. Edmund White, we recall, commenting on the extraordinary pressures that AIDS has put on gay fiction, writes: "Holocaust literature, exiles' literature, convicts' literature—these are the only possible parallels that spring to mind" (*Burning Library* 283). He also writes that his decision to collaborate with Adam Mars-Jones on a book of short stories about AIDS was prompted by the belief that he had something to contribute to a discourse that was losing sight of the fact that "actual human beings were suffering, watching their lives crumble, and having to confront very deep fears" (quoted in Dellamora 99). The suggestion here, then, is that gay fiction is under pressure from AIDS to adopt a positive social role, to respond with humanity and moral support.

Patrick Gale, speaking in an interview about his novel *The Facts of Life* (1995), explicitly endorses this viewpoint, although what is surprising here is his criticism of White and Mars-Jones for the inadequacy of their attempt to adopt such a role and give such support:

> *The Facts of Life* was written in a way as my response to what I saw as a failure in AIDS novels to date. They weren't speaking to me, giving me comfort. They were more like a brutal kind of journalism, if wonderfully written. The Anglican in me wanted to offer comfort, rather than just report from the battlefront. Take, for instance, Edmund White and Adam Mars-Jones's collection *The Darker Proof.* It was trailblazing when it came out. Adam's stories were breathtaking, but cold in a way. They were brutally accurate, but weren't giving the reader anything. They were just saying: "This is how it is," which is what was needed at the time. But I was writing *The Facts of Life* a good ten years on, and trying to put AIDS in perspective as the latest in a series of social diseases. Particularly the TB parallels seemed a way of doing that. Also, I wanted to put the gay characters with AIDS firmly back into a family context—once again, to show perspective; to say: "He's dying from AIDS, but ultimately he's just dying." People die of all manner of things. Families have a way of coping. The structure of a family will extend around and beyond death. (Canning, *Gay Fiction Speaks* 425)

These comments are surprising for at least two reasons. First, the objectification of AIDS that Gale is calling for here—the standing back, the sense of historical perspective—is, in my view, precisely what White and Mars-Jones attempt and achieve in their short stories, as I argue in Chapter 6. Second, Gale complains of brutal accuracy. But Joseph Cady, as I remark in the same chapter, criticizes these same stories for exactly the reverse reason: for failing to "report from the battlefront," for failing to say "how it is." In Cady's view, White and Mars-Jones, in their AIDS fiction, are not brutal enough; he sees their stories as counterimmersive, and thus evasive.

When it comes to the question of the function of literature, however, all these writers favor fiction about AIDS that is socially responsible. White, Mars-Jones, Gale, and Cady are in broad agreement with each other in seeing a need for fiction to act positively in addressing the anguish of people affected by AIDS, to show solidarity with this suffering group in face of the world's indifference. Their quarrel with each other is about the way to achieve this. But is it the function of art to give comfort? Where the great divide comes is with AIDS fiction that stares into the void. Thus in Oscar Moore's *A Matter of Life and Sex*, morality, reason, humanity, and positive social values are all beside the point. For here, the link between homosexuality and death represents bedrock reality: here, sex and self-destruction are inextricable, as well as compulsive and unavoidable. Moore's protagonist makes no attempt, shows no desire, to redeem or affirm his sexuality. Rather, he accepts it—fatalistically, and with a kind of dark pleasure—as an ineradicable and death-driven part of his personal makeup. Nor can this gay character be brought back into Gale's "family context": the family here is unsupportive and has no way of coping. In short, homosexual desire, in this novel, is a force beyond the reach of comfort or social responsibility.

## POSTGAY/POSTQUEER EXPLORATIONS

I have argued throughout this book that the conflict between assimilationism and radicalism is *the* fundamental antagonism of gay culture and politics, and my overriding aim here has been to show how this antagonism is reflected in gay male fiction of the post-Stonewall period. That this conflict, as I remarked earlier, is a continuing, ever-present tension is shown by the fact that since the early 1990s "gay" has been an identity under increasing pressure to change, and indeed in crisis. Alan Sinfield, for instance, suggests that "current changes in perceptions of bisexuals, along with other developments . . . indicate that we may now be entering the period of *the post-gay*—a period when it will not seem so necessary to define, and hence to limit, our sexualities" (*Gay and After* 14). I would therefore like to end this study with a brief indication of how the lines of inquiry I have pursued in this study—and my inevitably incomplete findings—might be extended in the light of current developments.

In this study I have explored fiction by writers who might be called the first generation of post-Stonewall gay novelists. Many of these are still very much alive and active. Indeed some of their finest work has appeared in recent years—for example, Edmund White's *The Married Man* (2000), Dennis Cooper's *My Loose Thread* (2003), Alan Hollinghurst's *The Line of Beauty* (2004), and Andrew Holleran's *Grief* (2007). However, the post-AIDS period has seen the emergence of a new and very different generation of gay fiction writers: a generation that includes such names as Randall Kenan, Dale Peck, Brian Keith Jackson, Scott Heim, and Michael Lowenthal. Too young to have experienced Stonewall or the freedoms of the pre-AIDS era, these writers do not look back to a lost paradise. For them, AIDS is simply a factor of the world they have inherited. Nor are they inclined to confine themselves to gay-themed fiction and the experiences of gay characters only. Rather, their tendency is to allow the imagination free play and thus extend the boundaries of gay fiction. For instance, Michael Lowenthal's most recent novel, *Charity Girl* (2007), is concerned with a dark episode in the history of the United States and focuses on the experience of Frieda Mintz, a charity girl who contracts venereal disease and is sent to a detention center. Lowenthal is explicit: "After a necessary period of 'gay literature' being a very specific and limited thing, it's now branching out to encompass all sorts of new possibilities . . . gay writers shouldn't be limited to writing *only* about gay characters or themes" (Gambone 331, 337). Dale Peck, too, writes about much more than gay lives, but insists that his understanding of others is always gay inflected: "So when I write about a fifty-year-old black lesbian in a small town in Kansas, I write it from the point of view of 'Dale Peck,' a thirty-year-old gay urban New Yorker" (Canning, *Hear Us Out* 347). However, he also seeks to extend the boundaries of gay fiction through new and experimental forms that foreground "the gap between language and reality" (329). One possible extension of my line of inquiry in this book, then, would be to ask how the conflict explored in this study is reflected in the work of this younger generation.

The continuing conflict between assimilationism and radicalism in lesbian and gay culture and politics is on clear display in Robert McRuer's book *The Queer Renaissance: Contemporary American Literature and the Reinvention of Lesbian and Gay Identities* (1997). McRuer opens his book with a discussion about the way that the debate about same-sex marriage rights in the United States (and, by extension, in the Western world generally) re-enacts this fundamental antagonism. He points out that the decision by the Hawaii Supreme Court to consider the extension of marriage rights to same-sex couples provoked a flurry of legislative activity elsewhere in the United States, defining marriage as exclusively a heterosexual union—activity that led eventually to the passing and signing into law of the Defense of Marriage Act (DOMA) in September 1996. But, McRuer asks, whence all this paranoia? What kind of a threat to civilization does lesbian and gay marriage constitute? The proponents of same-sex marriage, he argues, are not seeking to undermine heteronormative processes, but rather to uphold them. Moreover, the effect of an extension of marriage rights to lesbian and gay people would be further to distance, marginalize, and exoticize queer identities and communities that do not fit the "new and improved" model of family that such legislation would introduce. Hence, the debate over marriage rights in Hawaii, he claims, again makes visible "the crises that circulate around marriage and 'the family'" (viii).[1]

Accordingly, McRuer focuses on writing that seeks to challenge "dominant constructions of sex, sexuality, gender, class, and race" (ix). He brings together texts by Audre Lorde, Edmund White, Randall Kenan, Gloria Anzaldúa, Tony Kushner, and Sarah Schulman, and defends his decision to ignore the customary segregation of lesbian and gay writing in literary studies on the grounds that it is more representative of the way men and women have worked together in recent times: as partners in queer alliances and protests; as dissenters who refuse to be contained "by the model of a well-behaved same-sex dyad" (ix). Indeed, McRuer sees this breaking down of barriers as giving support to his project of examining the literary creation of fluid and disruptive identities and communities, and of thus staging a productive interchange of ideas that extends that fluidity and disruption. His example here might therefore serve as a model for future studies of lesbian and gay writing, even though, as he himself admits, his study unavoidably erects other barriers (which invite further disruption) and establishes other boundaries (which he hopes will in turn be crossed). *The Queer Renaissance* looks exclusively at the work of American writers, for instance; and thus a parallel study of British writers might bring together, say, Jeanette Winterson, Colm Tóibín, Jackie Kay, Hanif Kureishi, Sarah Waters, and Neil Bartlett. Moreover, such a study might in turn suggest further literary investigations that seek (on the basis that every inclusion implies an exclusion) to break through the cultural barriers of specific identities, communities, and locations, whether national, ethnic, gender based, or class based.

David Bergman finds McRuer's book "turgidly written" and "jargon-filled," and in his foreword to *Gay Fiction Speaks* takes McRuer to task for failing to separate fiction from political argument (xi). It is preposterous, Bergman implies, for McRuer to complain that Edmund White's novel *A Boy's Own Story* contains only two black characters, "as though novels operated as equal-opportunity employers" (xi). And in this respect, Bergman is of course right: it *is* absurd to expect fiction to respond to social demands, rather than to demands of the imagination. Nevertheless, it is not absurd to expect some attention to equal opportunities from *studies* of gay literature; and here McRuer's argument has some force. As my own study shows, there is a great temptation in writing about gay literature to focus on the work of prominent, well-established writers, who are also more likely to be part of the white male tradition. Such writers have a better chance with mainstream publishers, and hence of finding their way onto the shelves of main-street bookshops. This accessibility increases the appeal of their work as material for critical treatment.

The most radical and challenging gay fiction of our time is probably to be found on the lists of the smaller, more specialized publishing companies. Of course, we cannot and should not ignore the work of leading gay writers, whether or not of the white male tradition, but neither should we ignore the work of those who are less established, more marginalized, and possibly younger. Richard Canning acknowledges the problem in his introduction to *Gay Fiction Speaks,* where he reveals his concern about the extent to which his chosen interviewees "reflect the ethnic and cultural diversity of gay fictional voices that is today's reality" (xxiii). Canning admits that this first volume of interviews represents an almost entirely white tradition, but promises to try and rectify this in subsequent volumes. He remarks that his decision to focus exclusively on literary fiction for the sake of coherence (at least in this first volume) is partly responsible for the narrowness of his range here; many gay writers, after all, work in the field of popular literary genres, "such as the detective novel, romance, and science fiction" (xxiii).

I would like to add to these remarks that the lines of inquiry I have pursued in this study might also be fruitfully extended into the area of the gay short story. For short fiction, as many critics have argued, is the literary medium par excellence of the lonely, marginalized voice. P. P. Hartnett, for instance—himself a writer of radically queer fiction that is worthy of inclusion in a critical study of this kind—has recently edited a volume of short stories by younger gay men, some of whom have never appeared in print before. In this collection—*The Next Wave* (2002)—the voices of a generation, raised under Section 28 of the Local Government Act 1988, articulate their fears, hopes, dreams, and fantasies in the face of official homophobia and blundering attempts to silence them.

In his epilogue, McRuer considers whether the emergence and growing confidence of neoconservative gay commentators such as Bruce Bawer and Andrew Sullivan suggest that we have now moved to a postqueer moment. These considerations contrast significantly with Alan Sinfield's near-simultaneous reflections (from which I quote above) on whether we are now entering the period of the postgay. Are the times postqueer, or postgay? The confusion here underlines our current sense of instability: our sense of an identity—or rather, of identities—in flux. McRuer claims that the rise of gay neoconservatism, taken together with the current enthusiasm of some scientists in the United States to discover a genetic basis to homosexual orientation, at the very least highlights "the ongoing tension between liberal reformers and radical liberationists" (208). However, he concludes, as I do, with the proposition that this continuing conflict is to be welcomed as a fruitfully productive tension. Liberal reformers and radical liberationists need each other: their stand-off creates the energy that helps "to advance the gay and lesbian movement" and fires the imagination to produce the gay fiction that helps to shape "a queer world" (213).

Or as Blake puts it: "Without Contraries is no progression."

# Appendix
## An Interview with Edmund White

LES BROOKES

Edmund White was born in Cincinnati, Ohio, in 1940. He has been a teacher of writing at Columbia University and Executive Director of the New York Institute of Humanities. Among his nonfiction books are *States of Desire: Travels in Gay America* (1980) and *Genet* (1983), while his novels include *Forgetting Elena* (1973), *A Boy's Own Story* (1982), *The Beautiful Room Is Empty* (1988), *The Farewell Symphony* (1997), *The Married Man* (2000), and *Hotel de Dream* (2007). This interview took place in late March 1996 at the London home of Julia O'Faolain, where White was staying for a few weeks with his current partner, Michael Carroll.

LB: As you might expect, I'm interested in themes and thematic links. You have said, according to David Bergman, that all your work is about initiation and this seems true to me, but I wonder if you could say something more about that. Why, for instance, do you think initiation is such a strong theme in your work? Is it just that you've drawn on a central tradition in Western literature or might it have something to do, as Bergman suggests, with the vagaries of your childhood, where each movement to a new town involved you in a new process of learning?

EW: Well, I think it's a couple of things. Firstly, so much gay fiction is really about coming out, and coming-out stories are basically stories of initiation, whether it be into gay society or into gay sex or into the adult world or into the recognition of oppression or prejudice. But also it's true that in my case that I was born in Cincinnati to parents who were both Texans and then my parents got divorced when I was seven, so we tended to move almost every year, going back to the South but also going to various towns in the Midwest. And then when I was twenty-two I moved to New York and I think it might be hard for an Englishman to realize what a gulf lies really between *l'Amérique profonde* and the two coasts. I mean, it's really quite a different world and especially where I went, of course, which was *Time-Life* books—part of the whole Time Magazine/Life Magazine empire. That was a world that was entirely dominated by Ivy League/East Coast people and they were all named Auchincloss. So I think for somebody like me . . . I really *did* feel like an outsider. But I had always felt an outsider, because we were Yankees who had gone back to live in the South. And our mother, too, was very de-classed by the divorce and so she kind of went down several notches socially, and we with her, and yet because of the divorce agreement we had to spend the whole of every summer with our father, and so suddenly we were plunged into a world of debutante balls and all that stuff, but we never really had the proper clothes. And then again, I was sent to a "good" boarding school, Cranbrooke, which was trying to be very English with lots of sports that were unfamiliar to Americans, like Rugby, and even Christmas ceremonies where we had to carry in a boar and sing "The Boar's Head." Things like that. All this crazy Englishness. It was a real piece of Anglophiliac snobbery. Anyway, I'm just trying to give you some suggestion of all the ways in which I felt like an outcast. But primarily it was because I was a gay living in a straight world.

LB: So do you see this sense of outsidership as being the source or well-spring of much of your writing?

EW: Yes I do, definitely. Because my first published novel, *Forgetting Elena,* as you know, is so much about somebody who's lost his memory, therefore, doesn't know who he is or who anybody else is and yet is embarrassed by that, doesn't freely admit it to anybody and is constantly studying his own face in the mirror to see what kind of person he might be. Are there laugh lines or not? Is he a friendly kind of guy or not? And then he molds all of his responses on the kind of cues that he's receiving from other people. I was very interested at the time in a guy called Erving Goff[man] who had a sort of "theater" theory of human relationships. I think he must have been a sociologist, and I think he had this idea that all life is theater. It was a perfectly banal idea, but he kind of went into it to some degree and I think that that was probably a minor influence on *Forgetting Elena.* But I also felt that it was very true to my own experience, because one of the curious things is that, though I felt like a total outsider when I went to New York, I was almost immediately embraced by a lot of socially prominent people as being one of them and I've always had that kind of response from people. Even when I first started coming to England in the sixties people would say "Oh Edmund, you're not like all those other Americans, you're more like an Englishman." And the French think I'm terribly French. It's this awful chameleon-like quality that comes, I think, from someone who tries hard to imitate people and accommodate himself, without even really thinking about it.

LB: You have written that the island in *Forgetting Elena* "sometimes resembles Fire Island," though David Bergman suggests that the model for the island is Cincinnati, the Republican Valhalla. Is there some truth in both of these propositions?

EW: I don't agree with Bergman. I think that the topography of the island—that is, that kind of big sandbar where there are no cars and where there is a constant presence of nature and the ocean—that's all very much like Fire Island. And so it was a place where people lived in a fairly primitive way that was terribly expensive. I mean, in other words, you would have a little cottage built on stilts, but you would have spent half a million dollars for it. And, of course, because it was so close to New York, it was very valuable real estate. There were three things that came together when I wrote that book. One was that I had read a book about Louis XIV by a man called W. H. Lewis, which took a close look at the sociological underpinnings of Versailles. One of the things that I picked up from that was that all titles were banished because they seemed kind of clunky and Germanic and heavy-handed to the French. They were replaced by innocent-seeming words like Monsieur, which was reserved only for the King's brother, and La Grande Mademoiselle, who was the Monsieur's wife and so on. And in the same way, everyone in my book pretends to be egalitarian, although there are actually tremendous class differences between them and there's all this jockeying for power behind the scenes, which our poor narrator can't understand because he doesn't know who anybody is. So that was one thing. The second thing was *The Pillow Book of Sei Shonagan*, who was a late tenth-, early eleventh-century Japanese courtier. Again, his was a highly aestheticized court that pretended to be quite egalitarian but in fact was as stratified as you might expect. And I think the third source was Fire Island itself, which again was a place where everybody wore shorts or swimsuits and looked more or less the same, but in fact one person might be the president of a bank and another a gigolo out for the weekend. So you never quite knew who anybody was. And I remembered reading somewhere that De Tocqueville had said that, since all human beings are naturally very snobbish, in a democracy the signs of rank will be much more sinister and complicated than they are in a straightforward aristocracy.

LB: This is Bergman again: "Civilisation, for White, is both a mask to cover the corrupt interplay of power and sexuality and the means of uncovering the hypocrisy of that interplay." What do you think he means by that? Is he saying that, for you, the social codes of civilization—which are the mask—nevertheless permit a measure of artistic freedom—which is the means of stripping the mask away?

EW: That sounds right to me. But don't you think that Bergman takes a rather dark, cynical view of my work? On the other hand, I do feel that in social exchanges between people there is a tremendous amount of hypocrisy, usually, but not always, conscious. I mean, I think people are always jockeying for power and prestige, and ruled by love and self-love. I think one of the duties of the artist is to see through that.

LB: The encoding process in *A Boy's Own Story* leads eventually to betrayal, but the impulse to betray is there in the first chapter. The narrator feels he is not the son his father wants him to be and he writes: "Perhaps, despite my timidity, I was in a struggle against him. Did I want to hurt him because he didn't love me?" This suggests that the narrator's need to betray originates in his sense of rejection. Is this the central theme of the novel?

EW: I think it is. That passage that you've just cited is important. I went back and put it into the first chapter after I'd figured out what the book was about. I wrote the novel from the beginning to the end in a straightforward way, but when I got to the end I wondered if I'd been laying it on a bit too thick in making the boy seem so very appealing and charming. Because in real life I *did* do this thing of turning in this teacher and I kept thinking: "I wonder if I'll have the courage to say that? And if I do, it will repel many readers." But I was proud of myself that I was able to be honest about it because it felt to me like the worst thing I'd ever done. I think it is the worst thing I ever did. So I wondered if I would have the strength of character to acknowledge it and I did. But it always puzzled me and, I think, if betrayal is one of the deepest themes of my writing, and maybe my life, it's so deep that I don't understand it. I know, for instance, that I made everybody laugh when I wrote that Genet is always talking about his three cardinal virtues being homosexuality, theft, and betrayal. I thought: "Betrayal? I don't understand. Why would anybody want to do that?" But I had already written *A Boy's Own Story*, so clearly I had a blind spot to my own deepest compulsions.

LB: Catherine Stimpson, writing about *A Boy's Own Story*, suggests a link with Salinger, a writer much concerned with lost innocence. Would you say that lost innocence is a central concern of your writing?

EW: I don't know. I mean, I think that Salinger was an influence on *A Boy's Own Story* for sure, but with this difference: that *The Catcher in the Rye* is narrated by the teenage boy at the time that he is a teenager, whereas *A Boy's Own Story* is narrated by an adult narrator who's looking back on his younger self. So there's a very complex relationship between the older narrator and the younger protagonist, which I think is a healing one because I think it's clear, even though it's nowhere stated as such, that the adult narrator is really at ease with himself and looking back at all this from the great distance of twenty or thirty years. So, I think that there's a suggestion behind all the anguish that everything is going to turn out right, that there is going to be a kind of self-acceptance at the end of the road, which is implicit in the narrator's very Olympian kind of stance. But I think that innocence, as such, doesn't interest me very much. It's a great American theme and I find it very annoying. I mean, in that way, I'm much closer to the French, who, if they should happen to have, say, a girl who loses her innocence, she loses it on the first page so that she can get on with her life. Because the French think innocence is very boring and I think I do too. I mean, for instance, Holden Caulfield's way of feeling that everyone is "phoney" . . . that's not a word, I think, that the boy in *A Boy's Own Story* would use. I think he's rather steely-eyed and disabused. Of course, he gets taken in—by the hustler, for instance—and sometimes makes mistakes of judgment, but it's not a question of losing innocence, it's a question of gaining in cunning.

LB: One critic, James Levin, describes *A Boy's Own Story* as "brilliantly written" and even "dazzling" but "not totally satisfying as fiction." He complains that there is no plot, no clear exposition of the narrator's problems, and no discussion of "the usual difficulties of gay youth." What do you think about that? Is that a fair comment?

EW: Well, I think that last objection comes from an earlier period when gay critics tended to feel that gay fiction should be in some way representative of the tribe. It's the sort of pressure that was felt by a lot of black American writers earlier on. There was that feeling that you were always a spokesperson for your people. That was the kind of pressure that was exerted on the Violet Quill members and myself from the beginning and we all resisted it. Two or three of the members had gone to the Iowa workshop and some had gone to Harvard, and we all had exalted, elitist notions of art that weren't going to bend very easily to these much more utilitarian views of the early gay critics. But, to answer the other objections, I think that it's no accident that *The Beautiful Room Is Empty* is much more plotted, specific, and straightforward than *A Boy's Own Story* because my idea was that *A Boy's Own Story* is about childhood, and childhood is mainly about very strong mood states and not much about the particular historical moment that you are living in. Children, after all, live in a world apart and there's something, I think, gloomily eternal about childhood that I wanted to show. So the moodiness and atmospheric quality of *A Boy's Own Story* and its lack of narrative drive seemed to me coherent with my vision of childhood. On the other hand, if it doesn't much matter when you live as a child, it matters very much when you live as an adolescent, especially if you are a gay adolescent, because the experience of being gay in Ohio in 1960 is very different from the experience of being gay in London in 1996. In the first place, if you're living in London in 1996, you're going to hear the word *gay* pronounced a lot more often. No young gay person today would ever feel he's the only gay person in the whole world, whereas people of my generation did feel that. We do belong to an oppressed minority group that does have a history, and that has made some victories, and that has changed social attitudes. There is an actual evolution of our society. So I thought that it was very important to show that the narrator of *The Beautiful Room Is Empty* was living in the 1960s, first in the Midwest and then in New York, was in therapy, was middle-class, self-hating, conventional, going to a heterosexual therapist, trying to become straight, and then, almost in spite of himself, is caught up in the whirlwind of Stonewall.

**LB:** Bergman sees *The Beautiful Room Is Empty* as being about the beginning of the decoding process and he writes: "The encoders for White are school, family, and psychotherapy, but they are not without their benefit as they also give the narrator the means to decode their own constructions." But, as I read the novel, the means to decode the constructions of school, family and psychotherapy are provided not from within those institutions but from without—by art students, bohemians, and political activists. Is that the way that you see it?

**EW:** I hadn't thought about it, but I think you're absolutely right. I'm currently reviewing a new book by Martin Duberman called *Midlife Queer,* in which he says that being an intellectual has made him more self-oppressing than he would have been ordinarily. It rang a bell with me because I too was a good student and reading Freud from the time I was twelve and going to shrinks and having this steely-eyed zeal about going straight. And, probably, if I'd been a more average kid, I would have accepted my homosexuality more easily or not thought about it so much. But actually I thought about it all of the time and worried about it terribly. I think you're quite right that the decodings came from the bohemian/Beatnik world, which was really the only permissive society in the 1950s. And then later the political activism that came out of Stonewall. In general it was in the air in the late sixties because there was the antiwar protest movement, there was the

"Black is Beautiful" movement, there was the beginning of feminism and civil rights, and I knew all those people and was sort of in touch with them.

LB: Bergman explains the title *The Beautiful Room Is Empty* in terms of the narrator's love for Maria: "The beautiful room of their love is empty because their love was not made for a conventionally beautiful room. Such a love requires new and different accommodations." Is this a valuable insight?

EW: I didn't think of that. When I named it I was thinking not so much of any particular relationship as the narrator's inability to really connect intimately with anybody. I felt that it came from the fact that he was a self-hating gay. I mean, he couldn't love women because he was gay and he couldn't love other men because he didn't want to be gay. The same problem that was posed in *Boy's Own Story*—how to love a man without being a homosexual—is still being agonized over in this book. I think that the Kafka quote that the title comes from really suggests that every time the beloved takes a step toward you, you have to retreat behind your door. And since you have probably chosen a beloved who is very much like you, whenever you take a step toward him or her, she or he hides behind the door too. I think if I had one relationship in mind it was more the relationship with Sean than it was with Maria. Because it seems to me that Sean is the first real relationship that the narrator has with another man that promises to be a love relationship, though they are both so self-hating, and Sean especially, that Sean goes crazy and falls apart and so on.

LB: The narrator of *The Beautiful Room Is Empty*—perhaps speaking for gays generally—describes the Stonewall Riots as "the turning point of our lives." Was he right? And, if so, what kind of a turning point was it? How did it change things?

EW: I think the main thing is that if I look at the difference in my own life between group therapy before Stonewall and then conscience-raising sessions after, they really are two entirely different experiences. Whereas I was going to group therapy with almost all heterosexual people with the goal of becoming straight, and always feeling that I was out of step and that every action and every feeling was yet another symptom of my central neurosis, which was being gay, by 1972 the American Psychological Association had redefined homosexuality as no longer a pathology and as part of a normal range of behavior. Of course, in America homosexuality is still a crime in about twenty states. But still, if you look at a list of things that have happened in America since 1969, it's really quite extraordinary—even though all this crazy Christian stuff goes on, which is almost unimaginable to Europeans.

LB: Whatever the effect of Stonewall, gay literature of the seventies seems to me to reveal a deep ambivalence to seventies gay male culture. What do you think was the source of all this unease?

EW: I think it was that most of us who were movement gays were socialists and what made us uncomfortable was the feeling that the fruit of all this movement activity was simply to raise in status a small group of already fairly privileged gay white men. We felt that women really didn't have much parity, that most gay men were fairly irritable about the presence of lesbians and tended to understand women even less well than straight men did. Because straight men, at least, liked to go to bed with them, and so had to accommodate themselves to them to some degree, but gay men had all the misogyny of white men in general and an attitude of sexual indifference. And then, in my own case, it was just the consumerism of American society being applied to people sexually so that they became sexual objects. I used to say Fire Island is a race that nobody can win and everyone is unhappy running it. In the consumerism of the clone culture everything was quantified in terms of number of inches of penis, number of inches of chest size, number of inches of waist size, number of years of your age, number of dollars of your income. You were just a kind of sum total of all these figures and obviously, on some scales, you were inevitably sinking. [Laughter] And you were never as good as the next person; there was no way you could be. It was all calculated to make everybody miserable.

LB: Are you trying to do what you said you wouldn't do, which is to try to encompass the seventies and eighties in *The Farewell Symphony?*

EW: I am, but I'm not having much luck with it because I can't seem to get beyond the seventies. I'm supposed to finish it this summer, but I'm still mired in the seventies because it's all so interesting. I mean, sociologically interesting. One of the things I'm trying to do in this book is to try to show the whole world of sexual promiscuity as being this very poetic and often very emotional world. I'm sort of an apologist for promiscuity because it seems to me that promiscuity—or adventurism as they like to call it—has gotten such a bad name because of AIDS that it's seen as this terrible cynical libertinage. Whereas I want to show that there were many people who were quite liberal in their thinking and who didn't want to imitate heterosexual institutions. Young gay people now have no idea that our promiscuity then was actually a form of idealism, that we really wanted to find new ways of relating. That's one of the things that I'm trying to re-establish and clarify in *The Farewell Symphony*. That's the theme.

**LB:** You constantly stress in your writing that gay identity is founded on gay desire.

**EW:** I think what happened, with the coming of AIDS and a whole new more puritanical generation in America, was a de-sexualizing of gay literature. Older gay writers like Felice Picano have been especially virulent in objecting to this, because they feel that losing the very principle that brought gays together and gave them their sense of identity—namely, gay desire—is too high a price to pay. If you are going to get rid of that, then what's the point? I think that there have been two great strains in gay politics since Stonewall. One is assimilationism, which is the David Leavitt brand—and you see a lot of it now in the work of these new gay conservatives, like Andrew Sullivan and Bruce Bawer. Their effort is to say: "Well, really we should disband. There's no longer any reason for gays to be a political entity, or even a cultural entity. We should just melt back into the crowd. We have achieved what we want, which is to be accepted, and now we should just become ordinary bourgeois householders like everybody else, with our adopted children and our Volkswagen or whatever." But it seems to me that they're living in some sort of strange world if they really think that we've been assimilated. At the other extreme is someone like Martin Duberman, who feels that gays have a special mission and can teach heterosexual society something, that they're on the cutting edge of psychosexual and cultural exploration, that there are new forms of association, new forms of love or freedom from possessiveness and jealousy unique to gay society. I feel very torn by this dialectic. I suppose, politically, I would situate myself somewhere between the two, because in some ways I'm very middle-class and getting more so, so that part of me is assimilationist. But still, my blood boils when I see any sign of antigay prejudice.

**LB:** To write about AIDS at all is a difficult and brave undertaking, but particularly so in fiction, which, as you have noted, some writers have abandoned in favor of the essay.

**EW:** One of the things I want to show, in this book [*The Farewell Symphony*], is the kind of slowness with which it happened. In other words, I want to show all the complexity and richness of the promiscuous society of the seventies, and then show how sexual freedom was virtually interchangeable in our minds at that point in the late seventies with political freedom. So when, at the very beginning of the AIDS crisis, we seemed to be called upon to close the baths, close the backrooms, and become monogamous, that seemed like a terrible loss of the freedoms we'd fought for. Because you have to remember that the right to assemble in any way, especially for pleasure, had always been the target of police

attacks. So, for people of my generation in America it was a dizzying moment when gays themselves were asking you to be revi-
sionist about all these things.

LB: Were the seven years you spent writing you biography of Jean Genet
a form of textual resistance to AIDS, an attempt to remind
people that, in your own words, "there is more to gay culture
than disease"?

EW: There is a passage somewhere in *Caracole* where a writer says: "I like
to deal with old materials, materials that have already cooled off.
It's like I like to make quilts out of old dresses." Well, I have that
feeling too. I mean, I don't mind writing journalism about things
that are happening now, because that's obviously what journalism is about, but in fiction I don't like to deal with such hot material. I like to let it cool off a bit. Suddenly, about 1986—around
the time I started my research on Genet—there was this tremendous outburst of AIDS literature in America and everybody was
rushing in with their AIDS novel. And I just thought: "I don't
want to be part of this whole circus. If I could have been first it
would have been different, but now I'm just going to be last and
come at the end of it all, after everybody else has had their say."
Because a lot of the early AIDS novels would suddenly clear their
throat and give you a scientific explanation of what AIDS was.
There was a lot of that kind of getting-the-message-out quality,
and what I wanted was to come a long way after and see it more
as social history.

LB: Critics frequently comment on the opulence of your style and link your
work to Wilde, Firbank, and Proust. But Wilde has recently been
re-evaluated as a political writer and in one of your essays you
analyze the political content of your own work. Are your aestheticism and your political engagement necessarily at odds, as
some critics suggest?

EW: I don't think so. It's interesting that *The London Review of Books,*
maybe six months ago or more, had a very serious and intelligent article about my writing, in which the writer said that he
felt that my essays in *The Burning Library* were doing a terrible
disservice to my fiction. For instance, he felt that my account of
*A Boy's Own Story* in "The Personal Is Political" is a terrible
oversimplification of the novel and that the truth is that my fiction isn't really political at all, that my essays are simply my kind
of after-the-fact grandstanding, in which I make use of the texts
and vulgarize them in order to try to fit in with some popular
political movement. But I don't think that's true. I mean, I guess I
feel that there's a dialectic going on in my mind all the time about
how true to my own quirky experience I can be and still write
about somebody who is, at least to some extent, representative of

a gay man of my generation. In other words it seems to me that the trajectory that fate forced on me—of being oppressed in the fifties, liberated in the sixties, exalted in the seventies, and almost wiped out in the eighties—is the same trajectory that so many gay people have followed . . . that I'm a kind of Everyman . . . or Everyqueer. [Laughter] But, on the other hand, I don't want to overdo that. For instance, I've sometimes felt that Paul Monette, encouraged by Larry Kramer, had a sort of trumped-up politicized anger, which is no doubt very therapeutic in the sense that it's better to be angry than to be depressed. But the truth is that there aren't that many people to be angry at right now. The main thing to be angry at is a virus. So I feel that Paul Monette's writing is what's called author manipulated. In other words, you feel that the action is constantly being wrenched out of shape in order to make it express a politicized anger and to point up themes of oppression and so on in a kind of textbook way. It feels, in fact, very programmatic and I've always tried to avoid that. But, on the other hand, I think it would be frivolous and hypocritical to pretend that if you are a gay male writer of my prominence and my generation that your writing isn't going to be read as representative. And so you have to accept that responsibility. I mean, to choose a much more exalted example, I think that somebody like Toni Morrison, writing about black experience, can't just say anything. She knows that everyone is watching. She's not totally free, let's say, in the way that John Updike is. I mean, a white middle-class heterosexual male living in the northeast of America, like Updike, can say virtually anything. Nobody cares. He's not speaking for anybody.

# Notes

## NOTES TO THE INTRODUCTION

1. See Bergman, *Gaiety* 4–7.
2. Stonewall is the name given to the events of June 1969 in New York, which began when "the police raided a popular homosexual haunt—the Stonewall Inn in Christopher Street, a regular gay beat. This was a regular occurrence, but this time the reaction was different—the homosexuals fought back" (Weeks, *Coming Out* 188). The weekend of rioting that followed, described by Dennis Altman as the Boston Tea Party of the gay movement, is now seen as a turning point in gay consciousness, and the New York Gay Liberation Front (declaring commitment to revolution in its founding statement) was born in the immediate aftermath. There are numerous accounts of Stonewall, some by eyewitnesses and participants, others by social commentators and historians. For an accessible narrative, see N. Miller 365–87; for a scholarly analysis, see D'Emilio, *Sexual Politics;* for a full-length study, see Duberman, *Stonewall.*
3. For a bracing critique of sexual radicalism today, see Dollimore, *Sex, Literature and Censorship* 3–21. Dollimore argues that much of it is not radical at all, "but tendentious posturing symptomatic of the way that much critique has become relatively ineffectual because academic, metropolitan and professionalized" (5). One way in which queer radicals tame the dangerous potential of homosexuality, he suggests, is by representing themselves as "personally immune to the subversiveness of desire" (11). I return to these provocations in Chapter 1 and at later points in this study.
4. There is of course a tension here between the notion of an identity that has been repressed and an identity that has yet to be developed. For a penetrating discussion of this tension and related issues, see Fuss, *Essentially Speaking* 97–112. See also Weeks, *Sexuality and Its Discontents* 185–210; and D. E. Hall, "Identity."
5. For further reflections on the place of fiction in gay literary self-representation, see Bergman, *Gaiety;* White, *Faber Book of Gay Short Fiction* ix–xviii; White, *Burning Library* 275–83; Woods, *History of Gay Literature* 336–58; Woodhouse, *Unlimited Embrace;* Canning, *Gay Fiction Speaks* xvii–xxvii and *passim.*
6. My focus on internal tension in this study not only grows out of my earlier suggestion that most gay people are a mixture of assimilationist and radical impulses, but also relates to Jonathan Dollimore's discussion of what he calls "the paradoxical perverse" and "the perverse dynamic," categories that he describes as manifesting "not mere undecidability, but a field of cultural representation and social struggle at once brutally divided and violently implicated" (*Sexual Dissidence* 121).

7. See the interviews with Cooper and Leavitt in Canning, *Gay Fiction Speaks*, for an indication of the attitude of these two writers to the "gay fiction" category. Cooper comments: "Gay identity doesn't interest me . . . I've never been involved in gay culture, really" (308). Leavitt says: "Gay people are my constituency and form a part of my readership, but they're not who I write for. I don't think any serious writer writes for a particular readership" (379). And in *Hear Us Out*, Canning's follow-up volume, Cunningham remarks: "I want to write about the biggest world I possibly can. I know what I know about gay people, but I know a lot of other things. (Laughs). It would be a shame not to write about those as well" (101).

## NOTES TO CHAPTER 1

1. For social constructionist theory in respect of sexuality, see Foucault, *History of Sexuality*; Plummer, *Making of the Modern Homosexual*; Weeks, *Coming Out*; Weeks, *Sexuality and Its Discontents*.
2. See Weeks, *Sexuality* 11–18, for a summary of the critique of essentialism that underpins his work. See also Fuss, *Essentially Speaking*, for a crucial discussion of the relationship between essentialism and constructionism, and especially her suggestion that "essentialism and the theories of identity deriving from it must be neither sanctified nor vilified but simultaneously assumed and questioned" (Dollimore, *Sexual Dissidence* 26).
3. Altman's argument here thus links up with our contemporary retheorizing of bisexuality, or what Jonathan Dollimore calls "the complexity and diversity of human sexual practice; and yes: the mobility of human desire, the unpredictability of human fantasy and, above all, our capacity to make profoundly perverse identifications in the sexual imaginary" (*Sex, Literature and Censorship* 23). For further discussion of bisexuality see Eadie; Field; Garber.
4. For accounts of the homophile movement in the United States, see Katz, *Gay American History*; D'Emilio *Sexual Politics*. For the European movement, see Lauritsen and Thorstad.
5. For a brief account of lesbian-feminism in the 1970s, see Miller 374–78. For more detailed accounts, see Abbott and Love; Myron and Bunch.
6. For accounts of the pathologizing and/or moralistic reframing of Freud's insights by his followers in the United States, see Abelove, "Freud"; Dollimore, *Sexual Dissidence* 169–90.
7. See, for example, Weeks, *Sexuality and Its Discontents*; Bersani, *The Freudian Body*; Fletcher, "Freud and His Uses"; Lane, "Psychoanalysis and Sexual Identity."
8. See the Appendix for the edited version of my interview with White, as it appeared in Overhere 18.1 (Summer 1998).
9. For an analysis of these urgent considerations in the United States, see Altman, *AIDS and the New Puritanism*. For the British response, see Watney, *Policing Desire*; Carter and Watney, *Taking Liberties*.
10. As Eve Kosofsky Sedgwick writes: "Anyone who was at the Rutgers conference on Gay and Lesbian Studies, and heard *Gender Trouble* appealed to in paper after paper, couldn't help being awed by the productive impact this dense and even imposing work has had on the recent development of queer theory and reading" (*Tendencies* 1).
11. But see also David Oswell for his suggestion that queer notions of sexual identity are well exemplified in Hanif Kureishi's novel *The Buddha of Suburbia* (1990). Oswell argues that queer is about widening the articulation of sexual identities, and in this sense neither "assimilationist nor separatist"

("True Love"163). He sees Kureishi's novel as "both a critique of an essentialist politics of race, gender and sexuality and also a problematisation of fixed sexual identity" (170).

12. See Weeks, *Making Sexual History* 194–211, for an account of these developments in the 1980s and 1990s.

13. See Anzaldúa and Moraga; Lorde; Beam.

14. For some expressions of this challenge, see Däumer; George; Hemmings.

15. See, for example, the essays in Vance.

16. Jo Eadie, for instance, seems to represent this latter group when he takes issue with Wilson on the grounds that she can see "no place for bisexual people within lesbian and gay politics" ("Indigestion" 77).

## NOTES TO CHAPTER 2

1. For discussion of these ideas about realism in fiction, see E. Auerbach; Barthes, "Reality Effect"; Culler ch.7.

2. See Gelder; Punter; N. Auerbach.

3. See Sinfield, *Wilde Century* 109–60.

4. See Miller, *Out of the Past* 249–57.

5. For accounts of the place of Vedantism in Isherwood's work, see Summers, "Christopher Isherwood" and *Gay Fictions* 195–214. Summers writes: "The importance of Isherwood's conversion can hardly be overestimated, for all his later work is informed by Vedantism, most obviously *The World in the Evening* (1954) and *A Meeting by the River* (1967) but also *Prater Violet* (1945), *Down There on a Visit* (1962), and *A Single Man* (1964). In addition, he collaborated with Swami Prabhavananda on translations of several Hindu religious works, edited the journal Vedanta and the West, and wrote a biography of Ramakrishna (1965), as well as personal accounts of his religious experience, *An Approach to Vedanta* (1963) and *My Guru and His Disciple* (1980)" ("Christopher Isherwood" 213).

6. See, for example, Paul Hammond's comments about the novel's "diversion into romance" in his discussion of *Maurice* (195–203). Forster's failure of imagination in the depiction of sexual relations may be due to lack of experience, he argues, but whatever the case, "Alec remains not quite imaginable, a need rather than an individual" (200).

7. For the history of both versions, as well as a critical assessment of them, see Summers, *Gay Fictions* 112–29, especially 127–29. See also E. Miller. Miller writes: "The revision is more shocking because in it Bob is sodomized, not murdered. But the violence of this revised ending is better justified since Bob does not simply reject Jim as 'queer,' precipitating Jim's retaliation; he initiates the violence. There is a strong statement of how inflammatory such name-calling can be" (666).

8. For the history of this movement in Europe, see Lauritsen and Thorstad. For its history in the United States, see Katz; D'Emilio, *Sexual Politics*. For an accessible introduction to both histories, see N. Miller 13–28, 112–34, 333–62.

9. See Jagose 24–29.

10. For discussion of the minoritizing view, see Sedgwick, *Epistemology*, 1, 9, 82–86 and *passim*.

11. For accounts of both Symonds and Carpenter, and their influence on Forster, see Weeks, *Coming Out* 47–83.

12. As I comment earlier, this ending has been criticized for its "sentimentality" and "utopianism," and in this respect *Maurice* may be compared with

Alice Walker's *The Color Purple*, a novel that has been similarly faulted. For a stimulating discussion of this "fear" of the happy ending, see Light. Alison Light argues that all fictions are utopian, answering a need in all of us "to construct alternative histories of the world and of its power-relations . . . however much we must insist on the ultimate fictionality of these accounts" (95).

13. For further explorations of the psychology that Isherwood is delineating here, see Sedgwick, *Epistemology* 67–90; Craft; Nunokawa.

14. See Dollimore, *Sexual Dissidence* 103–65, for an attempt to retrieve what he calls "the lost histories of perversion" (27). This stimulating and wide-ranging retrospective forms the background to his development of the concept of "the perverse dynamic" (228–30 and *passim*).

15. For the background to the Labouchère Amendment, see Weeks, *Coming Out* 14–20. In writing about this change to British law, both Weeks and Bristow draw on Smith (1976). Weeks (249n) admits to finding Smith's view of Labouchère more convincing than that of H. Montgomery Hyde in *The Cleveland Street Scandal* (1976).

16. For accounts of the way *Naked Lunch* was assembled or composed, see Tytell 48–51 and 113–18.

17. See, for instance, Adams 83.

## NOTES TO CHAPTER 3

1. See the Appendix for the edited version of my interview with White, as it appeared in *Overhere* 18.1 (Summer 1998). It is reprinted here because the original publication is not widely available. The interview supplied the initial idea for this study, and I refer to it at a number of points.

2. For an account of the events that led to the American Psychiatric Association's decision to remove homosexuality from its official list of mental illnesses, see Bayer 101–54.

3. Bergman opens his anthology of Violet Quill writings, *The Violet Quill Reader* (1994), with a brief but useful profile of this group of gay writers and friends. However, he expands this into a much fuller account in *The Violet Hour: The Violet Quill and the Making of Gay Culture* (2004), a social history as well as literary study that looks set to become the standard reference work to this literary circle.

4. For Sedgwick's discussion of these oppositions, see note 6 below.

5. Quoted in Allen 63.

6. See Sedgwick, *Epistemology* 91–181. Sedgwick develops her argument, through a discussion of these extensions of the fundamental homo–hetero binarism, in an analysis of writings by Melville, Wilde, and Nietzsche.

7. For a discussion of Wilde's transgressive aesthetic, see Dollimore, *Sexual Dissidence*, especially Part 3.

8. See Sinfield, *Faultlines* 29–51, for a more detailed explanation of this term.

9. W. H. Auden, "September 1, 1939." In Edward Mendelson, ed., *Selected Poems*. London: Faber, 1979: 86–89.

10. In his interview with the novelist, Philip Gambone draws interesting reflections from Holleran on these aspects of his novel (172–92). Holleran remarks, for instance: "A part of me wants to believe that every gay generation is 'an improved generation' and is further along and is more evolved and is more at ease with their homosexuality; and another part of me thinks that nothing changes, that it's just as difficult for a gay man of nineteen now as it was twenty years ago" (184).

11. W. B. Yeats, "Among School Children." In A. Norman Jeffares, ed., *Selected Poems*. London: Macmillan, 1962: 127–30.
12. See Bergman, *Gaiety* 188–209. This final chapter of Bergman's study discusses literary representations of the relationship between gay life and family life, and with particular reference to Holleran's fiction. For Holleran's own reflections on this relationship, see Gambone 184–88.
13. There is a revealing comment in one of the letters framing the central narrative, which suggests Holleran's own view of his achievement in *Dancer:* "However, I don't think a novel is a historical record; all a piece of literature should do, I think, is tell you what it was like touching Frank Romero's lips for the first time on a hot afternoon in August in the bathroom of Les's Cafe on the way to Fire Island" (7–8).
14. Reed Woodhouse comments perceptively on this diverse reception: Jewish readers find the novel funny, he suggests, because they see it as an accurate reflection of the nagging preoccupations of a neurotic Jew (103).
15. Ben Gove, in a penetrating discussion of the novel (99–115), argues convincingly that "Faggots problematises its own governing demonisation of promiscuity through its conscious and subconscious depiction of Fred's paradoxical desires on Fire Island" (114).

## NOTES TO CHAPTER 4

1. See, for example, Rictor Norton, *The Myth of the Modern Homosexual: Queer History and the Search for Cultural Unity*, London and Washington: Continuum International, 1997. Norton argues that Foucauldian constructionism (which, in his view, should properly be called "social constructionism") is essentially a Marxist analysis of society, which simply ignores historical evidence that does not accord with its view of the rise of bourgeois social control in the nineteenth century.
2. For an account of Foucault's anticipation of queer work on the construction of sexuality, see Halperin, *One Hundred Years of Homosexuality* 1–53. For an attempt to get to the truth of Foucault through his sexuality, see Halperin, *Saint Foucault*. For queer challenges to notions of sexual identity, see Warner.
3. The question whether the constructionist account of sexuality (which underpins the queering of lesbian and gay identities that has occurred since the early 1990s) is assimilative in its consequences is the focus of an ongoing debate. The various positions are well set out in Jagose 101–26. For a well-argued case against the "de-gaying" of gay identity, see Bersani, *Homos* 31–76.
4. Despite or perhaps because of this critical presentation of Rose, Reed Woodhouse sees her as "the tough one . . . the 'moral center,' the one who's mature" (147). She is part of the novel's assimilative tendency, his comments suggest.
5. Reed Woodhouse reads the Philip–Eliot relationship as an inept portrayal of romantic love rather than as a critique of Philip's pursuit of it as an ideal. Leavitt has no insight into romantic love, Woodhouse implies: "It will be a novel, each sober patient page promises, not of ecstasy and despair, but of Freud's 'ordinary unhappiness'" (146). He finds the novel permeated and marred by Leavitt's cautiousness and moral decency. For a more sympathetic reading, see Lilly 206–19.
6. For logocentrism and *différence*, see Derrida, *Writing and Difference;* and for related essays on language and signifying systems, see Barthes, "Death of the Author"; Foucault, "What Is an Author?"; Lyotard, *The Postmodern Condition*.

7. Reed Woodhouse, prompted by a review of *Home*, suggests that Clare is the emotional center of the novel (184); and his remarks here, taken in conjunction with his comments about the centrality of Rose in *Cranes*, suggest that these novels reveal their assimilative tendencies in focusing centrally on mothers and homemakers.

8. Some of Cunningham's comments on his fiction seem pertinent here, particularly in their reflection of the queer/postmodern context of the AIDS epidemic. The following, for instance, comes from an interview with Richard Canning: "Both books [*A Home at the End of the World* and *Flesh and Blood*] were written during the first ten years of the AIDS epidemic, and they're meant to be books for people who are mortally ill. I found myself wanting to write for the friends I had who were very sick and who had time to read only five, maybe ten more books" (Canning, *Hear Us Out* 92).

9. See also Dollimore, *Sexual Dissidence* 169–90. Here, Dollimore examines Freud's theory of perversion within a general study of sexual dissidence, in the course of which he expounds his own theory of perversion as "a dynamic intrinsic to social process" (228).

10. In *Cranes* and *Home* the gay scene is scarcely mentioned, and in this respect these novels align with earlier fiction in which the subculture is presented as a scene to be avoided: Mary Renault's *The Charioteer*, for instance, and Radclyffe Hall's *The Well of Loneliness*. The subtext of both former novels is of course AIDS; but the accent here on personal integrity and retreat into private experience ignores the fact that the maintenance of that integrity, and indeed the viability of any kind of gay life, entails access to and even active participation in the gay network. For discussion of these issues, with reference to Renault, Radclyffe Hall, Holleran, and Leavitt, see Sinfield, *Gay and After* 116–28.

11. For an extended meditation on this theme, see Bartlett.

## NOTES TO CHAPTER 5

1. For a well-argued case in similar vein, see Watney, "Lesbian and Gay Studies in the Age of AIDS."

2. See Dyer; Case; Gelder; Palmer. See also Wisker, "If Looks Could Kill," for an accessible introduction to contemporary women's vampire fiction.

3. Palmer 131; Benjamin 40–44. For further discussion of this relationship, see Brand.

4. See Veeder; Bristow, "Wilde"; Craft.

5. For her exploration of this concept, see Sedgwick, *Between Men* 83–96; also Sedgwick, *Epistemology* 19–21 and 182–212.

6. Hollinghurst himself makes some interesting remarks on the obliqueness of the allusions to AIDS in *The Swimming-Pool Library* in his interview with Richard Canning (*Gay Fiction Speaks* 331–65). He comments: "I thought a good deal about this [the need for the narrator to have some excuse to tell his story] with *The Swimming-Pool Library*. It was really also to do with the AIDS epidemic blowing up while I was writing it, and wondering to what degree I should reposition the book and demonstrate within it that this crisis was going on in the world which the novel depicted. I decided not to at all, but to leave the story placed historically where it was, in 1983. Various ideas went through my head, though—having the whole thing written by Will when he was very ill, or a friend getting it off his hard disk after he'd died. They all seemed horribly corny and contrived. I think for aesthetic reasons as much as anything else I decided not to pursue them" (336–37).

7. See again Canning, *Gay Fiction Speaks*, for Hollinghurst's own comments on these aspects of his novel. "Part of the joke of *The Swimming-Pool Library*," he remarks, "[is] that Will's given the maximum opportunity to do as he wants. He's spoiled" (341). He also says: "Bringing to the center people who could acknowledge and fulfill themselves, however compromised or satirized it may be, was certainly part of my conscious intention in *The Swimming-Pool Library*" (345).
8. See Barthes, *S/Z*, for the author's statement and discussion of his concept of the distinction between readerly and writerly texts.
9. For further insight into this mentality in extension of this argument, see the section on Stephen King's vampire novel *'Salem's Lot* in Gelder. Gelder detects a certain homophobia in the novel, "which shows its German-born vampire to be 'almost effeminate' and presents Matt and Ben's amusement at the thought that the townspeople might regard then as 'a couple of queers'" (129).
10. As Diana Fuss remarks, many of the essays in her collection *Inside/Out* show a fascination with this theme; but see especially those by Patricia White and Ellis Hanson.
11. For a study of the portrayal of female monstrosity in horror film in relation to Kristeva's theory of the abject and the maternal, see Creed, *The Monstrous-Feminine* 8–15. Creed, drawing on Kristeva's theory, argues that when woman is represented as monstrous it is almost always in relation to her mothering and reproductive functions.
12. Charles Baudelaire, "Au Lecteur" in *Les Fleurs du Mal*, Club des Librairies de France, 1959: 29–30.
13. See Canning, *Gay Fiction Speaks* 306.
14. There are hints of these concerns in Cooper's interview with Richard Canning (*Gay Fiction Speaks* 297–330). Cooper remarks: "I remember a few years ago a friend chiding me for still loving Rimbaud's work. His idea was that one outgrew Rimbaud and his ridiculous ambitions. But I still feel connected to Rimbaud's idea of writing transcending writing's fundaments and accessing the sublime" (310). Canning also suggests at a later point in the interview that Cooper's novel *Guide* engages with the morality/aesthetics debate of Wilde's *The Picture of Dorian Gray*, to which Cooper responds: "That's always been there. I just found a way to articulate it with *Guide*. Ethics has been at the center of all the books from the beginning" (322).

## NOTES TO CHAPTER 6

1. As Mars-Jones points out in his introduction to *Monopolies of Loss*, the first edition of *The Darker Proof* (1987) contained four stories by himself—"Slim," "An Executor," "A Small Spade," and "The Brake"—and two by Edmund White—"Palace Days" and "An Oracle." This edition is no longer in print. A second edition, containing two additional stories—"Remission" by Mars-Jones and "Running on Empty" by White—appeared in 1988. The page references in my discussion of these stories refer to this edition. All eight, however, have been reprinted in later collections: the five by Mars-Jones in *Monopolies of Loss* (1992), and the three by White in *Skinned Alive* (1995). I sometimes refer to these, and *Monopolies of Loss* has an introduction by Mars-Jones from which I quote at some length. Hence, full details are given in my bibliography.
2. Sarah Schulman remarks: "You know there's this push for domestic partnership laws, for gay marriage. But if the gay community was divided up into

privatized marriage family units, and wasn't a community, the response to AIDS would never have been what it has been" (quoted in Sinfield, *Gay and After* 88).

3. Christopher Bram comments: "It would be interesting to see a novel where AIDS is present, but not in the foreground. . . . The AIDS epidemic right now is the most important thing happening in our lives. It can't help but affect us. And we do need to address it. It's very difficult to know how to address it. Do we address it head on? As I said in my essay for the *Lambda Book Report*, what can you do with this story except redo the death of Little Nell in Dickens' *The Old Curiosity Shop?* Well, we know that's not what we need. And what we need is ways to understand how we think about it, how we confront it, how we avoid it. What sort of emotions we're letting build up when we don't talk about it. . . . I think that AIDS can be louder in fiction that pretends it's not there than when it's openly addressed" (Gambone 102–03).

4. See, for example, Burton: "By the time he's reached Cambridge, Hugo is supporting himself with prostitution—which also gives him access to hedonistic late Seventies New York and a galloping heroin habit. This is Sin with a capital S and it's going to be punished by Death with a capital A."

5. For an authoritative account of the way AIDS was initially viewed by many gay men in Britain, see Garfield. Garfield reports on how the news of a charity to raise money for research, after the death of Terrence Higgins in 1982, was "announced in *Capital Gay* under the headline 'US Disease Hits London,'" and of how most people, according to *Gay News*, "still thought of Aids as 'a media import, like Hill Street Blues'" (19).

6. See Bergman, *Violet Hour* 238–45, for further discussion of these three stories by White.

7. For White's account of the genesis of two of these stories—"Palace Days" and "Running on Empty"—see Canning, *Gay Fiction Speaks* 82–83. White also makes some pertinent comments in this interview on his reasons for choosing a counterimmersive approach to his subject (88–89).

8. David Bergman writes: "Luke's clandestine communion with the piss-stained soil is both his reassertion of the liberating power of the sexual in the face of death and a way of incorporating the past's earthy best as ballast to the urbane weightlessness of Paris and New York . . . and while the story does not hold out much possibility for a medical miracle, it does suggest that a spiritual or psychological reconciliation fashioned in his own terms is yet possible" (*Violet Hour* 240–41).

9. White must have felt an even stronger identification with Ray in 1994, the year his own lover Hubert Sorin died of AIDS-related illness. Self-renewal through writing is suggested in the two memoirs of Sorin that followed: the first, a reminiscence of their life together in Paris, *Sketches from Memory* (1995); the second, a novel, *The Married Man* (2000).

## NOTES TO THE CODA

1. As I write, London is preparing to host its gay pride carnival for the first time ever in Hyde Park, permission to do so having been previously denied on the grounds that royal parks are "for families and not for homosexuals" (Summerskill). The event prompts Ben Summerskill to a classic statement of the liberal reformist position, his argument encapsulated in the headlines of his article: "We're so ordinary, it's frightening. With only a few embittered exceptions, society now recognizes that being gay is perfectly normal."

He writes: "Gay people no longer have to be 'flamboyant,' 'entertaining' or 'interesting' to satisfy other people's objectification of them." But this, to return to McRuer's point, ignores the problem of whether standards of perfect normality help to stigmatize those who *wish* to be flamboyant, entertaining, and interesting.

# Bibliography

Abbott, Sydney, and Barbara Love. *Sappho Was a Right-On Woman*. New York: Stein, 1972.

Abelove, Henry. "Freud, Male Homosexuality and the Americans." 1985. Abelove, Barale, and Halperin 381–93.

Abelove, Henry, Michèle Aina Barale, and David M. Halperin, eds. *The Lesbian and Gay Studies Reader*. New York: Routledge, 1993.

Adams, Stephen. *The Homosexual as Hero in Contemporary Fiction*. London: Vision, 1980.

Allen, Walter. *Tradition and Dream*. Harmondsworth, Eng.: Penguin, 1964.

Altman, Dennis. *AIDS and the New Puritanism*. London: Pluto, 1986.

———. *Homosexual: Oppression and Liberation*. 1971. London: Serpent's Tale, 1993.

Anzaldúa, Gloria, and Cherrie Moraga, eds. *This Bridge Called My Back*. New York: Kitchen Table, 1983.

Auerbach, Erich. *Mimesis*. Princeton: Princeton UP, 1968.

Auerbach, Nina. *Our Vampires Ourselves*. Chicago: U of Chicago P, 1995.

Baldick, Chris, and Robert Mighall. "Gothic Criticism." *A Companion to the Gothic*. Ed. Stephen Heath. Oxford: Blackwell, 2000. 209–28.

Barker, Clive. *Cabal*. London: Harper, 1988.

Barthes, Roland. "The Death of the Author." *Image Music Text*. Ed. and Trans. Stephen Heath. London: Fontana, 1977. 142–48.

———. "The Reality Effect." *French Literary Theory Today*. Ed. Tzetvan Todorov. Trans. R. Carter. Cambridge: Cambridge UP, 1982. 11–17.

———. *S/Z*. Trans. Richard Miller. London: Cape, 1975.

Bartlett, Neil. *Who Was That Man? A Present for Mr Oscar Wilde*. London: Serpent's Tale, 1988.

Bataille, Georges. *Literature and Evil*. Trans. Alastair Hamilton. London: Boyars, 1985.

Baudelaire, Charles. *Les Fleurs du Mal*. 1857. Paris: Club de Librairies de France, 1959.

Bawer, Bruce. *A Place at the Table: The Gay Individual in American Society*. New York: Touchstone, 1994.

Bayer, Ronald. *Homosexuality and American Psychiatry*. New York: Basic, 1981.

Beam, Joseph, ed. *In the Life: A Black Gay Anthology*. Boston: Alyson, 1986.

Benjamin, Walter. *Charles Baudelaire: A Lyric Poet in the Era of High Capitalism*. Trans. Harry Zohn. London: New Left Books, 1973.

Bergman, David. "Foreword." Canning, *Gay Fiction Speaks* ix–xv.

———. *Gaiety Transfigured: Gay Self-Representation in American Literature*. Madison: U of Wisconsin P, 1991.

————. *The Violet Hour: The Violet Quill and the Making of Gay Culture*. New York: Columbia UP, 2004.

————. *The Violet Quill Reader: The Emergence of Gay Writing After Stonewall*. New York: St. Martin's, 1994.

Bersani, Leo. *The Freudian Body: Psychoanalysis and Art*. New York: Columbia UP, 1986.

————. *Homos*. Cambridge: Harvard UP, 1995.

————. "Is the Rectum a Grave?" *AIDS: Cultural Analysis, Cultural Activism*. Ed. Douglas Crimp. Cambridge: MIT P, 1991. 197–222.

Blazdell, Julia. "AIDS and the Borders of Postmodernity: From discriminating bodies to disseminating information." Diss. U of London, 1994.

Bonetti, Kay. "An Interview with Edmund White." *The Missouri Review* 13 (1990): 89–110.

Brand, Dana. "From the Flâneur to the Detective: Interpreting the City of Poe." *Popular Fiction: Technology, Ideology, Production, Reading*. Ed. Tony Bennett. London: Routledge, 1990. 220–37.

Bredbeck, Gregory W. "Andrew Holleran." Nelson, *Contemporary Gay American Novelists* 197–203.

Bristow, Joseph. *Effeminate England: Homoerotic Writing after 1885*. Buckingham: Open UP, 1995.

————, ed. *Sexual Sameness: Textual Differences in Lesbian and Gay Writing*. London: Routledge, 1992.

————. "Wilde, *Dorian Gray* and Gross Indecency." Bristow, *Sexual Sameness* 44–63.

Bristow, Joseph, and Angelia R. Wilson, eds. *Activating Theory: Lesbian, Gay and Bisexual Politics*. London: Lawrence, 1993.

Brite, Poppy. Z. *Lost Souls*. 1992. Harmondsworth, Eng.: Penguin, 1994.

Brookes, Les. "An Interview with Edmund White." *Overhere: A European Journal of American Culture* 18.1 (1998): 30–40.

Burroughs, William. *Naked Lunch*. 1959. London: Flamingo, 1993.

Burton, Peter. "The Wages of Sin." *Gay Times* 155 (August 1991): 57.

Butler, Judith. *Gender Trouble: Feminism and the Subversion of Identity*. New York: Routledge, 1990.

————. "Imitation and Gender Insubordination." Fuss, *Inside/Out* 13–31.

Cady, Joseph. "Immersive and Counterimmersive Writing about AIDS: The Achievement of Paul Monette's *Love Alone*." Murphy and Poirier 244–64.

Canning, Richard. *Gay Fiction Speaks: Conversations with Gay Novelists*. New York: Columbia UP, 2000.

————. *Hear Us Out: Conversations with Gay Novelists*. New York: Columbia UP, 2003.

Carter, Erica, and Simon Watney, eds. *Taking Liberties: AIDS and Cultural Politics*. London: Serpent's Tail, 1989.

Case, Sue Ellen. (1991). "Tracking the Vampire." *Differences: A Journal of Feminist Cultural Studies* 3.2 (1991): 1–20.

Chambers, Ross. "Messing Around: Gayness and Literature in Alan Hollinghurst's *The Swimming-Pool Library*." *Textuality and Sexuality: Reading Theories and Practices*. Ed. Judith Still and Michael Worton. Manchester, Eng.: Manchester UP, 1993.

Cooper, Dennis. *Frisk*. London: Serpent's Tail, 1992.

Craft, Christopher. "'Kiss me with those red lips': Gender and Inversion in Bram Stoker's *Dracula*." *Speaking of Gender*. Ed. Elaine Showalter. New York: Routledge, 1989. 216–42.

Creed, Barbara. *The Monstrous-Feminine: Film, Feminism, Psychoanalysis*. London: Routledge, 1993.

Culler, Jonathan. *Structural Poetics*. London: Routledge, 1975.

Cunningham, Michael. *A Home at the End of the World*. 1990. Harmondsworth, Eng.: Penguin, 1991.

Curzon, Daniel. *Something You Do in the Dark*. 1971. Port Washington: Ashley, 1979.

Danforth, Laura M. *The Death Rituals of Rural Greece*. Princeton: Princeton UP, 1982.

Däumer, Elizabeth D. "Queer Ethics; or, the Challenge of Bisexuality to Lesbian Ethics." *Hypatia* 7.4 (1992): 91–105.

Deleuze, Gilles, and Félix Guattari. *Anti-Oedipus: Capitalism and Schizophrenia*. Trans. Robert Hurley et al. London: Athlone, 1984.

Dellamora, Richard. "Apocalyptic Utterance in Edmund White's 'An Oracle.'" Murphy and Poirier, 98–116.

D'Emilio, John. *Making Trouble: Essays on Gay History, Politics and the University*. New York: Routledge, 1992.

———. *Sexual Politics, Sexual Communities: The Making of a Homosexual Minority in the United States 1940–1970*. Chicago: U of Chicago P, 1983.

Derrida, Jacques. "Of an Apocalyptic Tone Recently Adopted in Philosophy." Trans. John P. Leavey. *Semeia* 23 (1982): 63–98.

———. *Writing and Difference*. Trans. Alan Bass. London: Routledge, 1978.

Dollimore, Jonathan. *Death, Desire and Loss in Western Culture*. Harmondsworth, Eng.: Penguin, 1998.

———. *Sex, Literature and Censorship*. Cambridge: Polity, 2001.

———. *Sexual Dissidence: Augustine to Wilde, Freud to Foucault*. Oxford: Oxford UP, 1991.

Doty, Mark. *Firefly: A Memoir*. London: Vintage, 2001.

Duberman, Martin. Review of *Faggots* by Larry Kramer. *The New Republic* 180.1 (6 January 1979): 30–32.

———. *Stonewall*. New York: Dutton, 1993.

Dyer, Richard. "Children of the Night: Vampirism as Homosexuality, Homosexuality as Vampirism." *Sweet Dreams: Sexuality, Gender and Popular Fiction*. Ed. Susannah Radstone. London: Lawrence, 1988. 47–72.

Eadie, Jo. "Activating Bisexuality: Towards a Bi/Sexual Politics." Bristow and Wilson 139–70.

———. "Indigestion." Simpson 66–83.

Felman, Soshana, and Dori Laub. *Testimony: Crises of Witnessing in Literature, Psychoanalysis and History*. London: Routledge, 1992.

Ferro, Robert. *The Family of Max Desir*. 1983. London: Arena, 1987.

Field, Nicola. *Over the Rainbow: Money, Class and Homophobia*. London: Pluto, 1995.

Fletcher, John. "Forster's Self-Erasure: *Maurice* and the Scene of Masculine Love." Bristow, *Sexual Sameness* 64–90.

———. "Freud and His Uses: Psychoanalysis and Gay Theory." Shepherd and Wallis 90–118.

Forster, E. M. *Maurice*. 1971. Harmondsworth, Eng.: Penguin, 1972.

Foucault, Michel. *The History of Sexuality: An Introduction*. 1976. Trans. Robert Hurley. Harmondsworth, Eng.: Penguin, 1981.

———. "On the Genealogy of Ethics: An Overview of Work in Progress." *The Foucault Reader*. Ed. Paul Rabinow. Harmondsworth, Eng.: Penguin, 1991. 340–72.

———. "Power and Sex." *Politics, Philosophy, Culture: Interviews and Other Writings, 1977–84*. Ed. Lawrence D. Kritzman. Trans. Alan Sheridan et al. New York: Routledge, 1988. 110–24.

———. *The Use of Pleasure*. Trans. Robert Hurley. New York: Vintage, 1986. Vol. 2 of *The History of Sexuality*. 3 Vols. 1978–86.

Foucault, Michel. "What Is an Author?" *Textual Strategies: Perspectives in Post-Structuralist Criticism.* Ed. Josué V. Harari. London: Methuen, 1980. 141–60.

Friedman, Sanford. *Still Life.* New York: Dutton, 1975.

Fuss, Diana. *Essentially Speaking: Feminism, Nature and Difference.* London: Routledge, 1989.

———, ed. *Inside/Out: Lesbian Theories, Gay Theories.* New York: Routledge, 1991.

Gambone, Philip. *Something Inside: Conversations with Gay Fiction Writers.* Madison: U of Wisconsin P, 1999.

Garber, Marjorie. *Vice Versa: Bisexuality and the Eroticism of Everyday Life.* New York: Simon, 1995.

Garfield, Simon. "AIDS: The First 20 Years." *Observer Magazine* 3 June 2001: 16–24.

Gelder, Ken. *Reading the Vampire.* London: Routledge, 1994.

Genet, Jean. *Funeral Rites.* Trans. Bernard Frechtman. London: Panther, 1971.

———. *Our Lady of the Flowers.* 1943. Trans. Bernard Frechtman. London: Faber, 1990.

George, Sue. *Women and Bisexuality.* London: Scarlet, 1993.

Gove, Ben. *Cruising Culture: Promiscuity, Desire and American Literature.* Edinburgh: Edinburgh UP, 2000.

Gray, Martin. *A Dictionary of Literary Terms.* Harlow, Eng.: Longman, 1994.

Gunn, Thom. *The Man with Night Sweats.* London: Faber, 1992.

———. *The Passages of Joy.* London: Faber, 1982.

Hall, Donald E. (2002). "Identity." Summers, *The Gay and Lesbian Literary Heritage* 355–58.

Hall, Radclyffe. *The Well of Loneliness.* 1928. London: Virago, 1982.

Hall, Richard. "Gay Fiction Comes Home." *The New York Times Book Review* (19 June 1988): 1, 25–27.

Hall, Stuart. "The Question of Cultural Identity." *The Polity Reader in Cultural Theory.* Ed. Polity. Cambridge: Polity, 1994. 119–25.

Halperin, David. *One Hundred Years of Homosexuality and Other Essays on Greek Love.* New York: Routledge, 1990.

———. *Saint Foucault: Towards a Gay Hagiography.* New York: Oxford UP, 1995.

Hammond, Paul. *Love Between Men in English Literature.* Basingstoke, Eng.: Macmillan, 1996.

Hanson, Ellis. "Undead." Fuss, *Inside/Out* 324–40.

Hartnett, P. P., ed. *The Gay Times Book of Short Stories: The New Wave.* London: Gay Times, 2002.

Hemmings, Clare. "Resituating the Bisexual Body." Bristow and Wilson 118–38.

Hocquenghem, Guy. *Homosexual Desire.* 1972. Durham: Duke UP, 1993.

Hodges, Andrew, and David Hutter. *With Downcast Gays: Aspects of Homosexual Self-Oppression.* 1974. Toronto: Pink Triangle, 1977.

Holleran, Andrew. *Dancer from the Dance.* 1978. London: Corgi, 1980.

———. *Nights in Aruba.* 1983. Harmondsworth, Eng.: Penguin, 1991.

Hollinghurst, Alan. *The Swimming-Pool Library.* 1988. Harmondsworth, Eng.: Penguin, 1989.

Isherwood, Christopher. *A Single Man.* 1964. London: Methuen, 1978.

Jackson. Earl., Jr. "Dennis Cooper." Nelson 77–82.

Jackson, Rosemary. *Fantasy: The Literature of Subversion.* London: Methuen, 1981.

Jagose, Annamarie. *Queer Theory: An Introduction.* New York: New York UP, 1996.

Jenkins, Alan. "Life before the Flood." *The Independent on Sunday* 30 May 1993: 32–35.

Katz, Jonathan. *Gay American History: Lesbians and Gay Men in the U.S.A.* New York: Crowell, 1976.

Kinsey, Alfred. C., Wardle B. Pomeroy, and Clyde C. Martin. *Sexual Behavior in the Human Male.* Philadelphia: Saunders, 1948.

Kopelson, Kevin. *Love's Litany: The Writing of Modern Homoerotics.* Stanford: Stanford UP, 1994.

Kramer, Larry. *Faggots.* 1978. London: Minerva, 1997.

———. *Reports from the Holocaust: The Making of an AIDS Activist.* New York: St. Martin's, 1989.

Kristeva, Julia. *Powers of Horror: An Essay on Abjection.* New York: Columbia UP, 1982.

Lane, Christopher. "Psychoanalysis and Sexual Identity." Medhurst and Munt 160–75.

Lauritsen, John, and David Thorstad. *The Early Homosexual Rights Movement.* New York: Times Change, 1974.

Lawrence, D. H. *Selected Letters.* Ed. Aldous Huxley. Harmondsworth, Eng.: Penguin, 1978.

Leavitt, David. *The Lost Language of Cranes.* 1986. Harmondsworth, Eng.: Penguin, 1987.

Leavitt, David, and Mark Mitchell, eds. *The Penguin Book of Gay Short Stories.* Harmondsworth, Eng.: Penguin, 1994.

Light, Alison. "Fear of the Happy Ending: *The Color Purple*, Reading and Racism." *Plotting Change: Contemporary Women's Fiction.* Ed. Linda Anderson. Sevenoaks, Eng.: Edward Arnold, 1990. 85–96.

Lilly, Mark. *Gay Men's Literature in the Twentieth Century.* New York: New York UP, 1993.

Lorde, Audre. *Sister Outsider.* Freedom: Crossing, 1984

Lyotard, Jean-Francois. *The Postmodern Condition: A Report on Knowledge.* 1979. Trans. Geoff Bennington and Brian Massumi. Manchester, Eng.: Manchester UP, 1984.

McCracken, Samuel. "Are Homosexuals Gay?" *Commentary* 67.1 (January 1979): 19–29.

McIntosh, Mary. "The Homosexual Role." 1968. Seidman, *Queer Theories/Sociology* 33–40.

McRuer, Robert. *The Queer Renaissance: Contemporary American Literature and the Reinvention of Lesbian and Gay Identities.* New York: New York UP, 1997.

Manning, Toby. "Gay Culture: Who Needs It?" Simpson 98–117.

Marshall, Rodney. "Voicing Lost Language: The Politics of Urban Gay Writing: American and British Fiction from the late 1970s to the early 1990s." Diss. University of Exeter, 1995.

Mars-Jones, Adam. *Monopolies of Loss.* London: Faber, 1992.

Mars-Jones, Adam, and Edmund White. *The Darker Proof: Stories from a Crisis.* London: Faber, 1988

Martin, Robert K. "Edward Carpenter and the Double Structure of *Maurice*." *Essays on Gay Literature.* Ed. Stuart Kellogg. New York: Harington Park Press, 1985. 35–46.

Mathews, Harry. "A Valentine for Elena." *The Review of Contemporary Fiction* (Fall 1996): 31–42.

Maupin, Armistead. *Tales of the City.* New York: Harper, 1978.

Mayer, Hans. *Outsiders: A Study in Life and Letters.* Trans. Dennis M. Sweet. Cambridge: MIT P, 1982.

Medhurst, Andy, and Sally R. Munt, eds. *Lesbian and Gay Studies: A Critical Introduction.* London: Cassell, 1997.

Meyers, Jeffrey. *Homosexuality and Literature 1890–1930.* London: Athlone, 1977.

Mieli, Mario. *Homosexuality and Liberation: Elements of a Gay Critique.* 1977. Trans. David Fernbach. London: Gay Men's, 1980.

Miller, Edmund. "Gore Vidal." Summers, *The Gay and Lesbian Literary Heritage* 665–67.

Miller, Neil. *Out of the Past: Gay and Lesbian History from 1869 to the Present.* London: Vintage, 1995.

Mitchell, Juliet. *Psychoanalysis and Feminism: Freud, Reich, Laing and Women.* London: Lane, 1974.

Monette, Paul. *Love Alone: Eighteen Elegies for Rog.* New York: St. Martin's, 1988.

Moon, Michael. "New Introduction." Hocquenghem 9–21.

Moore, Oscar. *A Matter of Life and Sex.* Harmondsworth, Eng.: Penguin, 1992.

———. *PWA: Looking AIDS in the Face.* London: Picador, 1996.

Morton, Donald. "Birth of the Cyberqueer." *PMLA* 110.3 (1995): 369–81.

Murphy, Timothy F., and Suzanne Poirier, eds. *Writing AIDS: Gay Literature, Language and Analysis.* New York: Columbia UP, 1993.

Myron, Nancy, and Charlotte Bunch, eds. *Lesbianism and the Women's Movement.* Baltimore: Diana, 1975.

Nelson, Emmanuel S., ed. *Contemporary Gay American Novelists: A Bio-Bibliographical Critical Sourcebook.* Westport: Greenwood, 1993.

Nunokawa, Jeff. "*In Memoriam* and the Extinction of the Homosexual." *Tennyson.* Ed. Rebecca Stott. London: Longman, 1996. 197–209.

Oswell, David. "True Love in Queer Times: Romance, Suburbia and Masculinity." Pearce and Wisker 157–71.

Palmer, Paulina. *Lesbian Gothic: Transgressive Fictions.* London: Cassell, 1999.

Pearce, Lynne, and Gina Wisker, eds. *Fatal Attractions: Rescripting Romance in Contemporary Literature and Film.* London: Pluto, 1998.

Picano, Felice. "The British Are Coming—Or Are They?" *The Gay and Lesbian Review Worldwide* 8.4 (2001): 38–39.

———. *The Lure.* New York: Delacorte, 1979.

Plummer, Kenneth. *The Making of the Modern Homosexual.* London: Hutchinson, 1981.

———. "Speaking Its Name: Inventing a Lesbian and Gay Studies." *Modern Homosexualities: Fragments of Lesbian and Gay Experiences.* Ed. Kenneth Plummer. London: Routledge, 1992. 3–25.

Poirier, Suzanne. "On Writing AIDS." Murphy and Poirier 1–8.

Punter, David, ed. *A Companion to the Gothic.* Oxford: Blackwell, 2000.

———. *The Modern Gothic.* London: Longman, 1996. Vol. 2 of *The Literature of Terror: A History of Gothic Fictions from 1765 to the Present Day.* 2 Vols. 1997.

Raschke, Debrah. "Breaking the Engagement with Philosophy: Re-envisioning Hetero/Homo Relations in *Maurice.*" *Queer Forster.* Ed. Robert K. Martin and George Piggford. Chicago: U of Chicago P. 151–65.

Renault, Mary. *The Charioteer.* 1953. London: New English Library, 1990.

Roof, Judith. "Postmodernism." Medhurst and Munt 176–85.

Sedgwick, Eve Kosofsky. *Between Men: English Literature and Male Homosocial Desire.* New York: Columbia UP, 1985.

———. *Epistemology of the Closet.* Hemel Hempstead, Eng.: Harvester, 1991.

———. *Tendencies.* Durham: Duke UP, 1993.

Seidman, Steven. "Identity and Politics in a 'Postmodern' Gay Culture." Warner 105–42.

———, ed. *Queer Theories/Sociology.* Oxford: Blackwell, 1996.

Shatzky, Joel. "Larry Kramer." Nelson 243–47.

Shepherd, Simon, and Mick Wallis, eds. *Coming on Strong: Gay Politics and Culture*. London: Unwin, 1989.

Simpson, Mark, ed. *Anti-Gay*. London: Cassell, 1996.

Sinfield, Alan. *Faultlines: Cultural Materialism and the Politics of Dissident Reading*. Oxford: Oxford UP, 1992.

———. *Gay and After*. London: Serpent's Tail, 1998.

———. *The Wilde Century: Effeminacy, Oscar Wilde and the Queer Moment*. London: Cassell, 1994.

Smith, F. B. "Labouchère's Amendment to the Criminal Law Amendment Bill." *Historical Studies* 17.67: University of Melbourne 165–75.

Stevenson, Robert Louis. *The Strange Case of Dr Jekyll and Mr Hyde*. 1886. Ed. Emma Letley. Oxford: Oxford UP, 1987.

Stoker, Bram. *Dracula*. 1897. Oxford: World's Classics, 1986.

Sullivan, Andrew. *Virtually Normal: An Argument about Homosexuality*. London: Picador, 1995.

Summers, Claude. "Christopher Isherwood." Nelson 211–19.

———, ed. *The Gay and Lesbian Literary Heritage: A Reader's Companion to the Writers and Their Works, from Antiquity to the Present*. Rev. ed. London: Routledge, 2002.

———. *Gay Fictions: Wilde to Stonewall: Studies in a Male Homosexual Literary Tradition*. New York: Continuum, 1990.

Summerskill, Ben. "We're so ordinary, it's frightening." *The Observer* (20 July 2003): 29

Tytell, John. *Naked Angels: The Lives and Literature of the Beat Generation*. New York: McGraw, 1976.

Vance, Carol S., ed. *Pleasure and Danger: Exploring Female Sexuality*. New York: Routledge, 1984.

Veeder, William. "Children of the Night: Stevenson and Patriarchy." *Dr Jekyll and Mr Hyde after One Hundred Years*. Ed. William Veeder and George Hirsch. Chicago: U of Chicago P, 1988. 107–60.

Vidal, Gore. Afterword. *The City and the Pillar*. By Gore Vidal. Rev. ed. London: Heinemann, 1965. 207–11.

———. *The City and the Pillar*. 1948. London: Abacus, 1997.

Warner, Michael, ed. *Fear of a Queer Planet: Queer Politics and Social Theory*. Minneapolis: U of Minnesota P, 1993.

Watney, Simon. "Lesbian and Gay Studies in the Age of AIDS." Medhurst and Munt 368–84.

———. *Policing Desire: Pornography, AIDS, and the Media*. Minneapolis: U of Minnesota P, 1987.

Weeks, Jeffrey. *Against Nature*. London: Rivers, 1991.

———. *Coming Out: Homosexual Politics in Britain from the Nineteenth Century to the Present*. London: Quartet, 1977.

———. Introduction. Altman, *Homosexual: Oppression and Liberation* 1–19.

———. *Making Sexual History*. Cambridge: Polity, 2000.

———. Preface. Hocquenghem, *Homosexual Desire* 23–47.

———. *Sexuality*. London: Routledge, 1986.

———. *Sexuality and Its Discontents: Meaning, Myths and Modern Sexualities*. London: Routledge, 1985.

Weir, John. "Going In." Simpson 26–34.

White, Edmund. *The Beautiful Room Is Empty*. London: Picador, 1988.

———. *A Boy's Own Story*. London: Picador, 1983.

———. *The Burning Library: Writings on Art, Politics and Sexuality 1969–1993*. Ed. David Bergman. London: Chatto, 1994.

———. "Esthetics and Loss." *The Burning Library* 211–17.

———, ed. *The Faber Book of Gay Short Fiction*. London: Faber, 1991.

———. *The Farewell Symphony*. London: Chatto, 1997.

———. *Forgetting Elena*. 1973. *Nocturnes for the King of Naples*. 1978. London: Picador, 1984.

———. *The Married Man*. London: Chatto, 2000.

———. "Paradise Found." *The Burning Library* 145–56.

———. *Skinned Alive*. London: Chatto, 1995.

———. *States of Desire: Travels in Gay America*. 1980. Rpt. with afterword. London: Picador, 1986.

White, Edmund, and Hubert Sorin. *Our Paris: Sketches from Memory*. New York: Knopf, 1994.

White, Patricia. "Female Spectator, Lesbian Spectator: *The Haunting*." Fuss, *Inside/Out* 142–72.

Wilde, Oscar. *The Letters of Oscar Wilde*. Ed. Rupert Hart-Davis. New York: Harcourt, 1962.

———. *The Picture of Dorian Gray*. 1891. Ed. Isobel Murray. Oxford: World's Classics, 1981.

Williams, Raymond. *Culture*. Glasgow: Fontana, 1981.

Wilson, Elizabeth. "Is Transgression Transgressive?" Bristow and Wilson 107–17.

Wisker, Gina. "If Looks Could Kill: Contemporary Women's Vampire Fictions." Pearce and Wisker 51–68.

———. "Queer Vampires in Contemporary American Women's Fiction." *Overhere: A European Journal of American Culture* 18.1 (1998): 75–90.

Woodhouse, Reed. *Unlimited Embrace: A Canon of Gay Fiction, 1945–1995*. Amherst: U of Massachusetts P, 1998.

Woods, Gregory. *Articulate Flesh: Male Homo-eroticism and Modern Poetry*. New Haven: Yale UP, 1987.

———. *A History of Gay Literature: The Male Tradition*. New Haven: Yale UP, 1998.

———. "William Seward Burroughs II." Nelson 37–45.

# Index